A Handbook *of* CLINICAL DIRECTORY *of* HOMOEOPATHY

AF623931

A Handbook *of* CLINICAL DIRECTORY *of* HOMOEOPATHY

Dr M B L Saxena

MSc, PhD, DHMB (Gold Medallist) RMP, MIHMF

New Central Book Agency (P) Ltd

LONDON

HYDERABAD ERNAKULAM BHUBANESWAR

DELHI KOLKATA PUNE

REGD OFFICE
8/1 Chintamoni Das Lane, Kolkata 700 009, India
email: ncbapvtltd@eth.net

OVERSEAS
NCBA (UK) Ltd, 149 Park Avenue North, Northampton, NN3 2HY, UK

EXPORT
NCBA Exports Pvt. Ltd, 212 Shahpur Jat, New Delhi 110 049
email: ncbaexp@ncbapvtltd.com

BRANCHES

208B Peacock Lane, Shahpur Jat
New Delhi 110 049
email: ncbadel@ncbapvtltd.com

Shop Nos. 3 & 4, Vinayak Towers
681/B Budhwar Peth, Appa Balwant Chowk
Pune 411 002
email: ncbapune@ncbapvtltd.com

Shop No. 15, Bharati Towers
Forest Park, **Bhubaneswar** 751 001

House No. 3-1-315, 1st Floor
Nimboliadda, Kachiguda, **Hyderabad** 500 027
email: ncbahydb@ncbapvtltd.com

GSS Shopping Complex, 1st Floor
Opposite College Post Office, Convent Road
Ernakulam 682 035
email: ncbaernk@ncbapvtltd.com

A HANDBOOK OF CLINICAL DIRECTORY OF HOMOEOPATHY

© Copyright reserved by the Author.

Publication, Distribution, and Promotion Rights reserved by the Publisher

All rights reserved. No part of the text in general, and the figures, diagrams, page layout, and cover design in particular, may be reproduced or transmitted in any form or by any means—electronic, mechanical, photocopying, recording, or by any information storage and retrieval system—without the prior written permission of the Publisher

First Published: 2011

PUBLISHER AND TYPESETTER
New Central Book Agency (P) Ltd
8/1 Chintamoni Das Lane, Kolkata 700 009

PRINTER
New Central Book Agency (P) Ltd
Web-Offset Division, Dhulagarh, Sankrail, Howrah

COVER DESIGNER
Soumen Paul

COVER PRINTER
Biswanath Studio, Kolkata

ISBN: 978-81-7381-665-9

Price: ₹ 125.00

Preface

The easy accessibility, efficacy and affordable prices of Homoeopathic system of treatment have made it as one of the leading system of therapeutics all over the world. It is coming up fast being the latest in medical science, which has natural law and successful cures of the diseases without side effects. All this made me interested to study the system and treatment of homoeopathy. After practising in this field for more than 30 years and getting success and acclaim, my patients, friends and students insisted that I should write a book on my experience and knowledge of this subject so that others also could benefit. This book is an outcome of it.

Homoeopathy - a system of medicine was first expounded in 1796 by a German Physician Dr. Christian Freidrich Samuel Hahnemann, a celebrated scientist, chemist and one of the leading physicians of his time. Homoeopathy came to India in 1839 when a French Homoeopath Dr. Johan Martin Honigberger, a disciple of Dr. Hahnemann visited India to treat Maharaja Ranjeet Singh in Lahore. He treated him successfully and cured him permanently. Since then homoeopathy has been accepted so well that it has become one of the national systems of medicine.

Homoeopathy is based upon the therapeutics known as "Similia Similibus Curentur" which means "like cures like". It is a law of nature as scientific and unfailiable as the law of gravitation.

The study of earlier medical history shows that "Similia Similibus Curentur" is not a new law but it was recognized 22 centuries ago by Hippocrates the father of modern medicine. According to him disease is produced by similars and when similars are administered the patient is restored to health, thus the medicine substance which produces sleeplessness cures sleeplessness and that which causes vomiting cures vomiting.

Nevertheless, this principle of homoeopathy has been well recognized in Ayurveda which is evident from the writing of Rishis. The aphorism "Samam Samena Shante", "Ushnam Ushnena Shante" are identical to the law of healing established by Dr. Hahnemann.

The meaning of this law is that a drug which is capable of producing a particular set of disease symptoms in a healthy human's body is also capable of curing the same symptoms in the sick person. This law has been verified by Dr. Hahnemann throughout his life time and also by others and therefore, is a fundamental principle of Homoeopathy (Law of healing).

Another revolutionary fact of Homoeopathy is the use of potentised drug. The potentised drugs have tremendous power actually to cure the ailments without any adverse action whereas the same drug cannot do so in the pure form. It has also been confirmed that greater the potency greater is the power to cure which is carried out by special process called potentisation. This process develops the medicinal power of the medicine hidden within it which can be said to be the spiritualization of the material itself. Under this, substances generally considered to be inert without any medicinal power in their natural form such as common salt, charcoal, sand wood etc. are converted into extremely efficacious medicines when potentised. As an example Natrum muriticum i.e. common salt when potentised becomes a great medicine in Homoeopathic doses for anaemia, for debility, for intermittent fevers like malaria and for coryza. This is a new path in the field of medicine.

The homoeopathic treatment is most natural, rational and scientific system of cure. Literally "scientific" means that any system which is based on rational, logical, realism is science. Homoeopathy stands for all these tests.

In Homoeopathy patient reactions and symptoms help the physician to select his remedy and steer his health quickly, gently and permanently.

The Homoeopathic system of administration of drug is to stimulate the natural and recuperative power of the ailing body and enable to defeat the disease in natural manner because homoeopathic drugs stimulate the natural inherent power or recuperation in the human body. In other words the drug mobilizes the defence mechanism of the body against the offending agents. The result is an ideal cure without any side effects.

Homoeopathy firmly believes in enhancing body's own defence mechanism to maintain the healthy status. The Homoeopathic treatment is aimed at enhancing body's own healing capacity so that human system does not react adversely to the allergens factors.

The main objective of homoeopathy is "complete therapy" or treatment of the patient as a whole goes far beyond the specific attack against the invading pathogens.

To make readers more acquainted with the principles of homoeopathic treatment for cure are given in the following paragraphs:

In homoeopathy only proven remedies are used. Proven remedies are those whose symptoms, indications, duration of action, depth of action are fully known. It has been observed and proved that proven medicines when administered act instantaneously, deeply and for a long time cures morbid condition as if by magic.

It advocates the use of single remedy at a time so that the true effects could be ascertained. If remedy shows adverse effects it can be antidoted. Each remedy has relationship with other remedies as complementary, supplementary and antidotal. This knowledge ensures a harmless treatment.

In Homoeopathy, use of minimum dose of the drug is advocated. The quantity of the drug should be very minute as to produce no aggravation or minimal aggravation and no side effects.

It advocates the use of potentised remedy which immediately produces effective results as soon as given. Potentisation of medicines are done at centesimal, decimal and 50 millesimal scale of potencies.

The medicines are given according to law of cure known as "Similia Similibus Curentur" or "like cures like". As per Homoeopathy, every powerful medicinal substance is capable of producing in a healthy human body a particular set of disease symptoms and each medicine is also capable of curing the symptoms which are similar to those that it can produce in the body in its healthy condition.

Homoeopathy recognizes the vital force on which depends the orderly state of health of the individual, which is brought in order by the dynamic medicine. The vital disorder is different in every patient, whereas, the disease may be the same. So, homoeopathy treats the peculiar vital force and individual disorder.

Homoeopathy supports that suppression is a fundamental cause of chronic diseases (miasmas) which may be due to maltreatment with crude and poisonous medicines and that health cannot be maintained unless these miasmas are cured.

To know complete Homoeopathic system and potentision it is suggested that the organon of medicine written by Dr. Hahnemann needs consultation. It deals with many of the questions which come in the mind on the system of healing such as like cures like, why does a drug cures the sickness, the significance of symptoms of the sickness, the miracles of small dose, how is a medicine proved? The significance of different lines of treatment in acute and chronic diseases, why the mental disposition of the patient be given importance, the homoeopathic aggravation and the necessity of diet restriction.

In this book diseases commonly named are arranged alphabetically together with the medicine to be used on the basis of specific guiding symptoms to help in selecting the correct medicine easily. Almost in all cases the symptoms of the medicine are given and in very few cases the symptoms of the medicine are not given but medicines are arranged in order of preference for convenience of the user.

The potency of medicine to be used is not mentioned in the book because the selection of potency is dependent on number of various factors which are discussed in on- going paragraphs.

It is suggested in general that 30th potency be used for each medicine otherwise 3rd or 6th potencies be used which act equally well. In particular cases when the potency does not show desired efficacy or when the improvement is slow or stops, it will become necessary to increase or decrease the potency of the medicine which can be ascertained from the recovery of the patient. In skin diseases, potencies 200 and above should be used. As a general rule for acute diseases lower potencies i.e. 30th and below be used and for chronic diseases potencies 200 and above be used. When selected remedy fails to cure or impairs the improvement, due to miasmatic effect, the homoeopathic miasmic remedies be given in between the current remedies to remove this effect. The miasmatic remedies always be given in 200 potency and above.

There are few considerations which also influence the choice of potency. Diseases characterised by diminished vital action require the use of lower potencies, while diseases characterised by increased vital action respond well to higher potencies. The stages and duration of disease is also important for consideration of the potencies. For symptoms of later stages of disease higher potencies are required.

There is no hard and fast rule for the administration of the Homoeopathic medicine. The homoeopathic medicines are given in trituration, tincture and mother tincture. The dose 2 grains is suggested for trituration. Tinctures are to be given in sugar globules of 30 number in size, four globules for adult and half the quantity to child and the infants half the quantity of the child. By my experience, the Homoeopathic medicine be given in cooled pre-boiled water to make the treatment effective and cheaper. In case of mother tincture 2-4 drops in 1/4 cup of water for adults and one drop for children will be sufficient.

Repetition of the dose be carried out in acute diseases namely cholera, diarrhea, inflammation etc. The dose may be repeated after 10-15 minutes intervals. In chronic diseases a dose in the morning and night be given at frequent intervals of 3-7 days in high potencies and when symptoms of improvement are noticed the interval between the dose be enhanced.

In this book the common and homoeopathic medicines effectively-tried by me and others have been suggested. But as detailed indications for the use of the medicines cannot be given in a book like this, only specific and precise indications are given to make their application easy. However, many ailments and emergencies can be met easily by Homoeopathic system of medicine with successful results.

I am highly indebted and record my gratitude to the learned authors whose knowledge has been shared in this book to make it more informative and useful. They have been referred in the bibliography section of the book. It is a known fact that a useful book cannot be complete without sharing the knowledge of other learned authors, to whom I again express my gratitude.

While writing the book, my wife Smt. Lajwanti Saxena all through encouraged and helped me at the time of necessity even facing all sorts of inconveniences in her daily domestic routine of work although, thanks are not enough, she deserves much more than it.

I express my thanks to Dr. Chitresh Bhargava and Shri Rameshwar Lal for the tedious work of spell check etc. and typing the book and to bring it in the present form.

Lastly, if this book helps in curing the suffering and restores the health to the user, I will consider my endeavours of writing this book have been amply rewarded.

Dr. M. B. L. Saxena

A

Abdomen (distended): *Sil., Sulph., Lyco., Ars.* (in tubercular children) *Cina* (from worries), *Iod., Phyto., Ferrum mur., Cal. carb., Ars. iod.* (*3x*), *Merc. iod., Baptisia* (Entric fever), *Dig., Terebenth., Ars.* (Dropsy) *Colocynth or Nux vom.* (tympanite), *Cimicifuga, China, Carb. veg., Iris.*

Abdomen (flatulence): *Carbo veg.* (from eructation the flatulence is subsided) *Lycopodium* (better by passing flatus) *China* (no relief by eructation and passing flatus).

Abdomen: *Ant crud., Acon, Bell, Merc., Nux.* (great soreness of the abdomen) *Ant crud* (sensation in the abdomen as if something tight would break, if much efforts are made to void stool) *Ars., Lach., Phos., Sec., Sepia* (burning in abdomen) *Bell.* (constriction of the abdomen around umbilicus as if ball is formed or clutching in the abdomen as if a spot has been seized by cloud or great tenderness and heat) *Cina* (abdomen bloated and hard in children) *Con.* (rumbling in the abdomen) *Lyco., China* (abdomen feels as if stuffed) *Lyco., China., Phos.* (constant sense of fermentation in the abdomen) *Mag. carb.* (contractive punching pain in the right iliac region, great heaviness in the abdomen) *Merc. v.* (stabbing punching pain in the abdomen, indurations of the liver) *Silicea, Lyco.* (burning in the bowels, much rumbling of flatulence in the abdomen).

Abortion: *Arnica.* (after a fall, blow or concussion) *Cantharis* (threatened abortion from congestion or ulceration of cervix uteri) *Chamomilla* (labour like pain, discharge dark colour, desire for frequent urination) *Crocus* (discharge consists of dark stringy blood, which is increased by least exertion) *Sabina* (dragging pain extending from back through to the pubis).

Abscess (brain): *Arnica* (abscess as a result of injury) *Bella.* (symptom develop fast, throbbing and burning pain causing delirium) *Crotalus* (abscess causes clouded perception and loss of memory, depressed, confused or sad, suffers from auditory vertigo, blood oozing from ears) *Heper. sulph* (temperature, discharge of fetid pus from the ear with shooting pain) *Myristica* (inflammation of middle ear leading to abscess).

Abscess (breast): *Bryo., Bell.* (breast red and swollen), *Phos* (during formation of abscess), *Phytolacca, Silicea or Heper. Sulph.* (imperfect suppuration).

Abscess (chronic): *Sil., China, Phos., Bary carb., Sulph., Heper. sulph., Cal. carb., Phosphoric acid.*

Abscess (liver): *Aco., Merc., Heper Sulph., Silicea.*

Abscess (threatened): *Bella., Apis., Merc. sol.* (acute) *Acon., Bell., Heper. Sulph., Arnica.*

Abscess (tubercula): *Cal. iod., Cal. carb., Sil., Sulph, Aur., Ars. iod., Carbolic acid.*

Abscesses (Gathering): *Arsenic* (great debility, parts burns like fire, great thirst but drinks little) *Bryonia* (hard swollen and feels heavy stitching aggravates by motion) *Lachesis* (when pus is formed, portion becomes purplish in colour) *Mercurius* (glandular abscesses, intense shining redness, beating and stinging) *Phosphorus* (in mammary abscesses).

Achalasia of the cardia (oesophagus muscles do not work properly): *Abies nigra* (pain after eating, feeling of hard boiled egg lodged in the stomach) *Carbo veg.* (digestion slow, simplest food distresses, food purtified before it is digested, difficulty in swallowing).

Aching or burning pains in the stomach with great distention: *Arn., Ars., Bella., Phos.* (sour stomach with sour belching and taste, heart burn, gulping up and vomiting of sour matter) *Calc. carb., Carbo veg., China, Nux vom., Phos., Sulphur* (sour stomach always after eating) *Nat mur., Nux vom., Phos., Sepia, Sulphur* (rancid belching) *Arn., Ars., Chin., Ferrum, Merc., Phos., Sepia* (foul belching) *Nux vom., Puls., Verat* (bitter taste, bitter belching bitter vomiting). *Ars., Chin., Nat mur., Nux vom., Sepia* (total loss of appetite) *Cal carb., Chin., Nat mur, Nux., Phos.* (ravenous hunger) *Ars., Chin., Ferr., Phos* (great weakness and loss of energy).

Aching, sore and bruised feeling all over the body: *Rhus tox.* (relieved by motion) *Phytolacea* (aggravated by movement).

Acidity (heart burn): *Nux vom., Bryo., Puls., Carbo veg., Iris vers., Anacard., Lyco.* (for elderly persons) *Cal. carb., Robina* (Chronic acidity).

Acids intolerable: *Antim. crud., Antim tart., Ferrum met., Merc. cor., Nux vom., Puls., Sepia.*

Acne (pimples): *Bella.* (in the plethoric) *Acid phos., Baryta carb., Cal. carb., Kali bromide, Carboic acid, Kali Hydro iod., Juglan, Ars.* (during menses), *Lappa.* (after menses).

Acne (rosa cea): *Ant. crud., Radium bromide, Rhus. or Merc.* (young persons) *Bella., Ars.* (severe and chronic cases).

Acne in beard: *Lyco., Graph., Merc. sol., Ant. tar., Merc. Iod., Sulphur, Acon., Ars.* (collapse condition).

Acrocyanosis (cold and blue hands and fingers): *Arsenic alb.* (blue and icy cold body, debility, exhaustion and restlessness) ***Carbo. veg.*** (blueness of the skin, poor digestion, hot perspiration) ***Nitric acid*** (cold blue nails, sweating of palms and hands).

Adenoids: *Agraphis nutans* (enlarged tonsils and otitis media) ***Bacilinum*** (treatment be started with this) *Calcarea carb.* (pale and fat children with adenoids and tonsils swollen) *Calcarea phos.* (swollen and painful tonsils, child peevish and obstinate, weak and thin with pale face).

Affections of the mouth, bad taste in the mouth: *Bryonia, Calcarea carb., Merc, vivus.* (bitter taste in the morning) *Bella., China, Ferrum, Pulsatilla* (sweet taste) *Ars., Cal. Carb., China, Nux vom., Phos., Acid sulph.* (sour taste) *Ars., Carb veg., Nux vom., Phos. acid* (salty taste) *Rux tox., Verat.* (acrid biting taste) *Arn., Cham., Merc. v., Puls.* (putrid taste) *Sabina, Silicea* (greasy oily taste) *Bryo., China, Puls., Staph., Sulph.* (insipid taste) *Bella., Canth., Heper., Lyco., Phos., Verat.* (loss of taste) *Bryo., Calo., Heper, Sulph.* (solid food taste bitter), *Bryo., China, Puls.* (all food and drinks taste bitter) *Lyco., Nux vom.* (all foods taste sour) *Ars., Bell., China, Sulph.* (all foods taste salty).

After acute ailment, there is excessive perspiration and then there is relief: *Caladium, Nat. mur., Psoranium.*

After operation of stomach, vomiting: *Bismith, Nux vom., Staph.*

Aggravation better from closing eyes: *Bryonia.*

Aggravation from anger: *Cham., Colocynth, Nux vom., Staph., Sulphur.*

Aggravation from noises: *Iod., Nat. mur.*

Aggravation in ailment from consolation: *Lilium ting., Nat. mur., Platinum.*

Aggravation in ailment from storm: *Rhododendron, R.T., Sepia, Lachesis, Lycopodoum, Tuberculin, Agarcius, Kali Bich., Nat. carb., Phos., Psoramium*

Aggravation in ailment from summer and heat: *Bryonia, Flouric acid, Iodin., Lach.*

Aggravation in ailments from warmth of the room: *Apis., Lyco., Nat. mur., Plat., Puls., Spon., Sulphur.*

Ague: *China, Ars.* (chronic and un-deformed cases) *Cedr., Nat. mur.* (after the abuse of quinine) *Carbo veg., Ipecac.* (much gastric disturbance with nausea) *Nux vom., Veratrum alb.* (chill predominating), *Bryonia, Gels., Acid phos., Terebentha.*

Ailment aggravates before menses flow: *Ammon. cast., Bovista, Cal. carb., Gels., Lachesis, Puls., Sepia.*

Ailment aggravates during full moon: *Alumina, Cal. carb., Graphites, Sabadilla, Silicea*

Ailment aggravates from light, sound and touch: *Bella.*

Ailment aggravates from lying on bed: *Ars. alb., Bella., Conium, Glonine, Hyocymus, Lach., Lyco., Phos., Puls., Rhus tox., Rumex.*

Ailment aggravates from mental work: *Anacardium, Argent., nit., Cal. carb., Coccolus ind., Gels., Nat. carb., Nux vom., Phos., Picric acid, Silicea.*

Ailment aggravates from the movements of feet: *Coffea.*

Ailment aggravates from the sound of carriages: *Nitric acid.*

Ailment aggravates from the sound of feet movement: *Nux vom.*

Ailment aggravates from warmth of the bed: *Led. pal., Merc., Mag. carb., Sulphur.*

Ailment aggravates, before mid night: *Phos., Puls., Rhus tox.*

Ailment aggravates, in the morning: *Nux vom., Lachesis, Nat. mur.*

Ailment aggravates, in warm room or in warm wind: *Apis., Puls., Sabina.*

Ailment aggravates, with slightest change in warm weather: *Bryo., Dulcamara.*

Ailment better by cold open air: *Antim. crud., Aco., Aloes, Alumen, Ambra., Amyl nit., Antim. tart., Apis., Argent. nit., Allium cepa, China, Glonine, Kali iod., Kali sulph., Lyco., Mag. carb., Merc. iod. rube., Nat. mur., Picric acid, Puls., Sabadilla, Secale, Sepia, Tabacum, Tarentula his.*

Ailment better by hot bath: *Antim. crud., Bufo., Strontsia.*

Ailment from cold drift: *Bella., Silicea, Capsicum, Drosera, Hepers, Kali bich., Mag. phos., Rhus tox.*

Ailment from eating heavy and fatty items: *Puls., Carbo veg.*

Ailment from excessive bleeding: *China, Hamamelis.*

Ailment from hair cutting: *Bella., Aco., Glonine.*

Ailment of fiber tissue: *Rhus tox., Rhododendron.*

Ailment repeats every year: *Ars. alb., Carbo veg., Lachesis, Sulphur, Thuja.*

Ailment subsides, in the open air: *Aco., Alumina, Mag. carb., Puls., Sabina, Nat. mur.*

Ailments aggravate during menses: *Cimicifuga, Puls., Tuberculinum, Hemamalis.*

Ailments due to change of weather: *Rhus tox., Sulphur, Psoranium.*

Ailments due to living in the damp places: *Ars. alb., Dulcamara, Nat. sulph.*

Ailments from dry cold wind: *Aconite* (ailments aggravate immediately after catching dry cold) *Bryonia* (the ailment gradually develops after catching dry cold) *Heper sulph* (the ailment gradually develops patient wants to keep his head warm so use the woolen scarf to cover his head) *Causticum* (feels better from drinking cold water urine passes with coughing) *Nux vom.* (wants to cover up the body and will not like to expose any part of the body).

Ailments of right side: *Bella., Bryo., Chelitonium, Kali carb., Mag. phos., Lyco., Podo.*

Ailments resulting from fear: *Aconite* (after fear the fever develops) *Ignitia* (immediately after fear develops sorrowness) *Belladona* (imaginary factors develop fear) *Gels.* (fear develops diarrhoea) *Veratrum album* (from fear cold sweat on forehead).

Albuminaria (bright disease): *Ars., Phos., Cantharis, Merc., Kreos., Nux vom., Acid phos., Terebintha, Apis mel., Ferrum met.*

Alcoholic effect of: *Nux vom., Bella, Capsicum* (large doses be given in sugar water), *Agaric., Opi., Ars., Digitalis, Kali brom., Strych., Sulphur.* (when there are tremors) *Ant. tar.* (gastric irritation).

Allergy from bread: *Antim. crud., Hydrastist, Lyco., Nat. mur., Nitric acid., Puls.*

Allergy from eating fruits: *Ars. alb., China, Puls.*

Allergy from fatty food: *Antim. crud., Cal. carb., Carbo veg., Cycla., Lyco., Puls., Thuja.*

Allergy from pastry: *Antim. crud., Lyco., Puls.*

Allergy from tomato: *Lyco.*

Allergy from vinegar: *Antim. crud., Carbo veg.*

Allergy: *Bromium* (from dust) *Capsicum* (from red pepper) *Lac. delf.* (from milk of children with nausea, vomiting and diarrhea) *Oxalic acid* (from coffee which produces diarrhoea) *Sambucus nig.* (from fruits) *Sepia* (during pregnancy allergic to cooking food smell) *Oxalic acid* (to sour fruits like strawberry, apples grapes etc) *Nat. mur.* (from egg, honey and onion) *Pulsatilla* (from flower smell), *Apium g.* (from walking in the garden) *Arsenic alb.* (from ice cream) *Thuja* (from onion) *Lycopodium* (from eating oyster) *Alumina* (from salt, wine, vinegar, pepper which produce immediately cough) *Histaminum* (in general).

Alone, cannot remains: *Ars. alb., Bismith, Lyco., Kali carb.*

Alopecia (falling of hair): *Cantharis* (internally) and externally in pomade, *Acid phos.* (after illness or from general debility) *Aloc., Acid flour., Iod., Ars., Cal. carb.,* Silicea, Sulph. (chronic headache).

Amblyopia (impaired vision): *Acid phos., China, Ferrum, Ars., Anacard., Phos.* (from debility) *Acon., Arnica, Ruta, Nux vom., Gels., Macrotin.* (from over use of eyes) *Cimici.* (aching in eye balls) *Spigelia, Colocynth.* (great pain in the eyes) *Cact.* (hyper anemia of the optic nerve).

Amblyopic (weakness of the sight): *Belladona* (pupil dilated, red rings around the candle light) *Hyoscyamus* (optical illusion, dark spots before the eyes) *Pulsatilla* (as if looking through mist, aggravation towards evening) *Stramonium* (dim sight with thirst and sweat on the forehead) *Sulphur* (intolerance of the light of the sun, constant heat on the top of the head).

Amennorhoea (Suppression of menses): *Bryonia* (bleeding from nose when the menses should appear, dry hard stool symptoms aggravates by motion) *Colocynth* (amenorhoea from anger and silent grief) *Dulcamara* (amenorrhoea from exposure to cold) *Pulsatilla* (suppression, specially from getting the feet wet) *Ferrum, Helonias* (with anaemia) *Bell., Acon.* (in full blooded patient) *Merc.* (yellow complexion, liver derangement) *Argent. nit.* (watery discharge), *Graphites* (constipation and unhealthy skin), *Sepia* (sclerotic appearance leucorrhoea) *Phos.* (diarrhoea tendency to chest disease), *Kali carb., Dulcamara, Sulphur, Cycl., Plat., Nat. mur., Baryta carb.* (functional disorder).

Amnesia (loss of memory due to various causes): *Anacardium* (due to brain fag causing impaired memory and absent mindedness, weakness of sense of sight and hearing, lack of self control aversion to work) *Lycopodium* (uses wrong words, wrong syllabus, spells wrongly, confused thoughts).

Anaemia: *Acetic acid* (profound anaemia in women where there has been unusal loss of blood after labour), *Arsenic alb.* (extreme prostration and anxiety) *Cal. phos.* (anaemia in children, child peevish, flabby, feeble digestion) *China* (anaemia caused by excessive loss of blood or other fluids of the body) *Ferrum aceticum* (patient is thin, pale weak, easily exhausted and suffer from shortness of breath) *Ferrum met.* (anaemia after intermittent fevers, pale face but at a time face is flushed red) *Ferrum phos.* (throbbing pain in head, with senstiveness of the scalp, marked prostration) *Iridium* (in anaemia to increase red capuscles) *Nat. mur.* (great debility and weakness particularly in the morning) *Phophorus* (due to long lasting depression) *Picric acid* (anaemia when bone narrow lacks vitamin B12 or other substances required for the formation of blood) *Silicea* (due to iron deficiency, nails become dry and brittle).

Anaemia: *Ferrum, Pyro., Phos., China* (from haemorrhage) *Helon., Acid phos., Ars., Iod., Merc., Macrot, Nat. mur, Silicea, Argent nit.*

Anaemia (perinecious): *Ars. alb., Mag. acet., Picric acid, Thyroidenum.*

Anaemia and debility: *China* (due to excessive loss of fluids, sexual excess and vices cause debility, sleeplessness and irritability) *Ars. alb.* (emaciation rapid, cold sweat) *Phosphorus* (sudden prostration nervous system is exhausted) *Ferrum met.* (anaemia with plethora) *Acid phos.* (for debility of nervous origin, burning in spine) *Zincum* (brain is the cause of debility).

Aneurisms: *Bar. c., Kali hydroiod, Cal. phos., Iod., Lyca., Aco., Vervir.*

Anger (effect of): *Aconite* (palpitation and arterial excitement) *Cham.* (bilious derangement) *Bryonia* (Headache) *Bell., Hyos.* (brain disturbance) *Nux vom., Staph.*

Anger in strong desire to kill others: *Nux vom., Cham., Ignatia, Staph., Bryo.*

Anger in, strong desire to jump from windows: *Argent, nit.*

Anger: *Bryonia* **(exceeding irritable, headache as if head will split open, constipation)** *Cham.* **(anger causes indigestion and derangement of the liver)** *Colycynth* **(during anger do not wish to talk or answer any question)** *Nux vom.* **(very irritable during anger and wishes to be alone).**

Angina pectoris (with pain in the right arm, heart feels as if tighten in a vice): *Merc. sol.* **(affecting the extremities or leading to paralyses, agitations, help in dissolving the blood clot).**

Angina pectoris: *Amyl nit., Ars., Cact., Dig.* **(very slow labourer pulse)** *Ver. vir., Ver. alb., Hep. sulph., Iod., Strych., Naja, China, Puls., Aurum, Strophanth.*

Angry on small matters: *Aurum, Causticum, Cocculus, Cyclamen, Nux vom., Zincum.*

Anguish: *Ammonium mur.* **(due to grief, desires to cry but can not cry, melancholy, apprehensive)** *Arnica* **(trauma of grief, after mental strain or shock or sudden loss of finance or human, indifferent, nervous, wants to be alone)** *Arsenic alb.* **(great anguish, restlessness, exhaustion by slightest exertion)** *Cocculus* **(profound sadness, absorbed in reveries)** *Ignitia* **(grief after shock and disappointment, sighs and shocks, joy and sorrow alternating, hysterical person),** *Phosphoric acid* **(apathetic, indifferent as a result of grief and mental shock, settled despair).**

Ankles (weak): *Cal. phos., Cal. iod., Cal. carb., Phos., Sulph., Thuja, Nat. carb.*

Ankles: *Ammon. carb.* **(tearing pain in ankles, in bones of feet)** *Agr. met.* **(ankles swollen, legs weak and trembling)** *Ledum pal.* **(gouty pain, ankles sweat, sole painful).**

Anorexia nervosa: *Carbo. veg.* **(appetite lost, it should be taken over a long period)** *Ipecac* **(loathing of food, persistent sensation of vomiting)** *Nux vom* **(finds fault in others and irritable, women with irregular menstruation or dysmenorrhoea with pain in sacrum).**

Anus (constricted): *Nux vom., Plumb., Bella., Graph., Nitric acid.*

Anus (fissured and sore): *Graph., Nit. acid, Aesculus, Kali hydroiod, Paeonia.*

Anus (fistula): *Silicea, Caust., Graph., Nitric acid, Sulph., Calc. carb., Nitric acid.*

Anus (itching of from worms): *Cina, Ign., Teucar.*

Anus (itching of): *Sulph., Nitric acid, Ignitia, Thuja, Ars, Ambra.*

Anus (pain in): Aesculus h.

Anus (prolapsed): *Podoph.* **(with squirreling diarrhoea)** *Ruta, Nux vom.* **(with constipation)** *Graphites* **(with constipation and piles),** *Aloe* **(with piles and great irritation),** *Lyco., Ign.* **(in children).**

Anxiety (effects of): *Ign., Phosphoric acid, Anac., China, Acon., Gels., Nux vom.*

Aortic incompetence: *Arsenic iod.* **(inflammation of aorta, senile heart, fatty degeneration)** *Aurum mur.* **(high blood pressure, arterio sclerosis).**

Aortic valve stenosis: *Arsenic iod.* **(senile heart, myocarditis, fatty degeneration, slow pulse, heart palpitates, breathlessness on climbing stairs),** *Aspidosperma* **(shortness of breath, thrombosis of pulmonary artery)** *Aurum met.* **(hardening of walls of the heart, angina pectoris, rheumatism pain wanders from joints and gouts).**

Apathae: *Merc., Borax, Kali chloride, Ant. tar.* **(with vomiting of milk after**

nursing) *Ars. alb.* (ulcerous) *Sulphuric acid* (in adults).

Apathies due to, cannot suck the mother's breast: *Ars. alb., Borax.*

Aphonia (chronic): *Phos., Carbo veg., Kali bich., Heper sulph.* (wheezing).

Aphonia (from over use of the voice): *Caust., Kali bich., Phos., Arn., Baryta carb.*

Aphonia: *Caust., Kali hydr iod* (syphilitic) *Phyto.* (complete or partial loss of voice), *Acon., Bella., Merc., Glonine, Carbo veg.* (Catarrhal) *Ant. tar.* (from cold with bronchial rales) *Ign., Nux vom.* (nervous and hysterical).

Apoplexy (fate of): *Acon.* (full, quick strong pulse), *Bella,* (great redness of the face and convulsive movements). *Opi.* (bloated, dusky red face, stupor and stator), *Phos., Cocculus, Rhus., Lyc., Arnica* (after effects).

Apoplexy: *Aconite* (pupils dilated fixed look and great difficulty in swallowing) *Arnica* (sighing, muttering and involuntary discharge of faeces and urine) *Belladona* (visible throbbing of carotid and temporal arteries, mouth drawn to one side, difficult or impossible digitations, loss of sight, smell and speech) *Cocculus* (head and face hot, feet cold, stupid feeling in the head and vertigo, paralysis of lower limbs) *Hyoscyamus* (sudden falling down with shriek twitching and jerking of body muscles) *Lachesis* (ailment of left side, mouth drawn to left side, cannot bear anything to touch his neck) *Nux vomica* (paralysis of the lower jaw and often of lower extremities which becomes cold) *Opium* (slow pulse, respiration labored, snoring and rattling, convulsive motions of the extremities or titanic stiffness of the whole body) *Glonine* (throbbing headache in temples and full sensation), *Amyl nit., Nux vom., Gel., Aster rubins.*

Appendicitis: *Bella., Merc. corr., Lach., Ars alb., Bryo., Crot. h., Iris tenex* (pain in appendix region after the attack of appendicitis).

Appetite (deprived): *Ars., China, Cal. Carb., Ferrum met., Nux vom., Acid nit.*

Appetite (excessive): *Cim.* (from worms) *Iod., China, Acid phos.* (after illness), *Merc., Silicea, Cal. carb., Gels., Ignitia.*

Appetite (lost or deficient): *China, Ferrum., Macrot., Acid phos., Nux vom., Ars., Merc., Puls., Uran. nit.*

Appetite (morbid): *China* (insatiable hunger especially during the night, great thirst, yet drinks little at a time) *Cina* (caused generally from trouble from worms, hunger soon after meal, urine turns milky after short time) *Silicea* (patient hungry but no appetite, constipation) *Staphysagria* (ravenous hunger, even when stomach is full).

Appetite (variable): *Cin., China, Iod., Cal. carb.*

Arrogant: *Platina* (haughty, proudly, contempt to others, indulges in self exhaustion).

Arterial thrombosis: *Apis* (thrombosis of middle or end of the thigh, feeling of string all along the inner side of the thigh) *Bothrops* (thrombosis in an artery of the heart, skin swollen, livid and cold with hemorrhagic infiltration) *Lachesis* (thrombosis with high blood pressure, ailment aggravates aduring sleep, worse on left side, pressure and constriction).

Arteries (disease of): *Baryta carb., Phos., Lyco.*

Arterio sclerosis (Atheroma): *Arnica* (cerebral arterial sclerosis, vertigo) *Bothrops* (sudden onset of excruciating pain in affected limb, the limb goes cold and turns pale) *Crataegus* (fatty, degeneration of the walls of the arteries, dyspnoea on exertion, blueness of finger and toes) *Baryta mur* (disease of the lungs, senile asthma) *Glonine* (disease of the brain, surging of blood to heart and head, pulsating pain, confusion and dizziness, fainting spell on exertion, limbs go numb) *Opium* (loss of consciousness) *Spigelia* (angina pectoris, neuralgia of arms, stitching pain, palpitation, dysponoea, chill in the affected parts).

Ascites: *Apocy, Apis., Ars., Eup. pur., Nux vom., China, Lyco., Crot. tig.* (from cirrhosis of the liver).

Asthama-bronchial: *Heper sulph.* (after suppressed eruptions, wheezing, rattling, suffocative during attack cannot lie down) *Hypericum perf.* (from foggy weather) *Ipecac.* (acute) *Arsenic alb* (between 1 to 3 AM) *Kali carb* (between 2 and 4 AM during attack sits with head low) *Ipecac.* (of children with rattling chest and vomiting) *Arsenic alb.* (with restlessness and difficulty in breathing) *Ferrum met.* (better by walking slowly worse after mid night) *Aralia racemosa* (after first sleep, loud wheezing, worse in the evening or night) *Thuja* (aggravated from vaccination or infection) *Lachesis* (aggravates before or after the break of the sleep) *Silicea* (aggravates during full moon or sudden change of weather) *Nux vom.* (aggravates from dyspepsia and food irregularities) *Nat. sulph.* (aggravates in cold wet weather, monsoon or near lake holds his chest with hand during coughing) *Heper sulph.* (aggravates in dry cold season but better in wet season) *Leuticum* (aggravates in summer at high attitude) *Kali carb.* (aggravates in summer or at high attitude) *Baryta carb.* (associated with high blood pressure) *Yerba santa Q* (associated with suffocation and pressure on chest) *Mag. mur.* (at sea shore or excessive eating of the salt) *Zinc met.* (cannot expel the phlegm and move the legs unconsciously) *Sambucus nigra* (attack comes suddenly in the night, turns blue, relief from profuse flow of the urine) *Ammon. carb.* (during attack desires for cool breeze) *Graphites* (better by eating) *Psoranium* (better by lying and keeping the hands open away from body) *Medorrhinum* (better lying on abdomen side and during wet weather) *Nat. sulph.* (better in dry cold weather, aggravation in wet weather) *Aurum met.* (better by cold) Causticum (better in monsoon season) *Atim. tart.* (better by sitting, cannot expel out the cough and lie down) *Nux vom.* (due to excessive eating) *Sulphuric acid* (due to pollution) *Aralia. r.* (during attack wants to sleep by keeping the head on hands) *Pulsatilla* (children allergic to rich food and women who have irregular menses) *Ambra grisea* (on attempting coition) *Spongia. t.* (severe dryness of respiratory passage, dyspnoea, better by bending forward) *Syphilinum* (attack starts immediately in night and ends early morning) *Zincum met.* (better by expectorant) *Ipecac.* (attack with constriction in chest, wheezing, suffocation and dysponea) *Carbo veg.* (during attack wants to be near to the fan), *Sulphur iod.* (with history of skin ailments) *Medorrhinum* (better by lying on knee chest position) *Hippozaenium* (suffocation with excessive secretion in old person) *Blatta orientalis* (associated with bronchitis) *Lycopodium* (attack comes in the evening) *Coffea* (attack comes in the morning) *Pathos foetidus* (aggravates from dust) *Guaiacum* (due to dust which subsides after passing stool) *Asafoetida* (excited by full meal) *Cannabis sativa* (can only breathe by standing up) *Sangunaria can.* (with dryness and burning in larynx, chest, sole and palm) *Kali mur.* (with gastric symptoms) *Lobelia inf.* (during attack excessive salivation associated with nausea and vomiting) *Chinunum ars.* (attack comes periodically with great prostration) *Kali sulph.* (with yellow expectoration).

Asthama-Cardic: *Aconite* (with palpitation and anxiety, irrational fear, numbness and tingling in fingers), *Aspidoderma Q* (breathlessness during exertion, stimulates the respiratory centre by absorbing oxygen in the blood) *Baryuta carb.* (with blood pressure, pulse full and hard) *Baryta mur.* (worse by every change of weather, cough suffocating and unable to take it out, high blood pressure in old person) *Digitalis* (weak heart, constant desire to breathe deeply, sensation as if heart will stop beating, pulse quickened by least motion) *Pyrogenium* (from septic condition) *Naja* (dysponea, attack begins with coryza and constriction in throat, better by sitting position).

Asthma (Chronic): *Ars., Sulph., Plumbum, Nux vom., Kali Iod., Thuja.*

Asthma (of children): *Sambucus* (profuse perspiration), *Ipecac.* (retching or sickness) *Ant. tar., Ars.*

Asthma (paroxysm of): *Aco.* (arterial excitement or from cold) *Ver. vir.* (laboured breathing, with cold sweat on the face) *Ipecac.* (spasmodic with retching) *Bella* (nightly spasm) *Phos., Cup. acet., Acid hydrocynic, Lob., Nux vom., Ars., Thuja, Nat. sulph.*

Asthma in, feels better by bending in front position: *Ars. alb.*

Asthma in, feels better on lying down: *Psoranium*

Asthma: *Arsenicum* (attacks of suffocation, especially at night cannot lie down for fear of sueffocation) *Ipecac.* (spasmodic asthma, with violent contraction in the throat and chest, rattling noise in the bronchial tube during inspiration) *Phosphorus* (complete loss of voice, sensation of weakness and emptiness in the abdomen). *Ipecac., Ars., Gels., Plumb., Cact., Lobilia, Cup. acetate., Nux vom., Carbo veg.* (with dyspepsia, flatulence etc) *Nat Sulph* (with diarrhoea).

Atrial fibrillation (irregular beating of heart): *Crataegus ox.* (irregularity of heart weak, extreme weakness, feeble and irregular heart action, breathlessness on least exertion, it be given in mother tincture, 15 drops dose four times a day) *Digitalis* (dilated heart, tired, irregular slow and feeble pulse, dropsy of parts).

Atrophy (General): *Ars., Znic, Iod., Cal. carb., Silicea, Phos., Sulphur.*

Atrophy of the optic nerve: *Nux vom., Argentum nit., Arsen., Veratrum vir.* (as per symptoms of the remedy).

Aversion (frigidity): *Berberis vulgaris* (desire diminished, cutting pain during intercourse, vagina tender and constricted, scanty menses) *Graphites* (aversion to coitus, constipation with late menses) *Ignitia* (sexual frigidity, women emotional and moody) *Onosmodium* (sexual desire completely lost, uterine pain early and prolonged menses, weak and tired, muscular prostation).

Aversion from fatty items: *Sulphur, Ars., Carbo veg., Petrolium, Heper.*

Aversion from fish eating: *Nat. mur. and sulphur.*

Aversion: *Arsenic alb* (cannot bear the sight of food, restlessness) *Carbo veg.* (aversion to fats, meat, etc. such foods distresses) *Nat. carb* (aversion to milk) *Pulsatilla* (aversion to fatty warm food and drinks) *Sulphur* (milk disagrees) *Berberis vulgaris* (desire diminished in women, vagina tender, scanty menses) *Ignitia* (sexual frigidity in hysterical women, who are emotional and moody) *Onosmodium* (sexual desire completely diminished, muscular prostration) *Graphites* (aversion to coition in man, early or no ejaculation) *Sepia* (aversion from husband and children in women) *Picric acid* (aversion from near relations) *Nat. mur.* (aversion from eating bread) *Alumina* (aversion from eating potatoes) *Puls* (aversion from marrying young) *Flouric acid* (aversion from wife and children in males) *Nat. phos.* (aversion from open air, bathing and company) *Adrenalinum* (aversion from mental work).

Awakening after, no freshness feelings: *Bryo., Conium, Heper., Mag. carb., Opium, Sulph.*

Awkward: *Apis* (drops things easily, apathetic) *Bovista* (things fall from hands)

B

Back (pain in): *Cimic* (Crack in the back), *Macrotin.*, *Ant. tar.*, *Aco.*, *Canth.*, *Terebintha* (with disease of kidney), *Ham.*, *Acon.*, *Nux*, *Aescul.* (from piles).

Back (aching of): *Arnica* (from over exertion), *Rhus*, *Bryo.*, *Nux vom.*, *Gels.*

Back (weakness of): *Silicea*, *Rhus.*, *Phos.*, *Ign.*, *China* (from nervous exhaustion)

Back: *Bell.* (back aches as if it would break) *Graph.*, *Phos.* (back aches as if broken) *Merc. vivus.* (bruised pain in the small of the back especially when sitting) *Graph* (bruised pain in the small of the back especially when touching the part) *Merc. vivus.* (cold clammy sweats on the thigh and legs at night) *Merc.*, *Nux.*, *Phos.* (bruised in the back worse from pressure and contact) *Rhus tox.* (Pain in the small of the back as if bruised, relieved by lying on something hard or by motion) *Rhus tox.* (pain between the shoulder when swallowing) *Cal. c.*, *Puls.*, *Silicea* (swelling and curvature of the vertebrae) *Sulphur* (sensation as if one vertebrae glided over the other).

Backache aggravates from rest and first movement: *Rhus tox.*, *Lac can.*

Backache, better by movement: *Cobalt.*, *Puls.*, *Rhus tox.*, *Zincum.*

Backache/Lumbage: *Cocculus ind.* (at small point of the back, hardly stand or walk, thigh ache as if pounded) *Berberis vul.* (pain both from sitting and standing) *Cobalt* (due to loss of vital fluid, worse from sitting better by walking) *Guaicum* (with stiffness, worse from warmth and motion) *Kali mur.* (better from lying) *Staphysagaria* (worse in bed at night and morning and also before rising from bed) *Aesculus h.* (constant dull pain at sacrum and hips, worse from walking) *Dulcumara* (due to exposure to cold) *Terebentha* (due to kidney and urinary trouble) *Nux vom.* (from sexual abuse, has to sit to turn in the bed) *Helonias d.* (after miscarriage) *Kali carb.* (with sweating or weakness, feels tired while walking or every time after taking food) *Medorrhinum* (pain between scapulae whole spine is sore to touch) *Viscum album* (from chill) *Colocynth* (with much muscular spasm and pain with least movement) *Ova tosta* (due to leucorrhoea feels as if back is broken in two parts) *Varolinum* (severe and painful) *Zincum met.* (better from emission) *Rhus tox.* (stiffness more on sitting or lying better by motion or lying on hard bed) *Ruta* (better on lying on the back) *Salix nigra* (cannot walk properly) *Ustilago* (extending to extreme end of the spine) *Symphytum* (worse from physical labour) *Carboneum sulph.* (worse getting up in morning and from walking) *Malandrinum* (pain severe in the sacral region) *Acetic acid* (better on lying on abdomen) *Agaricus* (pain in lumbar region with twitching of cervical muscles) *Ammonium mur.* (pain as if tightened in a vice when sitting) *Antim. tar.* (pain violent in sacra lumbar region), *Arnica* (injury to the back or spine) *Boryonia* (with pain and stiffness worse from movement) *Oxalic acid* (pain radiates to both kidneys and from there goes to legs, numbness and extremities) *Lac. con.* (across supra sacral region, extending to right sciatic nerve, worse by motion and first motion) *Variolinum* (with uterine hemorrhage) *Sepia* (worse from kneeling).

Bad effects of fear: *Aco., Ignitia, Lyco., Nat. mur., Opium, Phos., Puls., Silicea.*

Bad taste in the mouth: *Bryonia, Calcarea carb., Merc. vivus* (bitter taste in the morning) *Bella., China, Ferrum,* Pulsatilla (sweet taste) *Ars., Cal. carb., China, Nux vom., Phos., Acid sulph.* (sour taste) *Ars., Carb veg., Nux vom., Phos acid* (salty taste) *Arn, Cham, Merc v., Puls.* (putrid taste) *Sabina, Silicea* (greasy oily taste) *Bryo., China, Puls., Staph., Sulph.* (insipid taste) *Bella., Canth., Heper., Lyco., Phos., Verat.* (loss of taste) *Bryo., Calo., Heper Sulph.* (solid food taste bitter) *Bryo., China., Puls.* (all food and drinks taste bitter) *Lyco., Nux vom.* (all foods taste sour) *Ars., Bell., China, Sulph.* (all foods taste salty).

Balanitis (inflammation of the glands and lining of the prepuce with mucous purulent discharge): *Merc. cor., Calendula* (externally).

Barber's itch: *Graphites* (moist eczema around mouth and chin, itching and pimples) *Sulphur iod.* (weeping eczema, pus in hair follicles) *Rhus tox.* (skin red, swollen with intense itching).

Bashful: *Ambra grisea* (extremely nervous shy, hyper sensitive, timid) *Baryta carb.* (aversion to stranger, bashful) *Pulsatilla* (timid, gentle, mild, yielding disposition, highly emotional, thirst less).

Bathing causes illness: *Antim crud., Bellis., Cal. carb., Causticum, Rhus tox., Sepia, Sulph.*

Bed sores: *Bapt., Nux mosh., Arnica, Muratic acid, Pyrogenum.*

Bed wetting: *Belladona* (all of a sudden gets up from sleep and passes urine) *Causticum* (bed wetting in first sleep especially during winter, during summer ailment better) *Sepia* (during first sleep bed wetting particularly during winter season, better during summer, suits to thin weak young girls) *Ferrum phos* (in day time urine passes during coughing) *Plantago* (urine passes unconsciously during night) *Rhus aromatica* (diabetic patient passes urine unconsciously or urine passes in drops) *Kreosote* (during first part of the night, child cannot wake due to deep sleep, offensive odour) *Benzore acid* (foul smell cloth stain colour do not go, easily) *Causticum* (during first sleep, worse in dry clear weather) *Cina* (due to worms) *Sulphur* (in boys) *Kali phos.* (in grown up children urine dark yellow, itching in urinary tract) *Sepia* (in first phase of night by thin girls) *Ferrum met.* (more frequent in day time but also in the night) *Chloral* (child slept after urination and no liquid has been given to drink even then wets the bed in last spell of the night) *Ferrum phos.* (due to weakness of urinary muscles).

Before eyes feeling of opaque curtain: *Baryta carb., Cal. carb., Phos., Silicea, Baryta iod.*

Believe that he cannot be cured: *Ars. alb., Cal. carb., Psoranium.*

Bell's paralysis: *Aconite* (sudden attack of paralysis by exposure to dry cold wind, suppressed perspiration) *Cadium sulphate* (facial paralysis more on left side, distortion of mouth, swallowing difficult) *Causticum* (paralysis of face of right side, pain in facial bone, difficulty in opening the mouth) *Gelsemium* (facial muscles contracted around the mouth, lower jaw drooping, eye do not close) *Opium* (spasmodic facial twisting particularly the corners of mouth, distorted facial muscles).

Better by lying or rest: *Lyco., Nat. mur, Sulphur.*

Better by pressure: *Apis, Argn. nit., Bryonia, Lach., Mag. phos., Nat. mu., Puls., Sulphur.*

Better by sleeping on painful side: *Ambra gracia, Amm. carb., Borax, Bryo., Cal.carb., Colocynth, Puls.*

Better by warmth of the bed: *Bella., Graph., Heper, Psoranium, Sanicula, Silicea.*

Better from coffee drinking: *Colchicum.*

Bewildered: *Agaricus lamberti* (mental confusion and apathy, great depression, absent minded).

Bile stone pain: *Bella., Berberis vul., Cal. carb., Carduas mar., China, Cholesterinum 3X, Colocynth, Ipecac., Lyco., Manganum.*

Bilious colic: *Bryonia* (bitter bilious vomiting, particularly after eating and drinking, stool dry) *Chamomilla* (bitter bilious vomiting, patient very irritable) *Colocynth* (bitter taste, constrictive pain in the abdomen as if the intestine were squeezed between stones, compelling one to bend double, or due to abuse of opium) *Ipecac.* (constant and continual sick feeling in the stomach) *Nux vomica* (region of stomach very sensitive to pressure, gulping up bitter sour fluids, vomiting sour smelling and sour tasting mucous).

Bilious or gastric fever: *Aconite* (better taste of everything except water bitter bilious vomiting, pressure in the region of stomach) *Bryonia* (giddiness, nausea and faintness on rising up, fullness in the head, all foods and drinks taste bitter, vomiting immediately after eating, constipation, exceedingly irritable) *Chamomilla* (warm sweat about the head, bitter bilious vomiting, stools

green) *Mercurius* (fetid breath, bitter, sour putrid or sweet taste of the mouth, stomach sore to touch, diarrhoea, stools dark green frothy or yellow like sulphur) *Nux vomica* (irritable, bitter or sour taste and eructation, habitual constipation of large, difficult stools) *Pulsatilla* (beating pain in the head, worse in the evening, putrid taste, vomiting of mucus, nightly diarrhoea, stools watery or green like bile, fever induced from eating greasy rich food).

Biliousness (attack of): *Bryo., Puls.* (from indigestible food vomiting of bile and mucus): *Acon.* (from cold or excitement) *Cham.* (from worry or passion: *Veratrum alb., Iris vers.* (Sick headache with vomiting or diarrhea) *Nux vom.* (from stimulants, over eating etc. with constipation). : *Lept., Nux vom., Merc., Bryo., Mag. mur., Podo., Heper sulph., Ipecac., Iris vers.*

Black spots at different parts of the body: *Ars. alb., Cuprum, Merc., Opium, Secale cor., Veratrum alb.*

Bladder (catarrhal inflammation of): *Acon., Canth.* (from cold), *Dulc., Uva* (from damp), *Cannabis, Sat., Kali Iod., Chim.* (with mud, mucous or aluminous charge) *Eup. pur., Ammo mur., Ant crud., Puls., Terebinth, Zinc, Sulph.*

Bladder (irritability of): *Fer. met.*, (diurnal), *Bell., Canth., Sulph.* (nocturnal), *Nux vom.* (with spasm and in gouty person) *Lyco.* (with gavels) *Ac. Benzoic* (strong oudor, high coloured urine).

Bladder (paralysis of): *Cann. sat., Bella., Baryta carb., Acon., Nux vom.*

Bladder: *Taraxaccum* (cancer of bladder).

Bleeding/Haemorrhage Injury due to: *Arnica* (any injury external or internal)

Calendula Q (for external application for cuts, laceration and bruises) *Nitric acid* (wounds which do not heel).

Bleeding excessive: *Carbo veg.*, *Ferrum*, *Crotalus*, *Phos.*, *Sulph. acid.*

Bleeding of the nose (Epis taxis): *Aconite* (blood bright red) *Arnica* (after external injury) *Bryonia* (bleeding of nose at the approach of menses) *Nux vomica* (habitual drunkards) *Phosphorus* (profuse bleeding, frequently recurring attacks especially during stool).

Bleeding: *China* (bleeding from any orifices of the body, profuse flow, symptoms of collapse patient wants to be fanned) *Bell.* (blood bright red, frequent and profuse coagulates easily, feeling hot to the part it flows) *Ipecac.* (bright red blood), *Aconite* (continuous flow of blood with fever, anxiety and restlessness) *Carbo veg.* (continuous dark passive hemorrhage, patient wants to be fanned) *Secale cor.* (passive blood flow with tingling limbs) *Cyclamen* (profuse hemorrhage with dizziness and obscure vision) *Phosphorus* (for hemorrhage diathesis) *Hamma.* (passive venous bleeding with sere and bruise feeling), *Sabina* (profuse red worse from motion and pain in legs) *Millifolium* (profuse bright red without pain).

Blepharitis: *Graphites* (scrofulous subject with eczematous eruptions, moist, fissured and bleed easily) *Merc. sol.* (upper lids red swollen ulcerated, sensitive to heat or cold and touch) *Heper sulph.* (lids inflamed, with throbbing aching pain, ameliorated by warmth) *Pulsatilla* (discharge profuse and bland causing agglutination, itching burning, aggravated in the evening in warm room better by cold) *Calcarea carb.* (lids red swollen, and indurate, great itching worse in damp weather) *Calcarea iod.* (unhealthy children with enlargement of glands especially of the tonsils) *Rhus tox.* (upper lid swell up and profuse lachrymation, worse at night, cold damp weather) *Mezereum* (eczema of lids, thick hard scabs pus exudes on pressure) *Antimonium crud.* (pustules on the celery margins) *Arsenicum* (lids thick, red excoriated by the burning, acrid lachrymation, burning pain) *Sulphur* (pains sticking, itching, aversion to eye wash) *Psorinum* (strumous diathesis, offensive discharge from eyes) *Aconite* (lids red and swollen, tight feeling in them, dryness and burning) *Alumina* (dryness in lids in evening, itching excoriation at the acanthi) *Apis mel.* (puffiness of the lids especially upper lid, stitching pain) *Argentum nit.* (lids sore, very red and swollen, profuse discharge, firm agglutination in the morning relieved by cold application) *Causticum* (feeling of sand in the eye) *Cinnabaris* (dull pain over or around the eye) *Euphrasia* (lids swollen red, lachrymation acrid and burning) *Mercurius cor.* (pain severe, lachrymation profuse and acrid, secretion thin on excoriating) *Nux vom.* (worse in the evening associated with gastric problem) *Sepia* (pustules on lid margins, worse morning and evening) *Pulsatilla* (before formation of pus associated with gastric derangement or acne on face) *Heper sulph.* (after pus formation, throbbing pain, reat sensitiveness to touch better by warmth) *Rhus tox.* (lid swollen and lachrymation) *Graphites* (useful in recurrence sties) *Staphisagaria* (recurrence of sty especially in lower lid leave hard nodules in the lid) *Sulphur* (cannot bear to wash the eyes, restless feverish in the night) *Silicea* (sharp pain, better by warmth).

Blepharospasm (spasmodic closure of the lids): *Agaricus* (twitching of the lids, relieved during sleep or by washing with cold water) Other remedies are: *Alumina, Cicuta, Ignitia, Nux vom. . Physostigma, Puls as per symptoms.*

Blindness: *Bothrops* (day blindness due to hemorrhage into retina or conjunctiva hemorrhage) *Carbo. sulph.* (colour blindness) *China* (night blindness due to anaemia).

Blisters of eyes: *Euphrasia* (small blisters on cornea)

Blocking of nose of children: *Heper., Nux., Sambucus, Sticta, Ammon. carb., Lyco.*

Blocking of tear of eyes duct (continuously watering with): *Ambrosia* (copious flow with intolerable itching of the eye lids) *Euphrasia* (excoriating discharge from the eyes, continuously) *Pulsatilla* (inflamed lids, glued together, bland yellow thick dis-charge).

Blood in seminal discharge: *Canth., Led. pal., Merc., Petro., Sarsaparilla.*

Blood pressure (high): *Lachesis* (at the climacteric or otherwise, palpitation and irregular heart beating, oppressive sensation, suffocating attack, inability to lie down) *Lycopus virg.* (hyper-tension, tumultuous and forcible heart action, rheumatoid pain, cardiac asthma) *Plumbum met.* (with arterio sclerosis, pulse soft and small) *Sangunaria* (at the time of climacteric, flashes of heat, circumscribed redness of the cheeks, distention of temporal veins, headache in the occipital) *Veratrum viridi* (induces fall of both systolic and diastolic blood pressure, congestion of head, giddiness, blood shot eyes and bloated face) *Aurum met.* (sensation as if heart will stop beating for two or three second, palpitation, pulse feeble, rapid and irregular, alveolar lesion of arterio sclerotic nature, disgust for life, thoughts of suicide) *Glonine* (heat on the head) *Zincum met.* (forehead cool and base of brain hot) *Crataegus oxy.* (*Q*) (with disturb sleep) *Aurum muriticum natronatum* (with visible beating of caryatid and temporal arteries) *Sparitum scoparium* (to reduce and to increase the strength of heart).

Blood pressure (low): *Cactus* (pulse feeble, irregular quick, vertigo, flatulence face blue) *Carbo veg.* (imperfect oxygenation, craving for air, body icy cold) *China* (due to exhausting discharge from body, severe debility) *Crataegus Q* (heart dilated, breathlessness on least exertion) *Physostigma* (feeble pulse, palpitation, heart beat felt in chest), *Viscum alb.* (pulse small and weak, dyspnea lying on left side, weight and oppression of the heart) *Gelsemium* (sensation as if it is necessary to keep in motion or else the hearts action would cease, pulse soft and slow).

Bloody dysentery during summer season: *Aco., Merc., Ipecac.*

Bloody dysentery during winter season: *Ipecac., Merc., Dulcamra.*

Blotches: *Ant. crud., Graph., Lyco., Clemitis, Ars., Apis.*

Body tightness and restlessness: *Baptisia; Arnica; China; Phyto., Rhus tox, Ruta, Staph., Nux mosch.* (as per symptoms)

Boils (tendency to): *Sulphur, Heper sulph., Kali bromide, China, Sulph.*

Boils and itching on the parts where hairs are present: *Rhus tox., Baptisia, Coffea, Puls., Antim. crud.*

Boils/ulcer in mouth of children: *Borax* (blisters, ulcers on tongue) *Merc. sol.* (saliva flows copiously) *Nitric acid* (blisters, ulcers in the mouth, bleed easily).

Boils: *Aconite* **(the parts burn as if from hot coal)** *Arnica* **(bloody boils of dark colour, pain as if from bruise)** *Belladona* **(the parts have a hot, dry sensation, swelling of the glands under the arms and in the groups)** *Mercurius* **(matures slowly, profuse sweating without relief)** *Insulin* **(boils with enlarged liver)** *Cadmium sulph* **(red particularly on nose)** *Lachesis* **(red without opening, within tense pain)** *Secale cor.* **(small in crops with green fetid pus)** *Radium bromide* **(small on face, red swollen, burning and itching)** *Merc. sol.* **(with pus formation)** *Arnica* **(come one after another, small, painful and sore)** *Calcarea pic.* **(reoccurring)** *Tuberculinum* **(small in crops, intensely painful)** *Sarsaparilla* **(small painful with green content)** *Cuprum ars.* **(on scrotum associated with perspiration)** *Nat. sulph.* **(wet on whole body)** *Kali phos.* **(with foul smell)** *Calcarea picrata* **(in ear or nose)** *Gun powder* **(reoccurrence)** *Heper sulph.* **(very painful and sensitive to touch)** *Alumina* **(after itching, skin dry with cracks)** *Psorinum* **(appear in every winter and disappear in summer)** *Dulcamara* **(during menses)** *Belladona* **(develop all of a sudden, hard, intense burning and pain)** *Echinacea Q* **(lot of pus with fever)** *Silicea* **(with pus and take time to cure)** *Carbolic acid* **(watery, intense itching feels better on scratch-ing but later burning develops).**

Bone (contusion): *Ruta.*

Bone (exortosis): *Aur mur., Merc. Iod., Silicea.*

Bone (necrosis): *Merc. Prot. iod., Ars., Iod., Silicea, Acid flour, Symphytum, Phos., Ars., Asaf.*

Bone (nodes): *Sil., Kali Iod., Kali bich.* **(cranial)** *Merc. cor.,* **(tibia)** *Staph., Rhus* **(soft nodes),** *Aurum mur.* **(hard nodes).**

Bone (pain in): *Aur., Asaf., Merc., Ruta, Nitric acid, Fluoric acid., Phosphoric acid., Staph., Phyto., Eupatorium perf.*

Bone (porosities): *Silicea, Aur. mur., Merc., Kali iod.*

Bone (softening of): *Cali carb., Sili., Acid phos., Cal. phos., Phos., Merc., Sulph.*

Bowels: *Carbo veg* **(burning and flatulence in the upper part of the stomach)**

Brain (congestion of): *Bell., Apis., Opi., Gels.* **(cerebral depression)** *Glonine* **(cerebral exaltation),** *Ver. vir.,* **(children with gastric irritation),** *Acon., Nux vom., Bryo., Gels, Sulph* **(intermittent)** *Bacil* **(tubercular cases).**

Brain (concussion of): *Arn., Acon, Bella, Cicuta.*

Brain (meningitis): *Acon., Bell., Bry., Stram., Bacil* **(from tubercular deposit with convulsion)** *Cal. carb., Hell, Apis., Ver. vir., Gels, Sulph* **(mental excitement).**

Brain (softening of): *Merc., Bell., Bary. carb., Acid phos., Hypericum* **(pain and other nerve symptoms).**

Brain disorder: *Absinthium* **(epileptic seizures, nervous tremors with giddiness, delirium, hallucination, loss of consciousness, nervous excitement with sleeplessness, vertigo with tendency to fall backward.**

Brain fag: *Nux vom., Acid phos., Acid picric, Gels., Glonine, Strych., Phos., Cal. carb., Silicea, Anac., Staph., Zinc, Asar, Iris.*

Brain inflammation: *Aconite* **(high fever with hot and dry skin, great anxiety and fear of death, sleeplessness, restlessness, tossing from side to side)** *Belladona* **(red sparking of eyes, face red and blotted, furious delirium with desire to escape from bed, great intolerance to noise and light, startling and jumping during sleep)** *Bryonia* **(headache as if the skull was being pressed,**

delirious talks at night, wants to keep perfectly still as least motion makes him worse, sitting up in the bed causes nausea and fainting) *Hyoscymus* (white coated tongue, frothing at the mouth, staring distorted eyes, muttering with picking at the bed clothes) *Stromonium* (awakens with a shrinking look, grinding of the teeth, glistering eyes and staring look).

Branny tettr: *Ars., Graph, Lyco., Sulph.*

Breast (abscess of): *Bryo.* (earliest symptoms) *Bell.* (shining red and swollen), *Phos.* (during formation); *Silicea, Heper Sulph.* (torpidity or imperfect suppuration), *Phyto., Hydras.* (chronic tubular mastitis).

Breast (contusion of): *Conium.*

Breast (excoriation of): *Sulph., Hydras.*

Breast (tumor of): *Calc. Phos., Condurango, Conium, Lappa maj., Hydrastis, Aster rubens, Scrophularia.*

Breast: *Arsenic alb.* (severe burning and restlessness) *Asterias rubens* (acute lancinating pain, armpit gland swollen, hard and knotted) *Chimaphilla* (tumor painful, women have very large breast) *Carcinosin* (great pain an induration) *Phytolacca* (breast hard, painful and purple glands in armpit with retracted nipples) *Conium* (strong and hard tumor), *Carbo animalis* (darting and painful indurations in breast, great exhaustion) *Asterias rubens* (neuralgia of left breast and arm) *Bryonia* (hard, hot, pale and painful at menses) *Calcarea flour* (hard knots) *Carbo animalis* (painful indurations of right breast) *Chimaphila* (very large or painful tumor) *Chamomilla* (tender breast of infant) *Conium* (painful, wants to press to get relief) *Iodum* (dwindling of it) *Lac Can.* (swollen, painful before but better after menstruation) *Phytolacca* (inflammation hard, sore and sensitive to touch) *Sabal serrulata* (shriveled and undeveloped) *Silicea* (fistular ulcer type) *Medorrhinum* (and nipple are sore to touch) *Arsenic iod.* (lump painful and tender, nipple retracted) *Urtica urens Q* (milk to diminish) *Lac. defloratum* (milk to increase) *Phytolacca Q* (milk thick and stringy or thin mixed with blood) *Calcarea flour* (nodules stony and hard) *Phytolocca Q* (pain which extend up to back due to cold) *Calcarea iodata* (tumor nodular, freely moveable, painful when moving the arm, worse during menses) *Chimaphilla Q* (enlarged, out of proportion of the body) *Bryonia* (hard like stone hold it on movement to relieve from pain) *Lac. Con.* (inflamed, painful, hold when going up or down stairs) *Belladona* (reddish, painful during fever) *Sabal scrulata Q* (small do not develop properly) *Conium* (sore, painful during menses or lumps after contusion or bruises) *Silicea* (pain in it and uterus while feeding) *Carbo anamalis* (sensation of emptiness and sinking in the stomach while feeding) *Yohimbinum* (to increase quantity of milk in it) *Onosmodium Q* (if small to bring it in shape and size) *Urtica urens* (to increase milk) *Mammary 3X* (bring it to size and shape if small or enlarge or to increase the milk) *Bryo.* (stone like hardness of the breast which are hot, painful and not very red) *Bryo* (abscess of the breast) *Con* (indurations of mammas were painful just before menstruation) *Phyto.* (inflammation, swelling and suppuration of the breast).

Breast-painful and swollen, holds them while ascending the stairs: *Bryo., Lac.*

Breasts painful and feeling of wounds in them during menses: *Conium, Lac. can., Merc.*

Breath (fetid): *Merc., Carbo veg., Chin, Sulphur, Ant. crud., Aur.,* ***Acid*** *nitric, Aco., Acid carbol., Caps.*

Breathing (short and difficult): *Acon., Acid hydrocy., Ars,* **(tightness and debility), Ipecac. (wheezing dry and with nausea),** *Ant. tar.,* **(rattling-moist),** *Iod.,* **(emaciation),** *Ferr.,* **(anaemia),** *Heper sulph., Cup., Scill., Spong.*

Breathing difficulties on climbing at height: *Ars. alb., Coca.*

Breathing during rattling by elderly people: *Baryta carb., Senega, Baryta mur.*

Breathlessness and weakness while climbing stairs: *Cal. carb., Iodium.*

Bright's disease of kidney: *Aconite* **(dark scanty urine with stitches in the kidney caused by exposure to cold dry winds, nervous restlessness)** *Cantharis* **(constant desire to urinate but few drops at a time sometimes mixed with blood, the urine contains cylindrical casts and epithelial cells)** *Heper sulph.* **(sensation of throbbing in the region of the kidney, urine dark coloured or bloody)** *Apis mel.* **(scanty discharges of red urine, sometimes disease follows scarlet fever)** *Lycopodium* **(red sandy sediments in the urine, pain in the back before every urination relieved by urination)** *Ars., Phos., Canth., Merc., Phos., Kreas., Nux vom., Acid phos., Terebintha, Apis mel., Ferurm met.*

Bronchial catarrh (cold on the chest): *Bryo., Acon., Ars., Kali iod., Camphora, Kreos.*

Bronchitis (acute): *Acon., Ant tar.,* Kali *bich., Bryo, Ipecac, Phos.* **(cough, expectoration of strong nature).**

Bronchitis (chronic): *Ant. tar., Kali bich., Ars., Merc., Hyras., Phos., Scill., Stann., Senega, Sulph., Kali iod.* **(gouty bronchitis),** *Lobelia* **(obstinate bronchial cough with dipnoea).**

Bronchitis (in old person): *Ant. tar., Ammon. carb.* **(difficult expulsion of mucus),** *Con., Carb veg., Phos., Hydras., Kali bich., Senega.*

Bronchitis of children: *Aconite* **(feverishness and frontal headache)** *Bryonia* **(with little expectoration)** *Ipeeac.* **(wheezing and upper respiratory infection)** *Ant. tar.* **(rattling with mucus, cannot expel out)** *Kali bich.* **(ropy stringy mucus; difficult to take it out)** *Pulsatilla* **(with bland green mucus).**

Brow ague: *Sulph., Glon., Bella, Nux vom., Cheli., Ars., Thuja.*

Brown spots: *Lycopodium* **(on abdomen in chronic liver troubles with flatulence)** *Thuja* **(brown spots on nose and arms).**

Bruises and injury: *Conium* **(after bruises and injury to glands)**

Bubo: *Merc., Acid nit., Merc. bin. iod., Aurum mur., Phyto.*

Burning at fortaliae: *Cal. carb., Graph., Sulphur.*

Burning in soles during night, do not want to cover them: *Chamomilla,*

Burning like fire: *Apis., Ars. alb.*

Burning of eyes: *Allium cepa* **(smarting eyes with bland discharge nasal discharge acrid, sensitive to light, better open air)** *Arsenic alb.* **(acrid lachrymator, lids red ulcerated and granulated, swelling around eyes, photophobia, better by warmth)** *Merc.cor.* **(soreness of the eyes, lids edematous and excoriated, acrid discharge)** *Sulphur* **(ulceration of margins of lids, chronic ophthalmia, black floaters)** *Chalazion* **(swollen pockets on the eye lids)** *Staphysagaria* **(fatty deposits under the skin of the eye lids, forming heads on the outside)**

Burning sensation between both scapula and back: *Lyco., Phos.*

Burning sensation: *Arsenic album* **(burning aggravates during middle of night**

or day, better by warmth) *Sulphur* (burning in chronic ailments, burning in the soles or near heart or chest) *Phosphorus* (burning in back or stomach, may be in palms and arms, intense taking for cold drinks) *Aconite* (burning sensation before oedema, fever, restlessness and intense thirst) *Apis* (burning in oedema, no thirst during burning, biting pain, better by cold during burning) *Agaricus* (burning on skin from cold wind, better by warmth) *Cantharis* (burning while urination).

Burning sensations in all ailments if then: *Ars. alb., Phos., Sulph.*

Burning: *Cantharis* (and pain in burns) *Ars alb* (but better by warmth) Secale cor. (in feet) *Sulphur* (in sole and palm) *Picric acid* (in spinal cord due to mental fatigue) *Staphysagaria* (in urethera) (Canabis sativa (in urinary tract) *Berberis vul.* (in vagina) *Cantharis* (before and after urination) *Ars alb* (better by warmth) *Secale cor.* (in feet associated with cramps in calves does not wants to cover) *Sulphur* (in sole and palm) *Medorrhinum* (hand and feet wants to fan them) *Chamomilla* (soles at night, wants to take out from rag) *Plumbum met.* (of ulcer or gangrene) *Phosphorus* (with pain at small spot appears diagonally) *Aesculus h.* (with pain before and after passing stool) *Theridion* (below the lumbar region, cannot tolerate touch and noise) *Lycopodium* (sensation in between the shoulders) *Capsicum* (as if red pepper has been applied to the parts) *Kali phos* (below the shoulder blade, legs and fingers) *Oxalic acid* (in all parts of the body) *Lachnantes* (like fire in palms) *Rananculus b.* (at small spot) *Natrum phos.* (in spinal cord below the back) *Iris vers* (in whole alimentary canal, anus burns excessively) *Zinc met.* (in whole spinal cord) *Urtica urens Q* (external application of skin) *Allium cepa* (with smarting and bland discharge in eyes) *Merc. Cor.* (soreness of eyes) *Acetic acid* (burning pain in chest and stomach followed by coldness of skin and cold sweat on forehead) *Helonias* (constant burning in the region of kidneys) *Eupion* (in right ovary) *Hydrocotyle* (within vagina with severe itching) *Kreoosotum* (with swelling and itching between Libia) *Lycopodium* (of vagina during and after coition) *Terebintha* (intense burning of uterus region) *Electricity* (in feet up to the knees) *Colchicum* (in stomach and abdomen) *Magnetis poliombo* (from hand to feet) *Carbolicum acidum* (from mouth to stomach) *Theridon* (in liver region) *Malaria officinalis* (of hands and feet associated aching of hands and arms).

Burns and scalds (forms ulcers): *Kali bich., Sulph., Phos., Ars., Lach.*

Bursitis: *Arnica* (caused by injury) *Benzoic acid* (pain and swelling in knees, cracks on motion, tearing pain) *Cocculus* (inflammatory swelling of knees, intense pain) *Silicea* (pus is formed in the swelling, shooting pain) *Sticta* (house maid knee, caused by kneeling bursitis in elbow, heat and redness of joints).

Buzzing in the ear: *Belladona* (humming, roaring in the ear after scarlet fever) *China* (buzzing and lousing like a ringing or surging) *Carbo veg.* (caused by abuse of quinine) *Mercurius* (result of smallpox, patient perspire a lot) *Nux vomica* (result of a cold, worse in the morning) *Pulsatilla* (result of measles, worse towards evening).

C

Calcaneal spur: *Aranea diadema* **(pain in sole of the foot due to heel bone projection)** *Calcarea flour.* **(severe pain in the heel)** *Lycopodium* **(pain in the heel as if treading on pebble.**

Calculus (bilary): *Acid phos., Lyca, Berberis, Canth., Podophyllum., Dioscor.*

Calculus (spasm): *Nux vom., Dioscor., Gels, Aconite, Cham., Cal. carb., Ocimum can., Bella.*

Calculus (vesicle): *Lyco., Cann. sat., Canth., Merc.*

Callosities/corn: *Antim crud.* **(inflamed corns, large horny formation)** *Lycopodium* **(painful contracted)** *Sulphur* **(corns and callosities from pressure, formed by shoes)** *Thuja Q* **(corny skin, hard thick and insensitive.**

Calves (cramps) *Anacardium* **(as if paralyzed)** *Calcarea carb* **(knees cold)** *Cuprum ars.* **(better by standing)** *Cuprum* **(in calves, soles and palm also)** *Veratrum alb.* **(pain like a electric current)** *Conium* **(painful stiffness of calves, sudden loss of strength, muscular weakness, trembling).**

Can see only half portion of an article sometime of right side or sometime of left side: *Bella, Iris vers., Phosphorus, Spigellia.*

Cancer: *Ars. alb., Hydras.* **(of breast)** *Phos., Ornithogalum* **(of stomach),** *Thuja, Radium bromide, X' ray* **(epithelial),** *Symphytum* **(of bone);** *Ruta* **(of rectum),** *Condorango, Cicuta, Kreos., Aster rubens, Lobelia, Erimus, Hydrastis* **(of lips),** *Arnica* **(from injury).**

Cannot lie on painful side: *Aco., Ars. alb., Bella., Baryta carb., Hepar., Iodium, Kali carb., Nux mosch., Phos.*

Cannot tolerate sun heat: *Bryonia, Lach, Nat mur, Puls, Sulphur.*

Cannot tolerate the touch of someone: *Bryonia, Led Pal, Lyco, Nat mur, Sabina*

Cannot tolerate, light cloths on the waist: *Bovista, Cal. carb., Lachesis, Sulph.*

Carbuncle (Anthrax): *Apis mel* **(pains are stitching and burning, relieved by cold applications)** *Arsenic* **(burning in the parts, restlessness, extreme weakness, violent thirst, better in warm room and warm application) Belladona (bright redness of the parts, throbbing pain sleepy but cannot sleep)** *Carbo veg* **(has dark blackish appearance, great prostration, wants to be fanned)** *Lachesis* **(purplish colour, symptoms worse after sleep).** *Bell., Heper sulph.* **(at forming stage),** *Apis., Anthrac* **(much erysipelatoid swelling),** *Silicea* **(indolent)** *Ars., Lach.* **(severe or malignant).**

Caries (of nose): *Aurum met.* **(of nasal bones, of palate)** *Merc. sol.* **(nasal bone with swelling and pain).**

Caries, cavities dental: *Calcarea carb.* **(caries of teeth in fat children)** *Calcarea flour.* **(caries, necrosis and loss of enamel of teeth)** *Carbo veg.* **(teeth decay rapidly)** *Hekla lava* **(caries leading to facial neuralgia)** *Kreosotum* **(rapid decay of teeth)** *Merc. sol.* **(teeth loosen and decay)** *Staphysagaria* **(teeth black and crumbles).**

Cartilage damaged: *Aconite* (severe pain caused by sudden twist of the knee, joint inflammation, tendency of foot to bend) *Apis.* (swelling in knees with stinging pain) *Arnica* (due to injury) *Bryonia* (pain in knee, worse on movement, knee stiff and painful) *Casticum* (the knee is locked, does not strengthen fully tearing pain in knee joint).

Cataplexy: *Cann bis indica, Iod., Opi., Cup. act., Cic., Mosch.*

Cataract (medicines efficacious in arresting the progress of catract): *Causticum* (feeling as if there is sand in the eyes, pressure in the eyes, heaviness of the eye lids, burning, itching of the eyes, desire to keep them closed) *Idoform* (in senile catract, patches of flocculent masses in the cortex, rapidly progressing catract) *Sepia* (sharp pain in the eyes, heaviness of the lids, headaches worse morning and evening, perspire freely, useful in the catract of thin women) *Phosphorus* (colour before vision, black floating spots before the eyes, flashes of light) *Calcarea phos.* (headache especially of the right side pain around the right eye and tired feeling).

Cataract operation after eyes become red and with pus: *Rhus tox.*

Cataract: *Bella.* (from inflammation), *Cal. carb* (tubercular), *Sil., Coni., Euphr., Phos., Sulph., Dig., Bary. carb., Sanganaria* (for senile cataract).

Cellulitis orbitae (abscess or phlegm of the orbit): *Rhus tox.* (the lids are edematous swollen as well as the conjunctiva) *Heper sulph.* (after pus formation, lids swollen, sensitive to both touch and cold, throbbing pain) *Phytolacca* (eyes protruded, lids hard unyielding to touch) *Aconite* (heat and sensitiveness in around the eyes with fever) *Apis mel.* (lids edematous swollen with stinging and shooting pain, no thirst) *Lachesis* (black spot in the centre)

Cerebral palsy: *Agaricus* (palsy of upper and lower limbs from incipient softening of spinal cord, weakness all down the spine) *Arum sulph.* (paralysis agitates, constant nodding of head) *Bufo* (paralysis agitates, weak memory and extremities) *Causticum* (palsy of lips, of pharynx of vocal cords) Conium palsy after concussion of spine, palsy without spasm) *Hyosyamus* (epileptic attacks ending in deep sleep, spasms and convulsion) *Merc. sol.* (descending paralysis, upper extremities affected first, limbs rigid and immobile) *Plumbum* (multiple cerebra spinal meningitis tremors followed by paralysis).

Cerebra-spinal meningitis: *Arnica* (soreness in all the limbs as if bruised) *Belladona* (violent throbbing headache, dilated pupils with double vision) *Bryonia* (splitting headache worse from motion) Gelseminum (feels as if intoxicated, complete loss of muscular power) *Lycopodium* (fanlike motion of nostrils) *Opium* (very quick or very low pulse).

Cervical spondylosis: *Bryonia* (pain in the neck with stiffness also in the nape of the neck, worse on movement) *Chelidonium* (pain in nape, stiff neck, head drawn to left, fixed pain under inner and lower angle of right scapula) *Cicuta* (spasms and cramps in the muscles of nape of the neck) *Cimicifuga* (rheumatic pain in neck) *Belladona* (stiff neck, swelling of glands of neck) *Causticum* (stiffness and pain in the neck, muscles feel as if bound with ropes, can scarcely move his head, worst dry weather) *Dulcamara* (stiff neck from catching cold in damp and cold weather) *Lachenantes* (rheumatism of the neck, stiffness as if dis-located) *Strychininum* (cervical muscles rigid, sharp pain in neck, back stiff).

Cervicitis: *Hydrocotyle* (inflammation of the neck of the uterus, redness, ulceration of uterus, heat within vagina, intense itching) *Kreosotum* (ulcers on cervix which bleeds easily, fetid acrid discharge).

Chalazae (tarsal cyst): *Staphisagria* (induration of lids, resulting from sty or crops of small tarsal tumors) *Thuja* (chalazae appeArs like a condyloma) *Heper* (inflamed and sensitive to touch) *Zincum* (soreness and itching in the internal acanthi).

Chancre: *Merc., Nitric acid., Heper sulph., Kali iod., Phyto.*

Changeable mind: *Ignitia, Lyco., Nux mosh., Puls., Sarsaparilla, Zinc. met.*

Chapped nostrils: *Calend, also external application.*

Chest (aching, burning or weakness of): *Acon., Ars., Phos., Phos. acid, Sulph. Bryo.*

Chest (pain in): *Arn* (stitches in the side while walking), *Bryo., Canth* (pain catching the breath) *Phos* (slight wandering pain), *Acon.* (shooting and severe), *Puls., Sep., Cimic* (in inter-coastal rheumatism).

Chest (pleural effusion): *Bryo., Apis., Arn., Hep., Ars., Iod., Kali iod* (in the tubercular), *Dig., Apoc* (due to heart disease).

Chest (soreness): *Ars., Phos., Bryo., Hep. sulph., Sulph., Kali iod.*

Chest (tightness, oppression or weight): Ars., *Acon., Crot., Ign., Phos., Bryo., Cact., Ipecac., Sulphur, Camphora.*

Chest: Arnica (soreness in intercostals muscles after severe exertion, the ribs feel as if bruised) *Ars alb., Lach. Sulph* (sensation of coldness in the chest - *Cal. carb., Merc., Spong.* (burning) *Acon., Bell., Bryo Phos* (stitches in the chest when coughing or taking a deep breath) *Bryo, Aco., Bell* (quick anxious, difficult breathing caused by stitches in the chest aggravated by every movement) *Carbo veg.* (sensation of weakness in the chest) *Gels., Puls., Verat.* (sensation of constriction in the lower part of the chest) *Ign.* (oppression of the chest and breathing) *Ipecae.* (rattling in bronchial tube when breathing, the chest full of phlegm) *Calc. Puls., Sepia., Phos* (heaviness and fullness of the chest) *Rhus tox.* (stitches in the chest and in side of the chest, worse when at rest) *Lach., sulph., Sepia.* (feeling of heaviness in the chest).

Chicken pox: *Acon., Rhus, Bella.* (head symptoms), *Apis.* (excessive itching), *Canth., Ant. tar., Merc* (itching and inflammation) *Aconite* (fever with restlessness and anxiety) *Belladona* (congestion of the head, soreness of the throat, starting during sleep) *Pulsatilla* (catarrhal symptoms, watery eyes, tardy appearance of the eruption, diarrhea at night) *Atim tar* (child irritable, wants company) *Rhus tox* (severe itching) *Sulphur* (annoying rashness) *Variolinum* (a prophylatic).

Chilblain (inflamed): *Bell., Ver. vir., Rhus tox.*

Chilblain (tendency of formation): *Sulph., Cal. carb., Phos.*

Chilblain (ulcerated): *Ars., Petrol., Phos., Kreos., Nitric acid.*

Child bed fever (puerperal peritonits): *Arnica* (induced by external violence or operative manipulation during delivery, bed feels too hard) *Arsenic. alb.* (parts burn like fire, rapid prostration, craves for cold drinks) *Belladona* (great heat in the abdomen, which imparts burning sensation to the hand, intolerance to light and noise) *Bryonia* (Lucia suppressed with headache, cannot sit up from nausea and faintness).

Child weeps mostly in the night: *Nux.*, *Jalapa*, *Lac can.*, *Psoranium.*

Childish behaviour by elderly people: *Baryta carb.*, *Cicuta.*

Children dull minded: *Argent. nit.*, *Baryta carb.*, *Cal. phos.*, *Cal. carb.*, *Sulphur.*

Children wake up with screaming: *Apis.*, *Borax*, *Cina*, *Stromonium.*

Chill: *Cal. carb.* (chill at 2.00 AM, begins internally in the stomach region) *Camphor* (icy, coldness of the whole body, tongue cold, trembling) *China* (periodic chill at clear cut stages) *Gelsemium* (chill along spine in influenza, fever with shivering) *Merc. sol.* (creeping chilliness) *Natrum mur.* (periodic chill comes at 10.30 AM) *Pulsatilla* (chilliness even in the warm room with thirstlessness) *Veratrum album* (chill with extreme coldness and sweat).

Chilliness (constant): *China*, *Merc.*, *Sep.*

Chilliness and coldness: *Camphor.*, *Acon.*, *Bryo.*

Chlorosis (green sickness): *Arsenic* (pale face with puffiness of the eyelids, violent thirst, drinks often but little at a time, better in warm room) *China* (weak digestion, results from loss of blood) *Nux vom* (functions of the liver and stomach are affected, bitter sour eructation, habitual constipation of large difficult stools) *Pulsatilla* (frequent palpitation of the heart, cold hands and feet, bad taste in the morning, desire for spicy and stimulant things) *Sepia* (great sadness, weeps frequently, hoarse saddle, fetid urine with great tenacity).

Cholera (Asiatic cholera): *Aconite* (violent heat and dryness of skin, great fear and anxiety, bitter greenish vomiting) *Arsenic.* (vomiting and purging simultaneously, sudden prostration and great thirst, drinks little but often) *Camphor* (burning pain in the stomach and throat, icy coldness and blueness of the face and limbs), *Colocynth* (terrible cramp like pains which draw the patient nearly double, abdomen pain relieved by forcible pressure) *Ipecac.* (at early stage, nausea and vomiting are predominant symptoms) *Phosphoric acid* (watery slimy stools without pain, tenacious vise mucus in the mouth) *Secale cor.* (unquenchable thirst, heat and burning in the abdomen, thin scrawny persons) *Veratrum album* (unquenchable thirst for cold drinks, vomiting and purging simultaneously black vomit violent diarrhoea followed by rapid prostration, cold sweat over body).

Cholera (Asiatic or morbid): *Camphor*, *Acon.* (early stage), *Vert. alb.* (vomiting and diarrhoea predominate), *Cup. met.* (severe cramps), *Phos.*, *Ars.*, *Carbo veg.* (associated with typhoid conditions), *China*, *Phos. acid.* (convulsion), *Acon.*, *Ars.*, *Vert. alb* (collapse condition).

Cholera (simple, english or sporadic): *Camphor* (strong chills) *China* (simple and gripping), *Ver. alb.*, *Acon.*, *Ars.* (sudden and violent vomiting and purging).

Cholera infantum: *Aconite* (in the begging hot skin, quick pulse and sleeplessness before and during stool cutting pain and tandems, restlessness) *Apis mel.* (stool greenish, yellowish, shiny mucus, during stool griping and tandems, aggravation in the morning), *Arsenic.* (stools thick, dark green mucus or dark, watery offensive, vomiting immediately after drinking, restlessness and prostration, aggravation after midnight) *Belladona* (delirium worse during and after sleep, with desire to get out of the bed, sleepy but cannot sleep) *Bryonia* (thirst far large quantities of water at long intervals, gets faints and sick on sitting up, from cold drinks, fruits or getting overheated) *Calcarea carb.* (children with large heads and open fontanels, scrofulous stools chalk like, profuse sweat, cold damp feet) *Carbo veg.* (stools light coloured, involuntary putrid, cadaverous smelling) *Chamomilla* (green watery, corroding stools with colic, colic before and during stool) *Ipecac.* (stools grass green mucus or white, fermented, colic and sick stomach before and during stools, constant nausea and vomiting, after vomiting inclination to sleep) *Mercurius* (dry lips, tongue coated as with fur, violent tandems during and after stool) *Phosphoric acid* (stools whitish watery, light yellow painless, no debility though disease continue for long period) *Podophyllum* (gagging or empty retching stools smell like carrion) *Pulsatilla* (thirst less, stools changeable, before stool rumbling in the bowls, during stool chilliness) *Secale cor* (stools watery and slimy, involuntary, aversion to heat) *Sulphur* (stools changeable and excoriating worse in the morning) *Veratrum album* (stools greenish, watery with flakes, before stool severe colic, during stool cold sweat on the forehead, thirst for large quantity of cold water).

Cholera morbus (sporadic cholera): *Ant. crud.* (violent vomiting and diarrhoea cramp like pains in the stomach, tongue coated white, especially after drinking sour wine) *Arsenic.* (rapid prostration of strength, severe diarrhoea, renewed after drinking) *Chamamilla* (if attack was induced by a fit of passion) *China* (weakness which remains after an attack) *Ipecac.* (nausea and vomiting predominate, stools fermented) *Veratrum alb.* (violent vomiting with severe diarrhoea, excessive weakness and cramps in legs, eyes expressive of acute suffering).

Cholera: *Camphor* (body cool and bluish, no perspiration, do not want to be covered, vomiting and diarrhoea) *Veratrum alb.* (intense vomiting and diarrhoea, bluish body with cold body likes covering of body, cold perspiration on the forehead) *Cuprum met.* (vomiting and diarrhoea, chief symptom convulsion, cramps in calves, thigh muscles) *Arsenic alb.* (diarrhoea with stool blackish and foul smelling, restlessness and boring) *Carbo veg.* (after stoppage of vomiting and diarrhoea the patient becomes restless, flatulence in stomach, desires for fanning at nearby distance) *Camphor* (external coldness, cold sweaty skin and vertigo, collapse with painless stool or no stool, patient will not like to be covered even with feelings of coldness), *Ver. alb.* (External coldness, perspire more on forehead, profuse evacuation from stomach) *Secale cor.* (patient will not like to be covered along with other symptoms of the Secale be observed) *Cup. met.* (Cramps in stomach and in extremities).

Chordee: *Acon.* (internally and externally) *Gels* (violent painful nocturnal erection), *Bella.*, *Picric acid.*

Chorea (St vitus's dance): *Cina* (constant pricking at the nose, the urine turns milky after sometime) *Cocculus* (involuntary motions with the right arm and right leg, worse from riding in a carriage) *Ignitia* (caused by fright or other mental excitement, worse after eating) *Pulsatilla* (for young girls, where there is delayed and difficult first menstruation) *Stramonium* (extreme nervousness, loss of memory).

Chorea: *Agaricus* (cerebral chorea, twitching of eye balls and eye lids, upper side of one side and lower part of other side affected) *Causticum* (right side is worse affected than left) *Cup. met.* (starts from fingers, toes and extends to limb) *Ignitia* (due to fright, punishment, tingling in limbs) *Nux vom.*, (spinal chorea, unsteady drags feet) *Stromonium* (rotates arms, clasps hand over the head) *Zincum met.* (constant motion of the feet) *Viscum alb.* (with vertigo) *Cup. met.*, *Bell*, *Agar.*, *Stram.*, *Ars.*, *Cal. phos.*, *Ign.* (from fright), *Cina*, *Sant.*, *Merc* (from worms), *Vert. vir.*, *Strych.*, *Aur.*, *Cimici.*, *Spigelia*, *Ars.*, *Zinc. iod.* (chronic).

Choroiditis supportive: *Rhus tox.* (the lids are edematous swollen, with profuse gush of tears, conjunctiva edematous pain severe at night) *Aconite* (eye lids red, swollen, hot and dry high fever and much thirst) *Heper sulph.* (after suppuration has begun, eyes sensitive to touch, pain severe and throbbing better by warm application) *Phytolacca* (lids very hard, red and swollen) *Apis mel.* (lids edematous, chemo sis stinging pains through the eye)

Choroiditis: *Arum.* (there is exudation into the choroids and retina or into the vitreous causing haziness of vitreous) *Kali iod.* (syphilitic choroids-retinitis, great haziness and exudation into vitreous) *Mercurius* (iridous-choroids- iris is also involved, pains are intensive both in and around the eye, worse at night) *Phosphorus* (photo pries and chromo pries of various shapes and colour-red predominating, better in twilight) *Bryonia* (serous choroids, serous infiltration into the vitreous, the eyeball feels sore to touch and motion, while darting pains through the eye into the head) *Gelsemium* (serious inflammation of the vocal tract, pain better by hot applicatons, eye ball sore to touch, heaviness of the lids, headache, general depression, loss of muscular tone, fever thirst-less) *Belladona* (hyper anemia, optic disc deep red colour, eyes sensitive to light with feeling as if passed out of the head, flashes of light and sparks, headache) *Nux vom.* (eyes weak and sensitive to light in the morning, gastric derangements) *Prunus spin.* (pains severe, as if the eye ball were being pressed as under or else sharp, shooting and cutting through the eye and corresponding side of then head or crushing in character) *Sulphur* (sharp darting pains worse at night.

Chorosis: *Ferrum met.*, *Ferrum iod.*, *Puls.*, *Cal. carb.*, *Sepia*, *Nat. mur.*, *China*, *Petrol.*

Chronic catarrhal discharge: *Silicea* (old, chronic catarrh of the ear).

Chronic hepatitis (liver complaints): *Bryonia* (pains of a stitch like character, pain in the right shoulder and arm, constipation of dry, hard stool) *Calcarea carb.* (hard undigested stools, clay coloured cold damp feet scrofulous subjects) *China* (weak digestion and loss of appetite, liver painful to touch especially after abuse of quinine, painless undigested stool) *Mercurius* (fetid breath, dark green frothy stools with griping) *Nux vom.* (dizziness, great fullness in the stomach after eating, habitual constipation, luxurious or intemperate habits) *Podophyllum* (white tongue with foul taste, fullness and pain in the region of the liver, frequent chalk like stools, very offensive) *Silicea* (hardness of the region of liver with throbbing pains, the stools recede after being partially expelled) *Sulphur* (tongue white with red tip, constant heat on top of the head).

Chronic tonsils inflammation, associated with hard of hearing: *Baryta carb., Heper., Lyco., Plumb., Psoranium.*

Chronic vomiting in children: *Arsenic alb.* (after food with watery diarrhoea) *Veratrum alb.* (continuous retching, watery involuntary rice coloured stool) *Aesthusa cyn.* (of milk as soon as taken) *Phosphorus* (thirst for cold water but vomits as soon becomes warm in the stomach) *Ipecac.* (cold/coryza vomiting preceded by excessive nausea) *Aconite* (with fever) *Arsenic alb.* (watery copious excoriating discharge, sneezing) *Bryonia* (cold in chest and bronchitis) *Dulcamara* (caused by damp weather) *Euphrasia* (copious watering from eyes) *Gelsenium* (body ache, headache, pain at the base of the head) *Merc. sol.* (non stop flow of the mucus) *Nux vom.* (nose blocked, stuffy cold) *Pulsatilla* (greenish yellow discharge, nose stuffed).

Circulation (languid): *Lept.* (from liver disease) *Dig.* (from enfeebled heart) *Sepia, Ferr.* (women with scanty or deranged period) *Sulph., Bella., Rhus tox.*

Cirrhosis: *Merc. cor., Merc., Digi., Acid* nit., *Ars. Phyos., Phyto., Croton ting.* (with ascites clumsiness in use of hands, weakness of hands and joints).

Coccyx (inflammation etc.): *Cantharis* (pain in coccy bones, lancination tearing usually with urinary problems) *Cicuta* (tearing pain and jerking in coccyx especially during menses) *Hypericum* (spinal concussion, injury to coccyx) *Lachesis* (Neuralgic pain in coccyx, must sit still) *Bovista* (intolerable itching at the tip of coccyx).

Cold (in the head): *Camph., Gels.* (incipient cold with chills) *Acon.* (at an early stage with feverishness), *Dulc.* (from damp wet etc.), *Allium cepa* (worst in a warm room, better out doors), *Ars.* (thin acrid discharge with influenza taint) *Merc.* (sneezing with thick discharge sore throat, chilliness and perspiration), *Puls* (for females and children, thick foetid and loss of taste and smell) *Nux vom.* (stuffy cold), *Euphr.* (acrid fluent conyza, profuse lachorymation and redness of eyes) *Kali bich.* (tough stringy sputa associated with digestive derangement, *Ars. iod., Graphites, Ant. tar., Nat. mur.*

Cold (sensitiveness to it): *Camph., Rumex, Iod., Heper sulph., Kali iod., Sulphs., Gels., Nux vom., Phos., Sabadilla.*

Cold drinks not suitable: *Antim. crud., Argent. nit., Ars. alb., Cantharis, Croton tingl., Rhus tox.*

Cold effects, by wetting the feet: *Cal. carb., Sepia, Puls., Rhus tox., Silicea.*

Cold extremely any part of the body: *Cal. carb., Kali bich.*

Cold feeling in the abdomen: *Ambra, Cal. carb.*

Cold in the chest (catarrh fever, pulmonary catarrh): *Aconite* (attack induced by exposure to dry cold wind, stitches in the chst hindering respiration) *Belladona* (throbbing headache children cry and fret after coughing) Bryonia (dry or loose cough with stitches in chest, exceeing irritable patient) *Chamamilla* (fluent acrid discharge, irritable) *Dulcamara* (attack induced from exposure to wet or dampness, diarrhoea from taking cold) *Ipecac* (rattling of mucus in the bronchial tubes when breathing, cough suffocative) *Mercurius vivus* (fatiguing very dry cough, constant mingling of heat and chilliness) *Nux vom.* (cough is worse from reading, talking or reflecting, very irritable) *Pulsatillas* (loose cough with expectoration of yellow mucus, tightness across the chest, mild tearful disposition, aggravation in the evening).

Cold sensation, between both scapula and back: *Ammon. mur.*

Cold wet wind aggravates the ailment: *Cal. carb., Dulcamara, Manganum acet., Merc., Rhus tox.*

Cold wind intolerable and susceptible to cold: *Borax, Cal. carb., Graphites,*

Colic (in children) *Cham Bryo. Colocynth, Cina* (from worms) *Nux vom., Ipeeac., Caulo., Ignitia* (due to uterine problem).

Colic (in nervous women): *Coce., Plat., Secale, Caulo, Ignitia* (due to uterine problem).

Colic of children: *Colocynth* (doubles up in pain, better by pressure) *Chamomilla* (wants to be carried all time) *Magnesia carb.* (better by warmth and gentle pressure on the abdomen) *Bryonia* (worse from movement and touch, irritable) *Nux vom.* (spasmodic colic) *Chamomilla* (better when carried in laps) *Kali brom.* (pain at about 5 AM) *Stannum* (relieved by carrying with abdomen or mother's shoulder) *China* (simple and gripping), *Ver alb., Acon., Ars.* (sudden and violent vomiting and purging) *Iris vers.* (bilious motions and colic by pains) *Cup. met., Ver. alb.* (cramps and blueness), *Acon. Ars.* (collapse condition).

Colic of infants: *Chamomilla* (flatulent colic, loud screaming to be carried all the time) *China* (colic comes at certain hour) *Colocynth* (continuous crying, bend legs towards abdomen) *Ipecac.* (sharp out cries of the infants, cutting pains, green fermented stools of putrid odour) *Nux vom.* (colic from indigestion or use of improper food, strains to move the bowls).

Colic: *Colocynth* (paroxysmal with diarrhoea) *Discorea* (bilious) *Bell., Pumb.*

(with constipation) *Ver. alb.* (accompanied by vomiting of bilious matter), *Iris., Collin.*, (with flatulence) *Colch.* (in gouty patients) *Nux vom.* (from indulgence in food or fatigue). *Puls.* (colic with chilliness and rumbling of wind in the abdomen especially in the evening) *Rhus tox.* (colic compelling to walk bent) *Chin.*, Colo. (colic better but double) *Secale* (violent colic with convulsion).

Colica pictonum (lead colic): *Belladona* (clutching in the abdomen as if a point were with seized claws) *Colocynth* (feeling in the whole abdomen as if the intestines were squeezed between stones, relieved by bending double and with hard pressure great restlessness and lamentation) *Nux vom.* (gripping and clutching in the stomach, obstinate constipation) *Opium* (pain as if intestines were cut into pieces, pulse full and slow, constipation stool round hard black balls).

Colic-enteralgia: *Belladona* (constriction of the abdomen around the umbilicus, as if ball will be formed) *Carbo veg.* (constant pressure downward in the abdomen, worse from 4 to 6 PM) *Chamomilla* (flatulent colic distention of the abdomen, vomiting of sour food or of slimy substances) *Cocculus* (violent spasm of the stomach with a griping lacerating sensation abdomen distended) *Colocynth* (violent cutting, constrictive or spasmodic pains, feeling as if intestine were being squeezed between stones, compelling one to bend double) *Ipecac.* (constant nausea, after vomiting inclination to sleep) *Lycopodium* (colic with incarcerated flatulence, sensation as if abdomen burst) *Mercurius* (pains associated with chilliness and shuddering) *Nux vom.*

(pressure in the stomach as from a stone, colic from indigestion or use of improper food, malicious irritable disposition) *Pulsatilla* (after eating rich greasy food) *Veratrum album* (cold sweat over whole body, great weakness with very feeble pulse).

Colitis: *Acetic acid* (violent burning pain in stomach and chest, ulceration, burning thirst but cold water disagrees) *Lachesis* (colitis with offensive diarrhoea, haemorrhage from bowels like charred straw, black particles, pressure on rectum but no stool) *Sulphur* (great acidity, burning, painful weight like pressure) *Trilum* (chronic diarrhoea of mucus and blood).

Collapse (loss of consciousness due to any reason): *Camphor (Q)* (external surface cold throws off all covering) *Carbo veg.* (body becomes blue, icy cold, face puffy, pulse imperceptible, wants to be fanned) *Cuprum met.* (epileptic, collapse with jerking and twitching of muscles, eyes fixed, staring, sunken, turning upward).

Colour (of skin): *Acetic acid* (pale waxen, emaciated face, swelling) *Arnica* (skin black and blue on account of injury) *Belladona* (red shining, painful and throbbing) *Borax* (red swelling, erysipelas on face) *Calcarea carb.* (minute red spots, full of blood on skin) *Carbo veg.* (blue cold imperfect oxygenation, face blue, skin pale, pulse intermittent) *Chelidonium* (yellow, jaundiced skin, itching in liver disorders) *Colchicum* (pink spots on back chest abdomen) *Digitalia* (yellow with heart problems, slow plus) *Lachesis* (bluish, purple at appearance, hemorrhage below skin where the blood coagulates) *Mancinala* (intense erythema, red vesicles large blisters as from scalds) *Pulsatilla* (red raised rash) *Rhus tox.* (red swollen with intense itching) *Veratrum album* (blue, cold sweat and body) *Viola tricolour* (red spots blisters, on the face, hands knees of the children).

Colour (of the face): *Acetic acid* (face pale waxen, dark ring around eyes, anaemia) *Aconite* (red face becomes deathly pale on rising) *Antim crud.* (yellow, crusty eruption on cheeks, haggard face) *Ars. alb.* (pale yellow, swollen, lips black and livid) *Belladona* (red bluish, hot swollen and shining, throbbing and twisting) *Camphor* (pale blue cold body and sweat) *Cheledonium* (yellow jaundiced, eyes, tongue and urine yellow) *China* (pale sallow, eyes sunken, sweating on least exertion, indifferent) *Cina* (pale with dark rings around eyes, white and bluish about mouth) *Ferrum met.* (red and flushed from pain, emotion and exertion, red parts become white puffy) *Cuprum met.* (pale bluish, face distorted, lips blue) *Merc. cor.* (red with lips black swollen) *Opium* (face red, swollen, dark, suffused and hot) *Phosphorus* (blue rings around eyes) *Rhus. tox.* (purple, large burning blotches) *Sepia* (yellow blotches, saddle like yellow distribution of brown, yellow spots on nose and chicks) *Veratrum alb* (pale blue, cold in collapse).

Colour/sediment (of urine): *Aconite* (red hot, painful and scanty) *Arsenic alb.* (albuminous, globules of pus and blood) *Belladona* (dark turbid, loaded with phosphates) *Bryonia* (red, brown, scanty hot) *Calcarea carb.* (dark brown, fetid with white sediments and blood) *Carbolic acid* (almost black with diabetes) *Chelidonium* (yellow urine, profuse, foamy in jaundice, dark turbid) *Chionanthus* (very dark urine, bile and sugar in the urine, liver enlarged and jaundiced) *Cuprum ars.* (increased acetones and aceto acetic acid in urine) *Digitilis* (dark red sediment with throbbing pain at the neck of the bladder) *Lactic acid* (urine loaded with sugar, diabetes mellitus) *Lycopodium* (heavy red sediment with backache in renal region) *Merc. cor.* (bright red urine in the morning, copious, soon becomes turbid) *Ocimum canum* (brick dust red or yellow sediment, odor of musk) *Phosphoric acid* (profuse milky urine with diabetes).

Colour blindness: *Carbo. sulph.* (red and green colour lost white colour visible, cloudiness, atrophy of the optic nerve) *China* (night blindness due to anaemic retina, black spots before eyes, pressure in eyes better in open air) *Cicuta* (reading lines disappears, image moves away and comes near, wavering, squatness, spasm in the eyes) *Physostigma* (night blindness pupils contracted increasing myopia, photo-phobia).

Colour/mucus (of stool): *Aconite* (green like chopped herbs, small, frequent with tenesmus) *Aloe* (yellow bloody, transparent, jelly like mucus) *Arg. nit.* (watery noisy, flatulent, green like chopped spinach, has shredded mucus offence) *Arnica* (brown, bloody, putrid, looks like brown yeast) *Asarum europum* (strings of odorless, yellow mucus, diarrhoea of tough mucus) *Calc. phos.* (green slimy, hot, sputtering fetid flatus) *Carbo veg.* (acrid, corrosive, glutinous, moisture from rectum) *Chamomilla* (green, hot slimy, watery, fetid with colic) *Chelidonium* (bright yellow, pasty, clay coloured) *China* (light coloured, watery, painless, ingested) *Cina* (white mucus, like small pieces of popcorn) *Dulcamara* (green, watery, slimy mucus) *Ipecac* (pitch like green as grass, like frothy molasses) *Merc. sol.* (greenish, bloody and slimy, lot of mucus) *Podophyllum* (yellow, green, gushing, copious, rumbling, fetid with colic) *Secale cor.* (olive green, thin fetid, bloody).

Commit mistakes, while writing: *Lachesis*, *Lyco.* and *Thuja*.

Concussion of the brain: *Aconite* (high fever, with dry hot skin, violent thirst, shortness of breath, delirium especially in the night) *Belladona* (throbbing headache, dread from noise or light, sleepy but cannot sleep) *Opium* (delirious talking, eyes wide open, acuteness of hearing, stool round, hard, black balls).

Condylomata: *Nitric acid*, *Thuja*, *Merc. cor.*, *Sabi*.

Confusion of ideas: *Bapt.*, *Bell.*, *Gels.*, *Rhus tox.*

Conjunctivitis: *Aconite* (eye red, burning, very painful, great dryness pain burning and smarting) *Allium cepa* (lachrymation profuse non excoriating and nasal discharge is so) *Alumina* (dryness of lids and eyes especially in the evening, moderate discharge, heavy feeling of lids) *Antim. crud.* (postural conjunctivitis, moist eruptions behind the eArs, lids are excoriated by profuse mucus, discharges and lachrymation, excoriation of nostrils and swollen upper lips) *Apis mel.* (great swelling of the lids, pains stringing and shooting pain) *Acetic acid* (false membrane is dense, yellow white and tough, closely adherent removal very difficult) *Argentum nit.* (purulent discharge, causing haziness of cornea, acute granular) *Arsenic alb.* (acute catarrhal conjunctivitis, hot lachrymation, burning pain at night, granular lids, discharge thin and acrid, coryza acrid, great restlessness, better by warmth, burning pain at night) *Aurum met.* (scrofulous ophthalmia, photophobia, eyes sensitive to touch, irritable sensitive to noise) *Baryta iod.* (scrofulous ophthalmia with enlarged cervical gland) *Belladona* (catarrhal conjunctivitis, dryness of eye photophobia marked, headache, red face) *Calcarea carb.* (excessive photophobia, lachrymation worse during damp weather, purulent ophthalmia) *Calcarea iod.* (associated with tonsil and cervical glands) *Calcarea hypo phos.* (ulceration of the cornea, or gonorrheal ophthalmia) *Chamomilla* (scrofulous ophthalmia during dentition, redness and lachrymation, sometimes blood oozes out when opening the eyes) *Cinnabaris* (pain above the eye, extending from the internal to external acanthus) *Conium mac.* (photophobia and profuse, very slight or no redness of the conjunctiva) *Croton ting.* (vesicular eruption on face and lids, eye and face hot and burning, photophobia worse at night).

Constipation (chronic): *Sulph.*, *Nux vom.* (irregular action), *Bryo.*, *Opium.* (torpor) *Pulmb.* (obstinate, passes hard small balls), *Lyco.* (with flatulence), *Hydras* (with debility), *Aesculus h.* (with piles and much pain), *Collin.* (associated with piles or uterine disturbance). *Sulph.*, *Nux vom.*, (irregular action) *Bryo.*, *Opium.* (torpor) *Alum.*, *Graphites*, *Podophyllum*, *Nat. mur.*, *Sepia*, *Nitric acid.*

Constipation (in old persons) *Ant. crud.*, *Opium.*, *Hydrast.*, *Collinsonia*, *Alumina*, *Lyco.*, *Opium.*

Constipation of children: *Alumina* (even soft stool passes with great difficulty, stool sticky) *Bryonia* (stool large passes with great difficulty, stool dry and burnt) *Graphites* (no purging for days) *Lycopodium* (accompanied by passing wind downward) *Magnesia mur.* (hard stool crumble at anus) *Merc. sol.* (stool with mucus) *Natrum mur.* (hard, crumbling stool) *Nux vom.* (ineffectual urging for stool) *Silicea* (stool comes out but goes back) *Magnisium mur.* (during dentition, stool large and hard, difficult to pass, crumble at the verge of anus) *Podophyllum* (due to feeding by bottle) *Chelidonium* (with liver problem stool in round ball form) *Calcarea carb* (hard undigested stools, feel cold and damp, pale flabby skin) *Lycopodium* (stools very hard, scant and passed with great difficulty) *Nux vom* (stools large, hard and passes with great difficulty, frequent urging to stool).

Constipation, during journey: *Platina.*

Constipation, stool does not pass for few days, the stool is removed mechanically otherwise it recedes again: *Aloe.*, *Cal. carb.*, *Sanicula*, *Selinium*, *Sepia*, *Silicea.*

Constipation, with no desire for stool: *Bryo.*, *Opium*, *Sulph.*, *Veratrum alb.*

Constipation: *Antim. crud.* (a sensation of copious stool would take place, when only flatus is expelled, finally, a very hard stool is voided) *Bryonia* (hard dry stools as if burnt irritable mood) *Causticum* (stools tough, light coloured, whitish shining like grease) *Ignitia* (after stool a violent stabbing stitch from the anus upward into the rectum) *Lycopodium* (stool very hard, scanty and passed with great difficulty, great drowsiness after dinner, loud rumbling and gurgling in the bowels) *Nitric acid* (painless constipation, stools hard, dry and scanty, sour or bitter taste after eating) *Nux vom.* (stools large, hard and passed with difficulty, frequent urging to stool, sensation as if stone is in the stomach) *Opium* (stools small hard black balls, paralysis of the intestines) *Phosphorus* (stools long, narrow and hard, difficult to expel, belching up large quantities of wind after eating) *Pulsatilla* (constipation from eating rich greasy food) *Silicea* (stools as if the rectum has no power to expel it, stool recedes back into the rectum after having been partially expelled) *Sulphur* (the first effort at stool is often very painful compelling the patient to desist) *Veratrum album* (much straining during stool associated with cold perspiration on the forehead, great exhaustion after stool) *Nux vom.* (in effectual desire for stool sometime stool does not passes and has to come back without it) *Bryonia* (no desire for stool or stool dry, passes with difficulty in long stool form) *Alumina* (in effectiveness of abdomen causes constipation, even lose stool passes with great difficulty) *Carbo veg.* (constant feeling for passing the stool but only flatus passes on each attempt) *Lycopodium* (due to constriction of anus, the stool does not passes easily, first tight, dry stool comes out and then normal stool) *Opium.*, (paralytic condition of intestine causes constipation and no desire for stool, stool passes in round balls) *Nux vom.* (unsuccessful desire and sensation as if not finished for stool), *Alumina* (not attending the urging to stool inactivity of rectum, even soft stool requires great effort) *Bryo.* (no urging is caused by dryness of alimentary tract stool is loose and hard) *Carbo veg.* (urging of stool like *Nux vom.* (but relieved by passing flatus) *Lyco.* (has constriction of the rectum) *Opium* (from inactivity of the bowls, stool hard round black balls) *Nux vomica* (due to irregular function of intestine, has ineffectual desire for stool, passes little stool all the time) *Bryonia* (inactiveness of mucus membrane of intestine causes dryness and constipation, no desire for stool, stool dry, hard and as if burnt) *Alumina* (due to inactiveness of rectum, even soft stool passes with great difficulty only using force) *Carbo veg* (ineffectual desire for stool but only wind passes but not stool) *Lycopodium* (due to constriction of rectum the stool remains in the rectum first dry stool comes out and then soft stool) *Opium* (due to paralytic condition of the rectum the stool passes in form of hard, round and knotty balls).

Constriction (of anus): *Cactus* (*Q*) (in anus with severe constipation, with piles, feeling of an iron band, severe pain) *Ignitia* (painful constriction of anus after stool, stitches from anus deep into rectum, pressure as of sharp instrument digging from within outward).

Constriction of esophagus: *Abies nigra* (as if hard boiled egg is logged near the cardiac region, resistance for going down of solids, liquids) *Baptisia* (can swallow liquid only, vomiting due to spasm of esophagus) *Cactus* (due to heart problems).

Constriction of vagina: *Cactus* (*Q*) (constriction of vagina, prevents coitus, painful vaginismus) *Gelsemium* (vaginismus with prostration and weakness, wants to be left alone) *Lycopodium* (vagina dry, coitus painful, vagina constriction, mammae hardened).

Contusion: *Con.* (involving female breast) *Ruta* (the tibia) *Ham.* (with discolouration).

Convulsions (infantile): *Bell.*, Acon. (Bella. red swollen face and Acon. with frequently) *Cham.* (from indigestion colic etc.) *Ign. Cina* (from worms), *Glonine* (with hydrocephalus), *Cup. m. Ver. alb.* (with cramps) *Opium* (from fright) *Gels.* (rigidity), *Ver. vir.*, *Chloral hydrat*, *Zinc sulph.*

Convulsions-Uremia: *Cuprum arsenicum* (Uremia, brain edema, vertigo, increased acetones and aceto acetic acid in urine).

Corayza aggravates in closed warm room: *Puls., Allium cepa.*

Cornea (hard) *Sulph., Cal carb., Silicea.*

Cornea (inflamed) *Ver. vir.*

Cornea (opacity) *Phos. (6x) Sil (6x) Cal. carb. (30).*

Cornea (soft): *Ferrum pic.*

Coronary thrombosis: *Arnica* (tightness, constriction after over exertion, it heels affected lesions in the heart morose, irritable, wants to be left alone) *Borthrops* (helps in dissolution of a blood clot) *Cactus* (constriction in heart as if compressed or squeezed by a band, constant pain in cardiac region) *Lachesis* (terrible smothering feelings about heart, constriction in the chest, cannot bear any pressure on throat or chest) *Lilum tigrinum* (sensation as if the heart is grasped in a vice, feeling as if heart is stopped, coldness of body).

Coryza: *Carbo veg.* (watery discharge associated with lost of voice and scraping of throat). *Allium cepa* (irritable discharge from nose but non irritable discharge from eyes) *Euphorasia* (irritable discharge from eyes but non irritating discharge from nose) *Iodium* (thick and excroting discharge from nose, burning, yellowish or greenish, eats well even then weak) *Kali iod.* (thick yellow discharge from nose, burning and excroting, pain in the face) *Arsenic alb.* (thin burning and excreting discharge from nose, better by warmth) *Arsenic iod* (restlessness, weakness, burning in eyes with excreting discharge from nose like arsenic) *Nat. mur.* (thin excessive discharge in the morning, sleepy in day time) *Pulsatilla* (thick non excreting yellow or green, stringy discharge in the night, in spite of cleaning the nose it becomes full again, taste lost) *Nux vom.* (in the night or in warm room nose is chocked, nothing comes out on cleaning it again and again).

Cough or asthmatic attack on drinking or eating cold items: *Ars alb., Bryo., Puls.*

Cough (dry) during night: *Justica adha., Bella., Hyoscymus., Drosera, Manganum.*

Cough (dry): *Acon.* (recent, burning dryness in throat, in fever) *Bell.* (spasmodic with cerebral congestion, worse at night), *Bryo.* (hard, tight, irritating, shaking whole body, burning soreness under breast bone, stenches in chest) *Caust* (hoarseness, involuntary urination), *Lauro, Hyos.* (worse at night on lying down or coming on at 3 a.m.) *Sulph.* (obstinate tight following eruptions) *Iod., Brom., Spong., Acid nit., Acid sulph.* (laryngeal tickling) *Lach.* (as if something is in throat to be coughed out for relief) *Rumex* (worse when talking or in cold air soreness under breast bone) *Ipecac.* (recent wheezing, nausea or vomiting), *Phos.* (short laryngeal and bronchial tendency in limn disease, scariness in chest) *Graphites* (gruff voice) *Gels.* (severe in children) *Senega, Verbas.* (short harsh).

Cough (moist): *Ant. tar.* (profuse easy expectoration, vomiting), *Kali. bich.* (tough stringy mucous, difficult expectoration), *Puls.* (loose, worse on lying down), *Stannum, Merc.* (chronic purulent sputa, night sweat), *Hep. sulph.* (due to organic diseases chronic indigestion), *Nitric acid* (related to lungs diseases) *Phos* (bronchial and lung diseases, brown sputa), *Sulph.* (yellow mucous, Asthma following eruptions),

Ars. alb. (debility, tight chest difficult breathing at night), *Cact.* (spasmodic after midnight with vomiting, copious expectoration), *Sepia, Kali carb., Lyco., Scill., Crotalus, Naja, Senega, Sticta, Alum., Allium cepa., Capsicum, Viol. od.*

Cough (nervous and hysteric) *Hyos, Ign., Ambra., Agar., Corallium rubrum., Coni., Cup met., Rumex, Nux vom.*

Cough (spasmodic) *Drosera, Kali brom.* (tickling, retching worse at night), *Ipecac.* (vomiting), *Nux vom.* (headache as if bruised cough after meals), *Corall., Acid nit., Cup. met., Veratrum., Bella., Ambra., Euphor.*

Cough (spasmodic), associated with nausea and vomiting: *Bryo., Drosera, Kali carb.*

Cough continuous cannot breath for a single moment: *Drosera, Corallium rubrum.*

Cough from going to cold condition from warmth: *Phos.*

Cough in children: *Aconite* (dry harsh cough) *Belladona* (face red, burning hot), *Bryonia* (hard dry, pain in chest) *Antim. tar.* (rattling, accumulation of phlegm, difficult to take out) *Ipecac.* (wheezing, difficult respiration) *Heper sulph.* (sensitive to cold) *Kali bich.* (unable to clear throat) Nux vom. (dry cough) *Pulsatilla* (loose cough yellowish) *Mephitis* (all type of coughs):

Cough loose in the day time and dries up in the night but aggravates as soon as lies down: *Puls.*

Cough whooping: *Belladona* (hard barking like croup, child becomes red during coughing bleeding from nose) *Bryonia* (paroxysm sets in after eating or drinking with vomiting) *Drosear* (the paroxysms follow each other very rapidly, bleding from nose, deep hoArse voice, hoArseness) *Ipecac.* (suffocative cough, child becomes stiff and blue in the face the cough causes gagging and vomiting of phlegm) *Castanea vesca.* (early stage, with dry ringing violent spasmodic cough, very thirsty) *Pertussinum* (whooping cough when symptoms return again, Bronchitis-inflammation of bronchia) *Chamomilla* (scrapping dry cough from tickling in the larynx worse at night) *Kali bich.* (cough with expectoration of tough stringy mucus) *Phosphorus* (complete loss of voice) *Pulsatilla* (dry cough at night, going off when silting up in the bed).

Cough with pain in chest; while coughing tighten the chest with hands: *Bryo., Eupatorium, Nat. carb.*

Cough: *Acon.* (the child grasp at the throat with every coughing fit) *Lach.* (cough after sleeping) *Arnica* (whooping cough, every cough spell is preceded by crying) *Ant. tar.* (cough as if caused by the smoke of the sulphur with a sense of suffocation) *Ars alb. Bell* (cough from dust in the throat) *Ars alb., silicea* (dry backing cough with soreness of the chest) *Bell., Nit acid* and *Spong.* (barking cough pain in the larynx, headache fever) *Bell.* (dry spasmodic cough, worse at night and from motion) *Bell., Hyos.* (distressing dry cough excited by a tickling in the larynx) *Bryo.* (cough worse after eating or drinking with vomiting food) *Caust.* (cough relieved by taking a cup of cold water) *Bryo.* (cough at night in bed, compelling to assume erect posture at once) *Aconite* (short dry cough excited by smoking or drinking and at night) *Arnica* (dry short and tickling cough in the morning after rising, stitching pain in the side of the chest) *Belladona* (sensation as if dust in the throat causing a constant tickling) *Bryonia* (dry cough, during coughing a sensation that as if the head and chest will burst) *Calcarea carb.* (cough early in the morning with yellow expectoration) *Carbo veg.* (short dry cough, accompanied by stitches in the left side of the chest) *Causticum* (short dry cough relieved by drinking cold water cough with involuntary emission of urine) Chamomilla (dry tickling cough worse at night even during sleep) *China* (cough with expectoration of clear tenacious mucus or blood streaked mucus) *Cina* (dry spasmodic cough in children troubled with worms) *Heper sulph.* (croupy cough with loose rattling of phelm, also for dry hoarse cough worsen in the morning) *Ipecac.* (dry suffocative cough, with rattling of mucus in the bronchial tube when breathing) *Phosphorus* (dry tickling cough in the evening with tightness across the chest) *Pulsatilla* (cough during night going off when sitting up in the bed) *Antim. tar.* (loose cough without expectoration does not yield to coughing, thirst day and night) *Veratrum alb* (deep hollow cough, tickling low down in the bronchial tubes, excessive weakness) *Caust., Puls., Verat. alb.* (cough with pain in the hip and with involuntary emission of urine) *Cham.* (dry tickling cough at night even during sleep in children) *China* (cough with expectoration of clear transparent mucus or blood streak mucus) *Cimi* (cough particularly at night caused by tickling in the throat) *Cina* (short hacking cough, dry, spasmodic cough, preceded by rigidity of body and unconsciousness) *Con., Hyos., Puls.* (dry hacking cough at night worse while lying down) *Ferr., Chin., Silicea* (spasmodic cough with expectoration of tough, transparent cough) *Bell., Merc., Nux v., Phos.* (dry hoArse cough) *Heper sulph.* (cough excited whenever any part of the body gets cold or from anything eating cold) *Spon.* (dry barking, wheezing cough with rattling breathing) *Heper.* (rattling crocking cough, suffocative attacks, compelling to rise up and bend the head backward) *Hyos., Puls.* (the cough is relieved by setting up) *Ign.* (dry spasmodic cough day and night with fluent coryza) *Ipecae.* (suffocative cough, the child becomes quite stiff and blueness on the face) *Kali bich.* (true membranous cough, tickling in larynx, cough in the morning with expectoration of tough stringy mucus) *Lach.* (slight pressure on the throat produces long continued cough, worse after sleeping, oppression of the chest) *Lyco.* (cough with gray, salty expectoration, worse from 4 to 6 PM) *Merc vivus., Ars., Cal. carb.* (whooping cough shortness of breath when walking or going up stairs) *Nitric acid., Heper.* (dry barking cough in the evening after lying down) *Phos.* (cough from tickling in the throat, worse from cold air, reading aloud, talking, laughing, eating or drinking) *Phos.* acid, Ars. alb. Calc., Sulph. (cough with purulent offensive expectoration) *Phos. acid., Bell., Nit acid., Spon.* (dry barking cough) *Puls., Nitric acid* (cough with expectoration of black coagulated blood) *Rhus tox.* (cough with stitches in the chest) *Sepia, Merc., Phos.* (cough in the morning with profuse expectoration tasting very salty) *Silicea, Ars., Caust., Sepia, Staph.* (dry hacking cough with soreness of the chest) *Kali bich., Puls., Sulph.* (loose cough with soreness and pressure in the chest, talking excites the cough) *Ant. tar.* (loose rattling cough as if much would be expectorated but nothing comes up).

Coughing stoatps night: *Bryonia*, *Euphararasia*, *Manganum*.

Coward children: *Baryta carb.*, *Cal. carb.*, *Cal. sulph.*, *Gels.*, *Kali carb.*, *Lyco.*, *Nat. carb.*, *Phos.*, *Plumbum*, *Sepia*, *Sulphur*.

Coward persons for: *Gels.*, *Lyco.*

Coward, shy and undeceive women for: *Graph.*, *Puls.*

Cracking: *Cocculus* (cracking of cervical vertebrae when moving head).

Cracks in skin of hands and fingers: *Merc. cor.*, *Petro.*, *Cal carb.*, *Caust.*, *Graphites*, *Silicea*, *Heper sulph.*

Cracks in the back: *Acon.*, *Arn.*, *Ant tar.*, *Rhus.*, *Cimici.*, *Bryo.*, *Nux vom.*

Cracks of lips and nose: *Graph.*, *Cal carb.*, *Ars.*, *Ant. tar.*, *Nat. mur*, *Sepia.*

Cracks of mouth: *Antim crud* (in the corners of mouth, due to gastric disorder) *Arum triph.* (corners of mouth sore and cracked, lips cracked and burning) *Condorango* (Q) (due to stomach ulceration) *Nitric acid* (mouth corners cracked, ulcerated and scabby, stomatits excessive saliva)

Cramps (of finger of satirists, violinists, pianoist etc.): *Ruta* (stiffness of hands and wrist) *Aconite* (icy coldness of hands, numbness and tingling, shooting pain) *Apis* (numbness of hands and tips of fingers with dropsy) *Colchicum* (finger tips numb, pin pricking in hands and wrist) *Rhus tox* (paralysis of the arm leads to the numbness of hands on grasping) *Aconite* (eminence of redness on hands) *Causticum* (unsteadiness of muscles of hands and fore arm).

Cramps in the limbs: *Calcarea carb.* (violent cramp in the calf at night, especially when extending the legs, feet incline to be damp and cold scrofulous habit) *Carbo veg.* (cramp in the soles in the evening when lying down, profuse sweating of the feet) *Nux vomica* (persons of in temperate habit with high livers, contraction of soles when bending the legs) *Veratrum alb.* (relieves the predisposition to cramp to be taken in the night for few years).

Cramps in urethra: *Canth.*, *Lilium ting.*, *Merc. cor.*

Cramps: *Chamomilla* (cramps in calves, great irritability of temper) *Colocynth* (crampy pain in abdomen as if intestines were being squeezed between stones, also cramps in the muscles of the thigh) *Nux vom.* (cramps in calves when bending the legs) *Veratrum alb.* (for cramps, to be taken at night before going to bed and the repeated for few nights).

Craving: *Calcarea carb.* (for indigestible things like chalk, coal, pencil) *Staphysagria* (for tobacco, stimulants) *Sulphuric acid* (for alcohol).

Crick in the neck: *Aconite* (if caused by exposure to cold or suppressed perspiration) *Belladona* (sore throat with swelling of the glands of the neck) *Bryonia* (stiffness of the neck, aggravated by the least motion) *Rhus tox* (by getting drenched in the rain, the pains and soreness are relieved by continuously moving the neck) *Bell.*, *Ant. tar.*, *Dulc* (from damp) *Bryo.*, *Nux. vom.*, *Phyto.*

Cricks in the back: *Acon.*, *Arn.*, *Ant tar.*, *Rhus.*, *Cimici.*, *Bryo.*, *Nux. vom.*

Cries all of a sudden in sleep: *Borax*, *Lyco.*, *Apis.*, *Puls.*, *Zinc.*

Cries before urination: *Borax.*

Croup (Laryngitis) *Catarrhal Acon.* or *Spon.*, *Bryo.*, *Ipecac.*

Croup (spasmodic larynismus stridulus), *Acon.*, *Spon.*, *Bell.*, *Gels.*, *Kali brom.* (with convulsions).

Croup: *Acon.* (first stage of croup with dry cough and loud breathing during expiration, every expiration ends with hoarse, hacking cough) *Heper sulph.* (croup with loose rattling cough, worse in the morning).

Crowded and warm room develop faintness: *Lach.*, *Puls.*

Crista lactea (milk crust): *Calcarea carb.* (children of scrofulous habit, eruption is covered with thick scabs stools white, cold damp feet) *Graphites* (eruption exudes a sticky fluid, appears mostly chin and behind the ears, unhealthy skin) *Rhus tox.* (watery vesicles with red edges, eruption itches violent at night).

Crying of children: *Apis.* (from insect bites) *Arnica* (due to tiredness) *Belladona* (during head hot, cheeks flushed) *Bryonia* (from constipation, stool hard and dry) *Cantharis* (while passing urine) *Chamomilla* (wants to be carried away here and there) *Coffea* (due to sleeplessness) *Colocynth* (due to colic, bends double) *Antim crudum* (on looking of unknown person).

Crying of infants: *Belladona* (starts suddenly out of sleep and cries violently) *Coffea* (cries and laugh alternately, extreme wakefulness shows no inclination to sleep) *Nux vom* (due to constipation and flatulent colic, sleepless and restless).

Cyanosis: *Dig.*, *Cup. met.*, *Lach.*, *Ars.*, *Ver. alb.*, *Lauro.*

Cyst (ovarian): *Colocynth* (round, small cystic tumor in ovaries, boring pain must draw up double, restlessness) *Lycopodium* (ovarian cyst, vagina dry, coitus painful, worse right side).

Cystitis (inflammation of urinary bladder): *Asparagus* (cystitis with pus, mucus and tenesmus, stitches in the orifice of urethra has to pass urine again and again) *Cantharis* (intolerable tenesmus, cutting pain before during and after urine, bloody urine) *Tuberculinum* (in chronic cystitis).

D

Dacryoadentis (inflammation and abscess of the lachrymal glands): Remedies are: *Acon.*, *Apis.*, *Heper.*, *Rhus.* and *Silicea* as per symptoms.

Dacryocystitis catarrhalis (catarrhal inflammation of lachrymal sac): *Pulsatilla* **(discharge profuse and bland from the nose especially in children)** *Stannum* **(yellow white discharge from the lachrymal sac)** *Heper sulph.* **(profuse discharge, great sensitiveness to touch and cold)** *Euphrasia* **(thick yellow discharge, bland discharge from nose)** *Argentum nit.* **(carbuncular lachrymals swollen looking like a lump of red flash)** *Aconite* **(lids much swollen, great heat and dryness, general fever)** *Apis.* **(lids edematous swollen with stinging and shoot pain, no thirst)** *Mercurius* **(later stage when pus becomes thin and excoriating) Other medicines are:** *Bell.*, *Calc.*, *Cinnabaris*, *Hydrastis*, *Nat. mur.*, *Sulphur*, *Zinc. sulph.*

Dandruff: Ars., *Graph.*, *Sulph.*, *Lyco.*, *Sepia*, *Rhus.*

Deafness (after eruptive fevers) *Sulph.*, *Bell.*, *Merc.*

Deafness (from cold) *Acon.*, *Bell.*, *Merc.*, *Gels.*, *Dulc.*, *Puls.* **(Caused by draughts or wet).**

Deafness (from nervous causes) *Phos.*, *Petrol* **(noises in the ear)** *Acid phos.*, *China*, *Sulph.* **(perioidc or with roaring and buzzing noises in the head).**

Deafness chronic (from enlarged tonsils) *Baryta Iod.*, *Iod.*, *Sulph.*, *Merc. Iod.*, *Bell.*, *Kali iod.*, *Cal. phos.*, *Baryta carb.*

Deafness: *Belladona* **(deafness following scarlet fever)** *Calcarea carb.* **(after suppression of fever and ague by quinine)** *Conium* **(due to accumulation of wax in the ear)** *Gelsmium* **(sudden loss of hearing).**

Death time prediction: *Aco.*, *Argent, nit.* **(as per symptoms).**

Debility (constitutional) *Iod.* **(tendency to faint or to glandular enlargements)** *Aletris.*, *Helonias.*, *Avena sat.*, *Ars.*, *Merc.*, *Acid phos.*, *Cal. carb*, *Ferrum phos.*

Debility (from loss of body fluid) *China*, *Acid phos.*, *Ferr.* **(due to anaemia).**

Debility (nervous): *Acid phos.*, *Mosch.* **(feeble pulse cold extremities, defection),** *Ign.*, *Nux vom.* **(from bad habits).**

Decay (of bones): *Aurum met* **(soreness of affected bones).**

Decay (of teeth): *Kreosotum* **(very rapid decay of teeth)** *Phosphorus* **(necrosis of jaw bone).**

Decaying teeth in children: *Kreqsote* **(decay as soon as they appear; gums sore)** *Merc. sol.* **(teeth lose, gums bleed)** *Staphysagria* **(teeth black)** *Kali phos.* **(rotting with foul smell).**

Deformed (bones/joints): *Calcarea carb.* **(deformed extremities, crooked spine)** *Causticum* **(excessive deformities of joints in rheumatism joints enlarged, soft, painful)** *Kali mur.* **(enlarged joints in acute rheumatism)** *Sulphur* **(bones do not grow in under-developed child).**

Delay in learning for walking: *Cal. carb.*, *Phos.*, *Silicea.*

Delirium Tremens (Mania): *Belladona* (plethoric habit, boisterous delirium, frightful figure, sudden starting and jumping while sleeping), *Hyoscyamus* (furious delirium with wild staring look dilated pupils and throbbing of the carotids, grasping at imaginary objects, muttering) *Opium* (loud torturous breathing, complete loss of consciousness and sensation, delirious talking with eyes wide open, pulse in different) *Stromonium* (sings and prays most deviously, awakes with desire to escape from bed) *Nux., Agar., Ars., Kali Brom., Capsicum* (with dullness of sense, steeper and loud snoring) Acon., *Bryo.* (especially in the night) *Bell., Bryo., Opi.,* (delirium after suppressed scarlet eruptions) *Ars alb., Bell, Bryo.* (springs out of bed and tries to hide/ escape) *Bell.* (with wild manners such as tears clothes, try to injure himself or others, bites) *Hyos., Strom.* (fury with impulse to strike and kill), *Opi., Sram.* (with frightful figures and images before the eyes) *Bryo, Hyos, Stram* (Loquacious delirium with desire to escape) *Colcynth* (with open eyes and desire to escape) *Hyos.* (without consciousness does not know his own family, muttering, jerking of limbs) *Opi. Stram* (silent delirium with open eyes), *Hyos. Rhus.* (muttering delirium).

Dementia: *Anacardium* (Brain fag, impaired memory, absent minded) *Kali phos.* (nervous prostration, mental and physical depression) *Phosphoric acid* (mental debility followed by physical debility, nervous exhaustion).

Dentition (disorder during) *Cham.* (freakfulness and sour diarrhoea), *Acon* (feverishness) *Bell., Veratrum vir., Gels* (head symptoms and convulsions with redness of the face), *Kreos* (emaciation, great irritability wakefulness and constipation), *Cal. carb* (dentation too early or too late), *Phyto., Merc sol., Silicea* (in tubercular subjects) *Bael. Aconite* (has fever, restless, gums are inflamed)' *Chamomilla* (peevish, restless, wants to be carried) *Kreosote* (teeth decay as soon as they appear) *Podophyllum* (diarrhea during dentition) *Calcarea phos* (dentition difficult).

Dentition (teething): *Aconite* (green watery diarrhoea, great thirst dry hot skin, disturb sleep) *Apis mel* (green yellowish watery diarrhoea worse in the morning much yawning and uneasiness) *Belladona* (convulsions, followed by sound sleep, gums swollen and inflamed with numerous small blood vessels showing on the surface) *Chamomilla* (diarrhoea with greenish, yellowish or whitish, mucus stools smelling like bad eggs) *Coffea* (frets and worries in a pitiful manner, cries one moment and laughs the next) *Graphites* (unhealthy condition of the skin) *Hyoscymus* (yellow watery involuntary stools), *Ignitia* (the child is much distressed, sighs, soles and cries) *Mercurius* (diarrhoea greenish, slimy or bloody stools with much straining) *Nux vom* (very irritable and cross, loss of appetite with increased thirst, constipation with large difficult stools) *Podophyllum* (green, watery or whitish chalk like stools, very offensive with frequent gagging or empty retching) *Silicea* (constipation, the stool recedes after having been partially expelled).

Depression of spirits: *Ars.* (with emaciation) *Merc. Nux vom. Podophyllum* (with biliousness or liver derangement), *Ign* (from nervous causes, mental emotions), *Puls Plat. Cimici* (in females with deranged menstruation), *Aur. met., Kali brom.* (sucidial tendency) *Acid phos* (with nervous debility), *Arn.* (with much sighing and weak heart) *Secale.*, *Sulphur*, *China*, *Lyco.*, *Plumbum.*, *Spigilla*, *Helleborus.*

Desire constant for water, to keep the mouth wet: *Bella.*, *Ars. alb.*

Desire for taking indigestible items: *Alumina*, *Cal. carb.*, *Cimici.*, *Nitric acid.*, *Psoranium.*

Desire for to be alone: *Carbo. veg.*, *Ignitia*, *Rhus tox.*

Desire for weeping: *Rhus tox*, *Lyco.*, *Nat. mur.*, *Puls.*

Desire lost to move here and there: *Bryo.*, *Caladium.*

Desire to press head strongly with hard item: *Coffea*, *Nux.*, *Thuja.*

Desire to remain alone: *Ignitia*, *Nux.*, *Nat. mur.*, *Petrolium.*

Desires: *Bryo.*, *Cham.* (desire for things, but refused when offered) *Stram.* (desires to talk continuously), *Heper.*, *Nux.*, *Puls.* (desire to commit suicide) *Lyco.* (desire for solitude) *Stromon.* (desires light and company, aversion in Hyos.).

Detachment of the retina: *Gelsemium* (bluish haziness, pain serious infiltration beneath the retina) *Aurum* (upper half of the body not visible, lower half visible, retina inflamed opacity) *Arnica* (traumatic detachment of the retina) *Digitalis* (on walking in the evening the upper half is covered by dark cloud).

Diabetes: *Arsenic* (emaciation and rapid prostration of strength, extreme thirst drinks often but little at a time, great restlessness and fear of death).

Diabetes: *Phos. acid.*, *Lactic acid*, *Arsenic bromide*, *Mag. sulph. Uran. nit.*, *Acid phos.*, *Ars.*, *Nux vom.*, *Terebenth.*, *Helon.*, *Gentiana*, *Scill.*, *Nat. sulph.*, *Syzygium.*

Diarrhoea (chronic): *China* (in afternoon). *Ars.*, *Merc.*, *Con.*, *Podophyllum*, *Puls* (nocturnal) *Lept.*, *Aloe.*, *Merc. cor.* (dysenteric with piles) or *Oled.*, *Ricinus.*

Diarrhoea (during pregnancy): *Arsenic* (exhausting diarrhoea, great weakness vomiting after eating or drinking) *Bryonia* (diarrhoea in hot weather induced by taking cold drinks when system was heated) *Lycopodium* (diarrhoea with a constant sense of fermentation in the abdomen) *Podophyllum* (painless diarrhoea, profuse watery stools, yellow mucus, stool smelling like carrion, worse in the morning).

Diarrhoea (dysenteric): *Lept.*, *Merc. cor.*, *Coloc.*, *Aloe.* (with piles), *Merc. dulc.* (from diseases of the liver).

Diarrhoea (from cold): *Camphor* (sudden with chilliness) *Acon.*, *Merc.*, *Dulc.* (damp) *Colocynth.* (with colic).

Diarrhoea (from indigestible food): *Puls.*, *Nux vom.*, *Ant crud.*, *Ipecac.* (associated with vomiting then Ipecac.).

Diarrhoea (morning): *Apis.*, *Rumex.*, *Acid Phos.*, *Nuph.*

Diarrhoea (summer): *China*, *Iris vers.*, *Ver. alb.*, *Ars.*

Diarrhoea after eating or drinking: *Ars. alb.*, *Argent. nit.*, *Croton ting.*

Diarrhoea from drinking milk: *Cal. carb.*, *Nat. carb.*, *Niccolam met.*, *Sulphur.*

Diarrhoea from eating ice cream: *Arsenic.*, *Bryo.*, *Puls.*

Diarrhoea from eating onion: *Thuja.*

Diarrhoea from eating oster: *Bromium*, *Lyco.*

Diarrhoea immediately after drinking water: *Argent. nit.*, *Ars. alb.*, *Trombodium.*

Diarrhoea in children: *Arsenic alb.* (due to food poisoning or taking rotten food; unquenchable thirst) *Chamomilla* (dentition diarrhoea) *Merc. cor.* (bloody diarrhoea) *Colocynth* (with severe cramping colic) *Podophyllum* (sudden copious, fetid, discharge) *Veratram alb.* (pain less copious, pouring as if from hydrant). *Aconite* (dry hot skin, restlessness, stools white and watery) *Belladona* (small greenish discharges from the bowls) *Bryonia* (diarrhoea from the hot weather) *Calcarea carb* (stools whitish or watery, profuse sweat on the head) *Chamomilla* (stools green watery and corroding attended with colic, smelling like bad eggs) *Ipecac* (stools fermented, sometimes grass green mucus much nausea and vomiting with colic) *Magnesia carb* (sour smelling diarrhoea, stools green) *Mercurius* (stools dark green, much straining during and after stools, sore mouth) *Podophyllum* (profuse watery stools, smelling like carrion, chalk like fecal, worse in the morning) *Sulphur* (changeable stools, stools corroding, early morning diarrhoea).

Diarrhoea in summer season: *China*, *Bryo.*, *Camphor*, *Croton tingl.*, *Gambogia*, *Podo.*, *Olender.*

Diarrhoea of whitish colour: *Cal. carb.*, *Heper*, *Podo.*

Diarrhoea painless: *Bapt.*, *Bismath.*, *Borax*, *Ferrum met.*, *China*, *Phjos.*, *Podo.*

Diarrhoea, associated with cold perspiration on forehead: *Ars. alb.*, *Tabacum*, *Veratrum alb.*

Diarrhoea, from drinking milk: *Cal. carb.*, *Nat. carb.*, *Silicea.*

Diarrhoea, with the feeling that anus is wide open: *Apis.*, *Phos.*, *Secale cor.*

Diarrhoea: *Aconite* (frequent watery whitish or slimy, nausea and sweat before and tenesmus during stool) *Antimonium crud* (stools watery and profuse with deranged stomach, violent vomiting of bitter bilious or slimy mucus, worse after eating or drinking or overloading) *Apis mel.* (stools greenish yellowish, slimy mucus or yellow watery) *Arsenic* (stools thick dark green mucus or brown black watery, diarrhoea excoriating the parts, vomiting after eating or drinking) *Bryonia* (diarrhoea in hot weather or induce by taking cold drinks when the system was heated, thirst for large quantity of water, aggravation in the morning, from motion) *Calcarea carb.* (stool whitish or watery, chronic diarrhoea with clay like stools, feet cold and damp) *Chamomilla* (stools green, watery, corroding with colic, smelling like a bad egg) *China* (stools, yellowish watery, whitish or blackish, painless undigested offensive stools, emissions of large quantities of fetid flatus, aggravation at night, after eating and every other day) *Cina* (white pubescent stools, restless sleep, frequently changing position troubled with worms) *Colocynth* (stools saffron yellow, frothy or thin, slimy and watery before stool cutting colic, great urging, relieved by bending double) *Ferrum met.* (painless watery, undigested stools) *Gelseminum* (induced by sudden depressing emotions, fright, grief, bad news) *Heper sulph.* (chronic diarrhoea, stools light yellow, green slimy, undigested, sour smelling, fullness feeling in the stomach) *Hyoscymus* (painless yellow, watery diarrhoea, involuntary stools) *Ipecac.* (stools grass green mucus fermented, flatulent colic) *Mercurius* (stools dark green, slimy frothy or bloody, frequent urging and tentems during and after stool, sour smelling night sweat, particularly about the head, cold on the forehead) *Phosphorus* (chronic painless diarrhoea, stools undigested, watery with little white flakes or lumps like sago, sleepy in the day time particularly after meals) *Phosphoric acid* (painless diarrhoea, stools whitish watery or yellowish very offensive, frequent emission of pale watery urine) *Podophyllum* (profuse watery stools, smelling like carrion, before stool loud gurgling in the bowels as of water during stool prolapses and always worse in the morning) *Pulsatilla* (stools greenish, yellowish like bile or changeable stools, diarrhoea worse at night, craves cool) *Secale cor.* (painless, stools brown watery or slimy, discharged rapidly and with great force, aversion to heat or to cover up) *Sulphur* (stools yellow, brown green undigested, early morning diarrhoea, after suppressed eruptions) *Veratrum album* (stools profuse, watery blackish or greenish, colic before and during stool, after stool great weakness) *Ars., Carbo veg., Secale cor., Verat. album.* (acute diarrhoea with sudden prostration of strength) *Ant. crud., Bryo., Lach., Nux vom.* (alternating with constipation) *Ars., Cal. c., China, Ferrum, Heper., Lycoi., Phos., Phos. acid, Podophyllums, Rhus tox., Sulph., Verat. album.* (chronic diarrhoea) *Bell., Bry., Cham., China, Dulc., Merc., Puls., Verat. album.* (after a chill) *Acon., Bell., Bryo., Cham., Dul., Merc., Nux vom.* (after taking cold) *Ars. Bryo, Carbo veg., Dule., Puls.* (caused by cold drinks) *Carbo veg., Nux vom., Puls.* (after taking drugs) *Carbo veg., Puls.* (after eating fatty food) *Acon., Ant. crud., Coff., Verat.* (after fright) *Ar., Bryo., China, Colo., Puls.* (after eating fruit) *Colo., Gels., Ign., Phos. acid* (from grief) *Cham., Colo.* (from indigestion) *Coff., Opi.* (after sudden joy) *Ars., Cal. c., Sulph.* (from drinking milk) *Acon., Ant. crud., Bryo., Podo.* (after over heating) *Lyco.* (from eating oyster) *Apis., Ars., China, Colch., Ferr., Heper., Hyos., Phos. acid., Podo., Rhus tox.* (painless diarrhoea) *Ant. crud., Dulc., Hyos., Lyco., Phos.* (during pregnancy) *Acon., Rhus tox.* (after getting wet).

Diarrhoea Cont: *Bryo., Lach., Phos., Rhus* (watery Diarrhoea without pain in the bowls) *Antim. crud.* (watery Diarrhoea with cutting pain in the boewls, Diarrhoea and constipation alternate in aged persons) *Apis mel.* (greenish, yellow, slimy mucus or yellow watery, painless Diarrhoea worse in the morning), *Phos.* (Diarrhoea involuntary as if anus is wide open) *Arnica m.* (stools slimy mucus, brown fermented like yeast) *Baptisia* (exhausting excoriating stools and very fetid) *Bryonia* (Diarrhoea in hot weather or from taking cold drinks, worse in the morning and from motion, cutting colic before stool) *Cal. carb.* (stool whitish, watery, smelling sour during dentition), *Carbo veg.* (of thin pale mucus, involuntary cadaverous smelling stool) *Cham.* (stool hot, smelling like bad eggs) *Cham., Cal carb., Dulcamara, Merc., Podo., Sulph.* (Diarrhoea during dentition) *China* (stool watery, white blackish or yellow, worst after meal at night, painless debility Diarrhoea) *Cina* (involuntary white stools, stool mixed with worms, itching at the anus) *Colchicum* (with transparent, jelly like mucus stools, with tenesmus) *Colocynth* (after vexation, grief, stool green) *Gels., Opi.* (from fright) *Comphor* (from drinking limestone water), *Merc.* (bloody Diarrhoea with violent pain in the bowls extending down to thigh), *Ars., Ferrum* (dysentery like Diarrhoea, renewed each time after taking least food) *Con., Lyco., Nux.* (stool liquid, feacal mixed with hard lumps), *Digitalis* (watery Diarrhoea, white or ash coloured stools, chilliness before stool) *Dulcamara* (from taking cold, stools mucus green watery and whitish, weather suddenly becomes cool)

Ferrum (watery Diarrhoea burning corroding the anus) *China, Phos., Acid phos., Podo.* (painless Diarrhoea, stools of undigested food), *Gels.* (Diarrhoea from sudden depressing emotions, fright grief, bad news, stools yellow feacal cream coloured, bilious) *Graphites* (stools of brown fluid mixed with undigested substances, very fetid) *Heper.* (painless Diarrhoea, stool light yellow) *Hyoscy.* (painless Diarrhoea, stool yellow watery during lying in, Diarrhoea during typhoid fever) *Ipecac* (stool as if fermented, nausea and colic, stool green as grass) *Kali bich.* (morning Diarrhoea wakes up with urgent pressure to stool, stools watery with bloody jelly like, sensation of plug in the anus) *Lachesis* (chronic Diarrhoea, exhausting mostly in the evening or at night, alternate Diarrhoea and constipation, stool offensive) *Mag. carb.* (sour smelling Diarrhoea of children, cutting punching in the abdomen) *Merc vivus* (stool dark green frothy or yellowish like sulphur, tenesmus during after stool) *Nat. mur.* (stool thin watery with colic, excoriating stool only in the day time) *China* (stools are of undigested matter, worse at night and after eating, stools may be yellow watery or brown and offensive exhausting out weakness) *Ferr. met.* (profuse Diarrhoea coming on during or after eating) *Ars. alb.* (profuse Diarrhoea, thirst for small quantity of water at frequent intervals) *Acid phos.* (stools are frequent, copious and not attended with much debility) *Podophyllum* (profuse, gusting Diarrhoea coming on in the morning or more in day time than at night) *Iris.* (Diarrhoea in summer, stool copious and vomiting, patient worse at 2-3 in the morning) *Phos.* (constipation and Diarrhoea alternate, painless debility Diarrhoea, worse in the morning, stools white watery with little grain like sago, involuntary stool) *Phos. acid.* (copious watery whitish stools, painless not debilating) *Podophyllum* (chronic Diarrhoea, stools profuse gushing out like torrent, frequent chalk like stools very offensive with gagging and thrust smelling like carrion, during or after stool prolapsus of anus, Diarrhoea worst after eating or drinking) *Kali bich., Phos., Sulph.* (chronic diarrhoea worse in the morning) *Ars. alb., China, Puls., Verat.* (chronic Diarrhoea worse at night) *Puls.* (nightly Diarrhoea, stools watery or green like bile, preceded by grumbling and colic) *Ars., China., Colocynth* (Diarrhoea from eating fruits, Colocynth from eating peas) *Ipecac., Merc., Sulph.* (dysenteric Diarrhoea stools all mucus and blood, chilliness during stool) *Sabina* (Diarrhoea with pain extending from back throughout the pubis) *Secale cor.* (painful Diarrhoea with great prostration with sudden sinking of strength) *Antim. crud., Dulc., Hyos., Phos.* (Diarrhoea with green stool, smelling sour, very debility) *Sulph.* (painless morning Diarrhoea, has hardly tune to get out of the bed, watery green mucus, undigested changeable, before stool cutting colic, after stool tenesmus) *Verat. album* (Diarrhoea stool greenish watery with flakes or blackish watery stools, before stool severe colic during stool painless cold sweat on the forehead, after stool great sinking and empty feeling in the abdomen).

Digestive problems of children: *Antim. crud.* (white thickly furred tongue) *Carbo veg.* (slightest food distress) *Ipecac.* (nausea, vomiting) *Nux vom.* (constipation), *Pulsatilla* (due to heavy food) *Veratrum alb.* (loose rice colour stools).

Diphtheria acute: *Dipth., Lac. can., Merc. cyanatus.*

Diphtheria associated with croup cough: *Bromium, Iodium, Kali bich., Merc. cyanatus.*

Diphtheria associated with passing of little urine: *Apis., Ars. alb., Canth., Lac. can., Merc. cyanatus., Naja.*

Diphtheria covered with greenish membrane: *Phyto., Merc. proto.*

Diphtheria covered with white membrane: *Apis., Ars. alb.,* Kali *bich.,* Kali *chloride, Lac. can., Lach. Lyco., Merc., Merc. cyanatus., Merc. proto iodatus., Nitric acid., Phyto., Diptherium.*

Diphtheria covered with yellowish membrane: *Merc. cynatus., Merc. proto. iodatus., Nat. phos.*

Diphtheria extended to nose: *Kali bich., Lyco., Merc. cor., Merc. cyanatus.*

Diphtheria extends to ulvas: *Pyto.*

Diphtheria inflammation of left side in travels to right side also: *Lach., Lac. can.*

Diphtheria inflammation of right side travels to left side also: *Lyco., Lac. can.*

Diphtheria inflammation travels from one side to other side but return again to same side: *Lac. can.*

Diphtheria left sided: *Lachesis, Merc. bin. iod., Lac. can.*

Diphtheria of children: *Belladona* (red shining surface in the throat) *Ammonium carb.* (with burning sensation in the throat) *Gelsemium* (resulting into paralysis) *Ammonium carb.* (cannot sleep due to stoppage of nose) *Tarentula cubensis* (with dark coloured deposits).

Diphtheria of vocal chord: *Bromium, Diptherium, Heper., Kali bich., Merc. cyanatus., Spongia.*

Diphtheria right sided: *Apis., Lyco., Merc. proto iod., Lac. can.*

Diphtheria with red discharge: *Lac. can., Merc. cyanatus.*

Diphtheria: *Apis mel.* (puffiness arund the eyes, pain in the car when swallowing) *Kali biachrom* (stringy mucus) *Lachesis* (fauces covered with diptheric membreane) *Lycopodium* (right side first and spread to left, worse from warm and better by cold) *Mercurius* (tough feted mucus, breath very offensive).

Diphtheria (sequelae): *Phyto* (horseness) *Dig.* (enfeebled heart), *Gels., Ign., Coni., Strych.* (paralysis), *China, Sulph.* (debility), *Phos., Rhus., Sulph. Secale.* (Diarrhea) *Ars.* (albuminaria)

Diptheria: *Acon., Bella., Phyto.* (mild simple cases) Merc. *cyn.* (white membrane with depressed vital force), *Baptisia* (with typhoid symptoms), *Lachesis* (symptoms starts on left side and spread to right side), *Merc iod.* (much swelling of glands) *Kali bich., Iod., Acid mur., Ars., Ammon. carb.* (malignant with great prostration typhoid condition).

Discharge (from ears) *Arsenic album* (burning thin, excoriating and offence) *Calcarea carb.* (of mucus) *Heper. sulph.* (of fetid pus, pustules in auditory canal) *Pulsatilla* (thick bland green, offensive with pain).

Discharge (from nose): *Allium cepa* (exposure to damp cold weather, extremely acrid, copious, watery, drip like a tap) *Ambrosia* (lachrymation with intolerance, itching of eyelids) *Arsenic album* (excoriating thin watery, burning nose blocked, bleeding) *Arsenic iod.* (chronic nasal catarrh i.e. inflammation of mucus membrane with free discharge, from posterior and anterior naeres, profuse, thick, yellow with sneezing) *Aurum met.* (fetid, full of pus, blood, in caries of nasal bones) *Baryta carb* (thick yellow mucus with swelling of upper lip and nose) *Calcarea sulph.* (yellowish secretion, full of pus, tinged with blood, from posterior nacres) *Kali bich.* (thick ropy greenish or yellow discharge inwards fetid smell) *Merc. sol.* (yellow or greenish acrid and profuse, too thick to run down the lips, at times fluent, at a time blood comes) *Nat mur.* (violent, fluent, stoppage of nose) *Pulsatilla* (yellow, green mucus, bland, abundant in the morning coming out) *Sepia* (thick greenish discharge, thick plugs and crust blown out in the morning) *Spigelia* (bland, post nasal, chronic) *Phosphorus* (chronic, with small hemorrhages, handkerchief always full of blood).

Discharge from eyes: *Allium cepa* (eyes burn and smalrt, bland, copious acrid coryza) *Argentum nit.* (purulent abuncant, acanthi blood red, acute conjunctivitis ophthalmia) *Arsenic alb.* (eyes burn, lid ulcerated, edema around eyes, granulated and ulcerated eye lids, better by warmth, restlessness) *Cal. sulph.* (discharge yellow thick and dumpy, yellowish purulent mucus flows through nose inwardly tinged with blood) *Dulcamara* (discharge thick yellow, granulated lids, from exposure to damp cold weather) *Euphrasia* (acrid discharge from eyes and bland discharge from the nose, eyes water all the time, burning and swelling of the lids) *Merc. sol.* (discharge profuse and burning, swollen lids, iritis, inflammation of cornea) *Merc. cor.* (acrid discharge, photophobia, lids excoriated swollen and red severe burning) *Pulsatilla* (profuse, yellow thick bland, lids inflamed and glued together) *Silicea* (continuous watering due to swelling of lachrymal duet, sunlight causes pain in the eyes, due to abscess in the eye).

Dislike for milk: *Cal carb., Ignitia, Lac. defl., Nat. carb., Phos, Sepia, Silicea, Bryonia, Puls., Sulphur.*

Dislike for relations: *Phos., Sepia, Helleborus, Nat. carb.*

Double vision: *Gelsemium* (due to myopia, chill or congestive headache).

Doubts his ability, before taking up any work but when starts easily done: *Lyco., Silicea.*

Dream of, doing excessive labour: *Bryo., Rhus. tox.*

Drinks water in little quantity again and again: *Ars. alb.*

Dropsy (Ascites): *Apis mel.* (waxy paleness of the skin, urine scanty dark like coffee grounds, constipation with scarlet fever) *Arsenic.* (face livid, pale or greenish, debility and prostration, thirst but drinks little, anxiety, restlessness and fear of death, may be associated with heart disease) *China* (general debility, arises from loss of animal fluids) *Digitalis* (dropsy of knee joints and scrotum, strong visible pulsation of the heart) *Lacheses* (left ovary swollen with pressing and stitching pains, cannot bear pressure upon the uterine region, urine black and scanty) *Lycopodium* (upper body portion emaciated while lower greatly swollen, one feet cold and the other hot, urine scanty with red sediments like of sand).

Dropsy (General) *Dig.* (from heart disease) *Ars., Elat., Apis., Hellaborus., China, Apocy., Acon* (recent febrile).

Dropsy (Local) *Apoc., Ars., Apis.* (abdomen) *Ars., Bry., Dig., Hell.* (chest), *Ars., Apis., Ferr., Sulph., China* (extremities), *Apis., Ars.* (face), *Hell. Apoc., Bella., Sulph., Cal carb., Silicea.* (head) *Acon., Iod., Puls., Bryo.* (joints) *Iod., Rhod., Aur.* (Scrotum).

Dropsy (post scarelatinal): *Ars.*, *Apis.*, *Apoc.*, *Canth.*, *Herllob.*, *Terebenth.* (also after intermittent fevers) or *Sulph*, *Znic.*

Dropsy of hand: *Agaricus*, *Aethusa*, *Apis.*, · *Bovista*, *Hellaborus*, *Ignatia*, *Lachesis*, *Nat. mur. Nux vom.*, *Tarentula his.*

Drowsiness (Morbid) *Acon.* (with yawning and general weakness), *Lyco.* (after dinner with atony of the digestive system) *Opi.* (preceded by excitement)

Dubois (retinal vessels enlarged and tortuous, optic papilla swollen, haemorrhage in the retina, pains through the upper part of the eyeball just beneath the brow): *Phosphorus* (extraversion of blood, hole around the light)

Due to emptiness in stomach loss of hunger: *Agaricus*, *Alum.*, *Baryta carb.*, *Muratic acid*, *Rhus. tox.*, *Silicea*, *Sulphuric acid.*

Dwarf children: *Baryta carb.*, *Mendorrihnum.*

Dysentery in, only blood comes out: *Bapt.*, *Hamamalis*, *Merc. cor.*, *Variolinum.*

Dysentery: *Arnica* (caused by mechanical injury, stool clear mucus or bloody with tanesmas) *Arsenic* (stools dark of blackish fluid mixed with blood, of a putrid foul smell, during stool burning and tandems in the rectum, aggravation at night after eating or drinking) *Baptisia* (stool scanty with bloody mucus before and during stool colic pain in the hypogastria, all excretions extremely fetid) *Belladona* (stools greenish, slimy, bloody, great tandems during and after the stool, mouth and throat very dry, with little or no thirst) *Bryonia* (thin bloody stools induced by getting overheated) *Cantharis* (stool white or pale reddish like scrapings of the intestines burning thirst or no thirst at all) *Chamomilla* (stools frequent small, green or white mucus smelling like a bad eggs) *China* (stools chocolate colour smelling putrid, before stool colic relieved by double bending) *Colchicum* (stools jelly like mucus or bloody mixed with skinny substance severe colic and tandems autumnal dysentery) *Colocynth* (stool bloody mucus, or like scrapings, before stool cutting pain and great urging, violent colicky pains, mostly around the navel causing the patient to bend double) *Ipecac.* (stools bloody or bloody mucus much nausea and vomiting, caused by eating unripe sour fruit) *Mercurius viv.* (stools bloody mucus or green slimy, before stool violent and frequent urging during and after stool violent tandems) *Nux vom* (stools thin, bloody mucus sometimes mingled with lumps of feacal matter during stool violent tandems and cutting pain in the lower bowels, after stool relief, symptoms worse in the morning) *Podophyllum* (stools bloody and green mucus or jelly like mucus, prolapsis anus during and after stool, children toss their heads from side to side) *Pulsatilla* (before stool rumbling and cutting colic thirstlessness, worse towards evening and night) *Rhus tox.* (before and during stool cutting colic remission of the pains after stool and from moving about) *Sulphur* (before stool cutting colic painful sensitiveness of abdomen as if the internal parts were raw and sore) *Merc. sol.* (urging to stool continues and does not ceases with evacuation worse in the evening) *Nux vom.* (urging to stool, unsuccessful desire and sensation as if not finished better after stool) *Aloe* (griping pain in hypogastria before stool, stool coming out in jelly like masses; griping pain may or may not stop with stool) *Colo.*

(cutting pain causing the patient to bend double; pain urges to stool and urination) *Nux*, (relief after stool). *Colocynth*. *Canth.* (stool bloody slimy like scrupling with straining relief after stool) *Merc. vivus* (stool bloody mucus, dark green mucus or whitish green mucus, discharges are accompanied by chilliness, violent tenesmus during and after stool) *Nitric acid* (bloody stool and tenesmus) *Nux vom.* (with cutting at navel, pressure on the rectum, stools, bloody mucus with faeces, pitch like stools with blood) *Staph* (dysenteric stool with pressing and cutting in the abdomen before, during and after stool) *Baptisia* (stools of pure blood or bloody mucus, before stool severe colic, during and after stools tenesmus) *Bella.* (dysentery with bloody mucus stools griping colic and tenesmus during and after stool, griping pain in the lower abdomen, better from holding the breath and bearing down) *Canth.* (dysentery with white or pale reddish mucus or bloody mucus stools, stools like scraping of the intestines, before stool violent colic, during stool burning at the anus, after stool tenesmus, burning, biting, stinging at the anus).

Dysentry (chronic): *Aloe.* (with much straining also when piles are present), *Sulph., Chin.* (periodic) *Acid nit. Merc. cor., Nux vom., Ars., Sulph., Silicea.*

Dysentry bloody: *Nux vom.* (after passing stool the stomach pain goes off immediately for short while) Mercurius (stomach pain persists even after passing stool and ineffectual desire for stool continues) *Aloe* (severe stomach ache before passing stool but pain goes off after passing stool, but the patient is drenched with perispiration).

Dysmenorrhea (painful menstruation): *Belladona* (strong bearing down as if everything escape through vulva) *Cimicifiga* (severe pain in the back down the thighs, labour like pains) *Conium* (previous to menses the breast swells becomes hard and painful, much difficulty in voiding urine) *Nux vom.* (menses returns too soon, discharge thick and clotted, soreness across the pubis as if bruised, frequent desire to pass urine) *Pulsatilla* (pains so violent that she tosses about all direction with crush and tears, vertigo on rising up, worse in a warm room) *Sepia* (colicky pain and great bearing down obliging her to cross the legs, weight in the arms).

Dyspepsia (Acute): *Nux vom.* (from undigestible food, pain spasms or mental exertion) *Puls., Ant. crud.* (from rich, fatty food), *Carbo veg.* (in the aged), *Ipecac., Coff., Acon., Bryo.*

Dyspepsia (chronic): *Nux vom.* (pain after food, headache, flatulence and constipation with urging, piles etc) *Bryo.* (sense of pressure as if a stone in the stomach with tenderness congestive headache, head and stomach symptoms worse with every movement, constipation without any inclination to stool), *Puls.* (nausea heart burn, flatulence and vomiting of mucous or Diarrhoea) *Carbo veg.* (oppression of the chest or palpitation of heart from excessive foul flatulence, acidity and offensive Diarrhea), *Lyco.* (weakness much flatulence, sleepiness after even light meals chronic consitipation, acid rising especially in old persons), *Merc.* (depraved taste, offensive breath, water brash, oppression after food, biliousness, pale stool and depression of spirits), *Kali bich.* (chilliness sense of coldness in the stomach, yellow coated or red tongue, heat of hands, dryness of mouth), Rob. (acidity gasous eructation) *Ign.*, *Nux vom.* (from grief care etc. with nervous symptoms) *Cham.* (in children and females, from worry or from cold bilious headache, irritability), *Hydras.* (atonic dyspepsia, flatulence, turpidity of lever, constipation, all gone sensation), *Gels.*, *Sulph.* (chronic constipation, piles, eruptions), *Heper sulph.* (obstinate cases), *China*, *Sulph.* (flatulence anorexia, drowsiness and oppression after eating) *Ant. tar.*, *Ipecac.* (retching and vomiting) *Acon.*, *Ars* (from cold).

Dyspepsia (constitutional): *Cal. carb.*, *Puls.*, *Rob.* (chronic acidity, with tendency to Diarrhea) *Sulph.*, *Nux vom.* (flatulence, biliousness, tendency to constipation), *Ferr.*, *Helon.* (aneamic patients), *Phos.*, *Iod.*, *Ars.*, *Silicea.*

Dyspepsia: *Antimony erudum* (tongue coated white, eructation tasting of the food last taken, thirst worst at night) *Arsenic album* (nausea and vomiting after eating, heat or burning in the stomach) *Bryonia* (frequent eructation especially after a meal, everything tastes bitter, constipation) *Calcarea carb.* (can not bear anything tight around the waist, cold damp feet, profuse menstruation) *Carbo veg.* (frequent eructation without relief, sensation as if the stomach and abdomen would burst by eating and drinking) *China* (abdomen full and tight, eructation affords no relief, desire to be down after every meal) *Lycopodium* (after taking little feels full up to the throat, much rumbling particularly in the left side of the abdomen) *Mercurius* (pressure in the epigastria much saliva with saltiest metallic taste) *Nux vom.* (frequent sour eructation, cramp like pains in the stomach with pressure particularly after a meal, stool large hard) *Pulsatilla* (tongue coated white or yellow with bad taste in the morning, beating in the region of the stomach) *Silicea* (water tastes badly, constipation the stool recedes after having been partially expeled) *Staphysagria* (extreme hunger, even when the stomach is full of meal).

E

Ear (discharge from and soreness of): ***Merc.*****,** ***Acid carbolic*** **(thick bloody and foeted discharge)** ***Puls.*****,** ***Kali bich.*****,** ***Elaps.*** **(thin discharge),** ***Aur. met.*** **(yellow foeted discharge)** ***Acid mur.*** **(with burning and itching),** ***Cal. Carb.*****,** ***Ars.*****,** ***Hep.*****,** ***Sulph.*** **(chronic).**

Ear (inflammation of): ***Acon.*****,** ***Bell.*****,** ***Puls.*****,** ***Merc. sol.***

Ear (noises in): ***Sulph.*****,** ***Nat. Sabicyl.*****,** ***Acid phos.*** **(with deafness)** ***Nux vom.*****,** ***Ignitia*** **(sensitiveness to sound),** ***Bella.*****,** ***Veratrum vir.*** **(ringing noises from congestion with nausea),** ***Kali iod.*****,** ***Mosch.*****,** ***Puls.*****,** ***Acon.*****,** ***Macrot.*****,** ***Graph.*** **(roaring thundering).**

Ear ache (Otalgia): ***Belladona*** **(roaring and humming in the ear)** ***Chamomilla*** **(pain caused by taking cold, worse in cold and night, child extremely fretful)** ***Mercurious vivus*** **(pricking pain extending to cheeks, worst towards evening).**

Ear discharge in children: ***Heper Sulph.*** **(discharge of pus and blood)** ***Merc. cor.*** **(thick bloody, offensive discharge)** ***Pulsatilla*** **(green bland mucus)** ***Silicea*** **(chronic case).**

Ear injury: ***Arnica*** **(any kind of injury external or internal)** ***Ruta*** **(injury to the bone in the ear)** ***Ledum*** **(wound in the ear caused by a pointed article in an effort to remove wax or suppress itching)** ***Belladona*** **(injury, results into severe pain)** ***Heper. sulph.*** **(wound in the ear suppurates resulting in yellowish green pus flowing out).**

Ear wax: ***Conium*** **(helps in elimination of wax).**

Earache of children: ***Aconite*** **(acute pain with fever)** ***Belladona*** **(sudden on set particularly in right ear)** ***Chamomilla*** **(severe pain wants to be carried)** ***Merc. cor.*** **(if pus is formed)** ***Pulsatilla*** **(feeling of stuffing)** ***Plantago*** **(inflammation of middle ear)** ***Chamomilla*** **(of infants)** ***Valeriana*** **(from exposure to dry cold)** ***Chimaphilla*** **(severe in night and by warmth).**

Ears: ***Acon.*****,** ***China*** **(roaring in the ears)** ***Acon.*****,,** ***Acid Phos.*****,** ***Silicea*** **(acuteness of hearing, noise is intolerable)** ***Ars.*****,** ***Bell.*****,** ***Cal. Phos.*****,** ***Strom.*** **(dullness of hearing)** ***Bella, China*** **(inflammation of external and internal ear, stitches in the ear, humming, tingling in the ear)** ***Cham.*****,** ***China, Merc.*** **(stitches in the ear with hardness of hearing)** ***Puls*** **(shooting, darting, tearing pains)** ***Cal cab.*****,** ***Heper.*****,** ***Phos.*****,** ***Rhus tox.*** **(pulsation in the ears or heaviness of hearing after abuse of quinine)** ***Heper.*****,** ***Acid nit.*** **(hardness of heavy after abuse of mercury)** ***Caust*** **(buzzing and roaming in the ears and** ***head Bell.*****,** ***Lyco.*****,** ***Con.*** **(roaring and humming in ear)** ***Cham.*** **(Otalgia, swelling of parotid gland)** ***China, Calc c.*****,** ***Graph, Nux*** **(ringing in the ears)** ***Bell.*****,** ***Lyco.*****,** ***Nit. acid.*** **(singing afterward scrapping)** ***Cal c.*****,** ***Graph.*****,** ***Silicea*** **(stoppage of the ears, which open at times from loud noise)** ***Cal.*****,** ***Hep.*****, Phos. (hardness of hearing)** ***Graphites*** **(dryness of inner ear, cracking in the ear when chewing, hissing in the ear, detonation in the ears)** ***Kali bich.*** **(stitches in the left ear, discharge of thick yel-**

low fetid pus after scarlet fever) *Caust.*, *Con.*, *Croc.* (buzzing roaring) *Nit. acid.*, *Puls.*, *Merc.*, *Sulph.* (discharge of pus from ears) *Nat. mur.*, *Cham.*, *China.* (otalgia with stitches in the ears) *Merc.*, *Nitric acid.* (roaring, throbbing, cracking in the ears) *Bell.*, *Lyco.*, *Nitric acid.* (roaring in the ears in the morning), *Puls.* (otalgia, darting, stinging in the ears, discharge of pus, after measles, chicken pox etc.) *Puls.*, *Calc c.*, *Caust.*, *Sulph.* (hardness of hearing as if ears are stuffy) *Rhus tox.*, *Graph.*, *Merc.* (discharge of bloody pus, with hardness of hearing) *Heper.*, *Kali bich.*, *Merc.*, *Puls.* (discharge of thick yellow fetid pus) *Sulph.*, (wabbling in the ears, as if water is in them) *Calc c.*, *Graph.*, *Ńux vom.* (ringing in the ears): *Bella.*, *Lyco.*, *Nit acid.* (roaring, stitching, humming), *Cal c.* (singing after afterward snapping) *Nit. acid* (cracking in the ears), *Sil.* (stoppage of the ears, which opens at a time with a loud reports) *Calc carb.*, *Phos.*, *Rhus.* (pulsation throbbing in the ears), *Phos.*, *Rhus.*, *Sulph.* (whizzing in the ears), *Aco.*, *China* (roaring in the ears), *Phos.*, *ac.*, *Aco.*, *Sil.* (acuteness of hearing; noise is intolerable) *Cal Phos.*, *Stram.* (Dullness of hearing).

Ecchymoses (discolouration of skin from a bruise): *Arn.* (in recent case), *Ham.* (much discoloration) *Acid mur.*, *Rhus.*, *Ruta.*

Ecchymoses (effusion of blood beneath the conjunctiva): *Arnica mont.* (following blow and various injuries of the eye) *Ledum pal.* (inflammation of conjunctiva in which extrascavenger of blood predominate) *Hamamelis virg.* (Consequent upon burns or other injuries) *Aconite* (inflammatory conditions of the eye resulting from the irritant action of the force in body, dryness, heat and burning) *Calendula* (following any operation or resulting from cut wound of any type) Cantharis (from any burn, such as flame, exposure to fire works etc. burning pain in the eye).

Ecthyma (a cutaneous pustular disease): *Ant. tar.*, *Ars.*, *Merc.*, *Rhus.*

Eczema (scalled head and milk crust): *Merc. cor.*, *Rhus ven.*, *Graph.*, *Mezer.*, *Ant. tar.*, *Cal carb.*, *Kali bich.*, *Silicea*, *Heper Sulph.*, *Nux. juglans.*

Eczema (simple): *Rhus.*, *Merc.*, *Heper.*, *Sepia.*, *Led.*, *Croton ting.*, *Sulphur.*, *Clem.*, *Juglans.*

Eczema (with great redness and burning): *Ars.*, *Ant. tar.*, *Nux juglans.*, *Rhus ver.*, *Crot ting.*, *Merc.*, *Kali bich.*, *Phos.*

Eczema of children: *Antim. tar.* (vesicles surrounded by red areola about nose, ears, neck and shoulders) *Arsenic alb.* (burning corrosive discharge) *Cal. carb.* (thick scales, pus underneath) *Merc. sol.* (bright red shining eruptions) *Rhus tox.* (intense itching worse at night) *Sulphur* (on head or vulva with itching and burning).

Edema of the body: *Ars. alb.*, *Apis.*, *Apocynum*, *Helloborus*, *Lyco.*, *Acetic acid.*

Ejaculation: *Acid phos.* (deficient, sexual power, penis relaxed during intercourse) *Calcarea carb.* (semen ejected too soon, weakness after intercourse) *Selenium* (emission too rapid, increased desire, decreased ability) *Sulphur* (discharge on mere contact of bodies or of penis with vulva).

Elbows: *Arg. met.* (rheumatic affections of elbows, writers cramps, partial paralysisof forearm) *Arnica* (tennis elbow, sprain, injury) *Phosphorus* (stitches in elbow joint, numbness, can scarcely hold anything with hand) *Pulsatilla* (numbness around elbow).

Emaciation: *Ars.*, *Iod.*, *Ferr.*, *Merc.*, *Chin.*, *Kali iod.*, *Cal carb.*

Emphysema: *Ammonium carb.* (lack of strength of bronchial tubes, oppression of breathing, great accumulation of mucus in lungs, pain in chest) *Arsenic album* (great difficulty in breathing, suffocation, face turns blue, cold perspiration, anxiety and restlessness) *Carbo veg.* (bronchitis, cough spasmodic violent, total breathlessness, coldness of body, skin blue) *Ipecac.* (dry spasmodic cough in old persons, difficulty in expectorating mucus, difficulty in inspiration and expiration, wheezing).

Emptiness in stomach at 11 AM: *Nat carb.*, *Phos.*, *Zinc.*

Encephalitis (inflammation within the cranium): *Acon alternate with Arn* (if from an injury) *Bell.*, *Ver ver.*, *Hyos.*, *Opi.* (according to brain symptoms) *Bry.*, *Hell Apis.* (effusion) *Bacil* (tuberculosis).

Endocarditis: *Aconite* (palpitation with anxiety, brief loss of consciousness, high temperature, congestion of both heart and lungs, sudden lowering of blood pressure) *Cactus* (constriction severe, obstructed breathing, face blue, pulse quick, throbbing tense and hard) *Kalmia lat.* (severe pain in the heart region and shoulder blades, difficult breathing, shifting pain, better sitting erect) *Naja* (palpitation, gasping for breath, body cold, pulse slow, weak, irregular, tremulous better walking in open air, angina pain extends to left shoulder and arms).

Enlargement of tonsils: *Belladona* (enlarged, inflamed and painful) *Calcarea* (tonsils in persons of scrofulus habit) *Heper Sulph.* (as if caused by a splinter, incline to suprate) *Lycopodium* (throat feels contracted, red sand in urine) *Mercurius* (dullness of hearing).

Ennui: *Aurum met.* (disgusted with life talks of committing suicide).

Enteric fever (typhoid fever): *Bapt.*, *Gels.* (earliest symptomns) *Ars. alb.* (developed disease) *Ipecac.* (excessive Diarrhoea, also with epistaxsis) *Ver ver.* (involuntary Diarrhoea), *Ars. alb.*, *Acid mur.*, *Rhus tox.* (extreme prostration), *Terebenth. or Acid nit.* (intestinal haemorrhage), *Phos.*, *Bryo.* (lungs complication) *Acid phos.*, *China*, *Ammon. carb.*, *Nux vom.* (Debility following).

Enteritis: *Aconite* (abdomen swollen and tender to touch, cutting burning and tearing pains in the umbilical region) *Arsenic* (sudden sinking of strength, great restlessness, vomiting and worse after eating or drinking) *Belladona* (heat and tenderness of the abdomen) *Bryonia* (lips parched dry and cracked, very sensitive to pressure, anxious restlessness) *Mercurius* (abdomen painful to contact, restless sleep).

Enuresis (in continuance of urine): *Cina* (disease from the irritation of worms in the intestine) *Conium* (frequent micturition during the night, suitable to old men) *Phosphorus acid* (in children and young persons who grow too fast) *Pulsatilla* (involuntary emission of urine when coughing and during sleep) *Sepia* (the urine is very offensive and deposits of clay coloured sediment) *Sulph.*, *ur* (wetting the bed at night).

Epilepsy (recent): *Ign.* (in children and females), *Viscum.*, *Acid hydrocy.*, *Kali iod.*, *Bella.*, *Strom.*, *Oenanthe.*, *Croc.*, *Ver vir.*, *Argent. nit.*

Epilepsy in children: *Belladona* (jumps in sleep, loss of consciousness, foams from mouth) *Cina* (convulsion due to worms) *Cuprum met.* (convulsion, aura begins at knee) *Stramonium* (caused by fright).

Epilepsy (chronic): *Bella.*, *Bufo.*, *Cup met.*, *Arg. nit.*, *Hyos.*, *Stronònium*, *Znic.*, *Cal carb.*, *Sulph.*, *Opium* (fits in sleep) *Cina.*, *Teuc.*, *Ign.* (from worms), *Nux vom.*, *Agar.*, *Oenanthe.*, *Croc.*, *Opi.*, *Cocc.*, (from alcohol), Phos., *Acid Phos.*, *China*, *Nuphur.*, *Argn. nit.*, *Ferrum.* (from sexual excesses), *Plumb.*, *Ars. alb.*, *Cic.*, *Zizia*, *Scutel.*, *Kali brom.*

Epistaxis (bleeding of the nose): *Aconite* (blood bright red) *Aranea dia.* (after external injury) *Bryonia* (bleeding of nose at the approach of menses) *Nux vomica* (habitual drunkards *Phosphorus* (profuse bleeding, frequently recurring attacks especially during stool) *Ipec.*, *Acid Sulph.*, *Arnica.* (from a blow), *Aco.* (full pulse and in the plethoric) *Bell.* (flowing free with congestion), *Croc.* (dark stringy blood) *Bryo.* (preceded or accompanied by severe headache) *Ham.* (dark fluid frequent), *Mill.*, *China.* (frequent recurrence), *Phos.*, *Nux vom.*, *Ferr. Phos.*

Erection in penis (abnormal): *Acid Phos.*, *Acid picr.*, *Lyco.*, *Nuphar* (feeble and painful), *Acon.*, *Bell.*, *Gels.* (spasmodic).

Eructation tastes like that of the food taken: *Antim. crud.* (tongue thickly white, aggravation after vomiting) *Bryonia* (ailment develops from moving here and there, better by lying down tongue white in the middle) *Pulsitulla* (after eructation the mouth has taste and sticky feeling).

Eructation: *Arg. nit.* (difficulty in eructation despite of efforts cannot belch) *Lycopodium* (burning eructation near pharynx). *Cal. c.*, *China*, *Puls.* (fluid eructation tasting of the food) *Arnica.*, *Sep.*, *Sulph.* (eructation tasting rotten eggs) *Carbo v.* (eructation of sour rancid food).

Eruptions (General): *Rhus tox.* (vesicular with much itching) *Sulph.*, *Merc.* (nonvesicular with excessive itchng, worse in warmth) *Bryo* (popular, burning itching) *Acon.*, (recent burning itching, dryness of the skin) *Ars.*, *Phyto.* (Chronic much burning and formation of scales) *Ant. tar.*, *Heper.*, *Senaga.* (pustular), *Apis*, *Led.* (similar to bee stings, with itching and oedematus swelling) *Canth.* (patchy eruptions with superficial redness and burning). *Bella.* (bright red patches) *Puls.* (like that of measles) *Cal. carb.*, *Rhus.*, *Voila tricolor.*, *Graphites* (formation of scabs) *Staph.* (stinking) *Sil.*, *Sepia*, *Phyto.*, *Lyco.*, *Phos.*, *Clem.*

Eruptions (suppressed): *Sulph.*, *Bryo.*, *Ant. tar.*, *Camphora*, *Puls.*

Eruptions very small and red: *Bella.*

Erysipelas: *Acon.*, *Ver. vir.* (at commencement and during its course), *Bell.* (bright redness with little swelling also when brain is involved) *Apis.* (much swelling) *Rhus.* (simple vesicular), *Canth.* (vesicular with much burning) *Ver. vir.* (vesicular with severe head symptoms) *Ars.*, *Lach.*, (much prostration) *Sulph.* (chronic) *Apis mel.* (burning and stinging pain in the affected parts, chilies from least motion, dryness of throat) *Arsenic* (affected part assume a blackish hue with a tendency to gangrene, burning pain, rapid prostration, great anguish, intense thirst, worse after mid night) *Belladona* (smooth red shining skin, redness begins in a small spot, congestion of blood, throbbing headache, intolerance to light or noise) *Bryonia* (pain stitching burning and stinging, wants to remain quite, lips parched, dry and cracked dry hard stools as if burnt) *Heper Sulph.* (eruption is sensitive to touch, empty feeling at the stomach) *Pulsatilla* (erotic erysipelas, vertigo when rising bad taste in the morning, mild tearful person) *Rhus tox.* (vesicular erysipelas covered with watery vesicles, intolerable, itching and burning and tingling) *Sulphur* (vesicular eruptions filled with pus, scrofulous diathesis).

Erythema (a superficial inflammatory redness of the skin): *Bella., Acon., Apis., Kali bich., Nux vom., Ferrum., Rhus.*

Eustachian tube (obstruction of): *Belladona* (when the pain is intolerable) *Kali bich.* (chronic sinusitis therein a drip of stringy green mucus into the throat, difficult to take it out, pain in the bone above the eyes) *Pulsatilla* (chronic cold results in bland, thick greenish mucus coming out, sense of smell diminished).

Excessive discharge from the posterior portion of the nose: *Hydrastis, Corallium.*

Excessive hunger, feels hungry as that early in spite of taking food: *Cal. carb., Cina, Lyco., Strontium carb.*

Excessive sweating on head: *Cal. carb., Mag. mur., Sanicula, Silicea.*

Excitements (mental effect of): *Acon., Bell.* (headache and palpitation) *Coff.* (sleeplessness) *Cham.* (with bilious derangement).

Excoctions: *Cham.* (in infants) *Lyco., Sulph., Merc. sol., Cal. carb.* (in healthy subjects).

Excoriation (chafing) in children: *Chamomilla* (red rashes in clusters, fretful) *Graphites* (sores behind the ears, sticky transplant fluid oozes out) *Lycopodium* (excoriation becomes offensive, bleeds easily, constipation) *Sulphur* (small watery pimples over the body, much itching).

Excrescence (in wounds etc): *Acid nit., Carbo ani., Silicea, Acid carbolic, Arn., Ant. crud., Phos., Lach., Thuja, Phyto.*

Exhaustion (muscular or physical): *Arn., Ruta, Rhus, Hydras.*

Exhaustion: *Phos.* (lungs implications); *Merc. bin. iod., Phyto* (grandular enlargements) *Ars., Bapt., Rhus tox., Acid mur.* (much taxasmia), *Tereb.* (1 x)(purplish petchiac about the 12th day) *Acid Phos., China, Sulph., Psorinum* (convalescene).

Exhaustion and fatigue (mental): *Acid Phos., Nux vom., Gels., Cal. carb., Ign., Anacardium, Sil., Acid pic.*

Expectoration: *Agaricus* (little balls of mucus with cough, which ends in a sneeze) *Antim tar.* (difficulty in expectoration through the bronchial tubes are filled with mucus) *Bicillinum* (in humid asthma expectoration is full of pus) *Calcarea acetica* (expectoration has large pieces of casts of bronchial tube, loose cough) *Calcarea iod* (green purulent expectoration, with fever) *Calcarea sulph.* (white or yellow, thick, lumpy secretions from lungs or pleural cavaties) *Coccus cacti* (white tough mucus) *Ferrum phos.* (expectoration of blood, in pneumonia) *Millifolium* (spitting of blood while coughing) *Ipecac.* (bleeding from lungs with nausea, in bronchitis, in asthma) *Kali bichrom.* (glutinous and sticky yellow/green expectoration, coming out in a long stringy and tenacious mass) *Kali sulph.* (in bronchial asthma yellow expectoration) *Pulsatilla* (thick yellow/green, bland, loose cough in the morning) *Silicea* (violent cough with thick yellow lumpy expectoration) *Tuberculinum* (thick but easy expectoration, profuse bronchorhoea).

Extremely cold any part of the body: *Cal. carb., Kali bich.*

Extremities: *Arnica* (sensation as if the joints of the arms and wrist are sprained) *Bryo., Merc.* (sensation as if dislocated) *Arnica* (gout cannot afford to be touched) *Ars. alb.* (arms swollen with back blisters having fetid) *Ars., Bell., Calc. c., Nit. acid, Rhus.* (legs feels so heavy can hardly raise them) *Graph., Lyco., Nux.* (numbness) *Ars., Lach., Lyco., Merc.* (ulcers on the legs with burning, lacerating pain) *Bapt.* (the hands and feet too large) *Bryo., Puls.* (the hands and feet too heavy) *Bell., Nat. mur., Puls., Stromorium* (feling of weight in both arms) *Bell., Bryo., Rhus.* (lameness with tearing pain in the arm) *Bell., Bryo., Calc. carb., Puls.* (hip disease with stinging pain or burning in the hip joint, worse at night and from least motion) *Arnica, Bryo., Cocc., Puls.* (hot, inflammatory swelling of the feet) *Cal. c.* (children late learning to walk) *Cal. c., Caust.* (cold feet, feels as if they have damp stocking) *Cham.* (cramps in calves) *Cimici., Lyco.* (heat of one foot and coldness of the other) *Digitalis*(dropsy of the knee joint, swelling of the feet during the day time diminishes in the night) *Ferrum.* (stitching and tearing in the shoulder joints) *Graph.* (tatter in the bend of the knees and groins) *Heper.* (early stage of whitlow) *Merc., Silicea.* (when the pain is violent and throbbing in the whitlow) *Kali bich.* (stitches at the lower angle of the left scapula) *Lachesis* (caries of the bones of the left leg) *Mag. carb.* (pain as from a sprain in the right shoulder when moving the arm) *Nat mur* (great heaviness of the legs and feet) *Nux., Lyco.* (numbness and paralysis of the lower limbs) *Phos.* (stitches in the elbow and shoulder joints) *Cal. c., Phosphorus, Sulphur* (burning of the feet) *Rhus tox.* (tearing in all the joints of the fingers) *Rhus tox.* (rheumatism with or without swelling and redness caused by damp weather, bathing or straining) *Sepia* (heaviness of the legs, profuse sweat on the feet) *Silicea, Nit. ac.* (fetid sweating of the feet) *Ars., Lyco., Silicea* (Old ulcers with burning and lacerating pains) *Sepia, Veratrum alb.* (cramps in the calves) *Bryo., Nat. mur., Puls., Stram.* (feeling of weight in both arms) *Apis., Lach., Opi., Stram., Verat. alb.* (aggravation, after sleep) *Calc. c.* (great emaciation with swollen abdomen and good appetite) *Cimi., Gels.* (prostration of the whole muscular system) *Phos., Verat.* (prostration of the whole of the nervous system) *Ant. tar., Ipecac., Verat.* (nausea and vomiting with almost all ailments) *Phos. acid, Gels., Ign.* (bad effects from grief chagrin, unhappy love) *Ars., Bell., Ign., Puls., Sepia* (the pains are accompanied with chilliness) *Strom.* (convulsion with consciousness) *Bell., Hyos.* (convulsion without consciousness).

Eye (catarrhal infection of children): *Argent. nit.* (discharge of mucus) *Apis mel.* (chronic case, swelling prominent) *Aconite* (with fever) *Arnica* (inflammation caused in injured cases) *Belladona* (with throbbing in temple) *Euphrasia* (inflamed conjunctiva) *Merc. cor.* (pain with excoriating discharge) *Mercurius* (discharge thin, pain around eye worse at night), *caries* and *necrosis* (of the orbital wall due to injury or other factors) *Kali. iod.* (adopted to syphilitic variety, pain or absent) *Aurum.* (dependent upon or complicated with a mercurio syphilitic dyscrasia) *Silicea* (in caries of orbit of the eye, roughed bone, yellow discharge, better by warmth) *Cal. hypophos.* (for scrofulous subjects) *Pulsatilla* (inflammation of optic nerve and retina accompanied by more or less, severe pains in the head always relieved in open air) *Bryonia* (severe and sharp pain through the eye, eyes feel full and sore on motion) *Mercurius* (sensitiveness of the eyes to glare of the fire) *Conium* (much photophobia) *Nux vom.* (retinitis with gastric disturbance aggravated in the morning) *Veratrum viride* (enlarged disc).

Eye lashes (ectropion, entropion): *Apis.* (eye lashes turn outwards) *Borax* (eye lashes turn inwards) *Petroleum* (loss of eye lashes, marginal telepharitis, acanthi fissured).

Eyelid (sty on): *Puls.* altenate with *Acon., Hep., Sulph., Cal. carb., Apis., Merc. iod.* (in general) *Thuja* (chronic) *Sulph.* or *Staph.* (to prevent recurrence).

Eyelids (agglutination of): *Merc. cor., Cal. carb., Heper Sulph., Sulph., Kali bich., Puls., Graph.*

Eyelids (granular): *Merc. cor., Ars., Kali bich., Graph., Heper Sulph., Sulph., Cal. sulph., Puls., Phyto., Zinc.*

Eyelids swollen and glueing in the morning: *Apis., Argent. nit., Merc. sol., Rhus tox.*

Eyes (aching pain in): *Spig., Cimici., Ruta, Eupha., Jaborandi., Arn.* (from overuse), *Nux vom.* (by over use in artificial light), *Gels.* (pain in eyes with dizziness), *Euphr.* (profuse lachrymation) *Aco., Bell.* (burning in eye ball with frontal headache).

Eyes (blood shot): *Acon* (recent from cold) *Bell., Arn.* (from mechanical causes or foreign bodies) *Ars.* (chronic also from ulceration of cornea), *Spig., Cact., Sulph.* (tubercular ophthalmia).

Eyes (inflammation of): *Acon., Eupha. Merc., Arg. nit., Macrot., Sulph.,* (catarrhal) *Merc. cor., Bella., Conium, Nux vom., Spig., Gels.* (great intolerance of light) *Ars., Ant. tar.* (great intolerance with tubercular ophthalmia) *Clem., Cal carb., Heper Sulph., Iod., Hydras., Sulph.* (chronic tubercular), *Merc Acid nit., Aur., Kali iod., Thuja* (sphilitic) *Arg. nit. Cal. carb.* (in infants) *Ars.* (corneal ulceration) *Sulph.* (following the eruptive fevers), *Euphr.* (profuse lachrymation).

Eyes (Spots floating before): *Hyos., Bell., Coçc., Coni., Merc., Ruta, Chel., Solanum.* (rings and gauze before the eyes), *Ferr.* (from anaemia) *Kali iod.* (chronic).

Eyes (vesicles on) *Rhus., Heper sulph.*

Eyes (weakness of): *Ruta., Phos., Iod., Ver. vir.* (dimness from congestion), *Bapt., Acid oxalic, Nux mosch.*

Eyes (wound of): *Acon., Arn.*

Eyes feel stiff and weak: Other remedies are *Argent. nit., Cal. carb., China Ars., Con., Ignat., Kali iod., Kali mur., Lach., Lyco., Mag. carb., Natr. mur., Nitric acid, Nux vom., Puls., Senega, Silicea* and *Sulph., ur.*

Eyes inflammation with aversion to light: *Bell.* (eyes red, glistering and sparkling wild and unsteady) *Con.* (things look red, coldness in the eyes, obstruction of sight) *Gels.* (aversion to especially candle light).

Eyes: *Ars., Apis, Bell., Merc.* (inflammation of eyes with intolerance to light and increased secretions) *Ars* (oedematous swelling of eyelids) *Ars., Phos.* (contraction of pupils, eyes half closed) *Bell., Hyos., Opi., Stram.* (pupils dilated) *Apis., Calc.* (inflammation of eyes with stringing pain) *Hep., Merc., Sulph.,* (scrofulous ophthalmic) *Ars., Cal. carb., Merc., Sil, Sulph.* (ulceration or speaks on the cornea), *Bell.* (objects appear inverted) *Hyos., Stram.* (objects appear double) *Acon., Hyos., Opi., Stram.* (pupils dilated), *Ars., Phos.* (pupils contracted), *Caust., Ign., Sulph.* (eyes feels as if sand is in them) *Caust.* (cannot keep the upper lids of the eyes up) *Caust., Gels.* (sudden loss of sight as if a film is before the eyes) *Acon., Merc., Phos.* (movements before the eyes as of a swarm, insect, black motes), *Cham.*, *China.* (yellowish of white of the eyes, twitching of the eyelids, bleeding from eyes), *Cina* (dilation of pupils, squinting, dullness of the object which is relieved by wiping the eyes) *Con.*, *Lyco.* (sensation of coldness in the eyes, obstruction of sight) *Ars.*, *Caust.* (burning and itching of eyes), *Con.*, *Bell.* (things look red) *Canth.* (things look yellow) *Digitalis* (various colours before the eyes, things appear green or yellow), *Gels.*, *Rhus.*, *Sepia.* (great heaviness of the eye lids, cannot keep them open), *Graph.* (dryness of eyelids, eye lids red and swollen), *Heper.* (boring pain in the upper bones of the orbit), *Hyos.* (objects look red and large), *Stram.* (objects appear too small), *Ign.* (cannot bear the glare of the light) *Nat. mur.* (flickering zigzag before the eyes) *Bryo.*, *Lyco.* (stitches in the eyes without any redness), *Mag carb.*, *Cal c.*, *Merc.*, *Sulph.* (agglutination of lids in the morning) *Acon.*, *Merc.*, *Phos.*, *Sulph.* (black motes before the eyes) *Bell.* (stars before the eyes) *Bell.*, *Calc c.*, *Merc.*, *Phos.* (scrofulous ophthalmia, lid swollen, edges ulcerated and scabby) *Nat. mur.*, *China*, *Coc.* (letters run together when reading) *Nit. acid.* (for short sight) *Nat. mur.*, *Calc.* (for long sight) *Opi.* (pupils dilated and insensible to light) *Styes.*, *Puls.*, *Phos.* and *Lyco.* (especially on the upper lid) *Rhus tox.*, *Staph.* (on the lower lid) *Rhus tox.* (Erysiphelatous swelling of the eye and adjacent parts) *Secale cor.*, *Hyos.* (double vision) *Sepia*, *Gels.*, *Rhus.* (pain in the eye lids when waking, as if too heavy, cannot keep them open) *Silicea* (agglutination at night, eyes are dazzled by light) *Ars.*, *Bell.*, *Caust.*, *Sulph.* (burning in the eyes) *Merc.*, *Nat. mur.*, *Sulph.* (ulceration of the margin of the lids) *Euphrasia* (catarrhal conjunctivitis or phlyetenular or trachoma, lachryma-tion excessive, acrid and burning, discharge profuse thick yellow, micro purulent and acrid making the lids sore and excoriated) *Graphites* (eruptions are glutinous, fissure and bleed easily, intense photophobia, profuse lachrymation, external acanthi cracked and bleed easily upon opening the eye, thin acrid discharge from the nose) *Heper sulph* (intense photophobia, lachryma- tion and redness of eyes, lids swollen bleed on opening and sensitive to touch, discharge of yellowish white colour throbbing and stinging pains) *Ignitia* (catarrhal conjunctivities in nervous hysterical subjects, sensation as if sand is in the eyes) *Kali bichrom* (shreds or strings float loose in the eye, stringy dishcarge mixed with tears, absence of photophobia and redness of eyes) *Lachesis* (tendency of hemorr-hage on removing any membrane) *Mercurius* (thin excoriating, mico-purulent discharges are thin and acrid, severe pain, worse at night and by light) *Mercurius cor.* (all symptoms are intense in it all in the mercurial salts) *Mercurius prot.* (eye red and painful with photophobia, tongue coated yellow at the base) *Natrum mur.* (skin around the eyes glossy and shining) *Nitric acid* (copious yellow discharge of pus which flows down the cheeks which are swollen and painful) *Nux vom* (morning aggravation of all symptoms relieved by cold) *Phytolacca* (firm, hard swelling of lids) *Pulsatilla* (catarrhal and purulent conjunctivitis, discharge bland and profuse yellow or white, better in open air) *Rhus tox.* (lids red, edematous, intense photophobia, worse at night and damp weather) *Sanguinaria* (catarrhal condition with junctivitis, better by cold application, worse morning and evening) *Sulphur* (chronic occurring in scrofulous children covered with eruptions, pain sharp and lancinating as if needle or splinter is piercing, pain through back of eye to head, worse on application of water) *Terebintha* (severe pain in the eye and corresponding side of the head, urine dark in colour) *Zincum.* (conjunctivitis confined to the inner half of the eye, worse in evening and in cool air itching pain in the internal acanthus) *Thuja* (syphilitic iritic with gummite on the iris, large wart like stitching pain in the eye aggravated into night better by warmth) *Cendron* celery neuralgia following the course of orbital nerve) *China* (due to loss of vital fluid or mataria with chill and fever) *Arsenic alb.* (periodic burning pains worse after mid night, better by warmth) *Aconite* (at first state or sudden appearance of the disease due to exposure to cold draught of air, traumatic iritic, great heat, burning and dryness of the eye) *Belladona* (severe throbbing pain in the eye at head worse at night) *Clematis* (great sensitivenes to cold air) *Conium* (excessive photophobia with little redness) *Hamamelis* (hemorrhage has taken place into the iris or interior chamber) *Spigeli* (sharp and shooting pain both in and around the eye especially it has radiated from a point) *Terebintha* (iritic with intense pain in the eye and head, urine dark).

F

Face (ache): *Acon.* (from cold or depression influence) *Bell.* (redness of the face and mental disturbance) *Cham alt* with *Merc. sol.* (one side face ache from cold) *Colocynth, cimicifuga* (severe neuralgic pain) *Ars.* (periodical), *Spigelia pain* extends to the left orbit) *Gels.* (twitching of the face) *Chels.* (morning neuralgia with hepatic disorder) *Cimicifuga* (with uterine disorder) *Cham.* (with swelling and irritability) *Chin. Sulph.* (face ache is relieved by pressing a cold object on the face or by walking up and down a room).

Face (Pale and sunken): *Ars.* (emaciation), *Helon* (with anaemia) *Cal. Carb. Iod.*, *Acid Phos.*, *China* or *Cina* (from worms).

Face (redness of): *Nux vom.* (flushing after meals) *Acon.* (from excitement) or *Bell.* (scarlet red), *Melilotus, Sepia* (flushes) *Ferrum.*, *Carbo veg.*

Face: *Acon.* (swollen, red and hot face) *Bell.*, *Hyos.*, *Opi.* (dark red blotted, swollen face) *Ferr.* (least emotion produces a red flushed face) Ars., *Canth.*, *Chin.* (pale face with distorted features) *Bell.*, *Acon.*, *Bryo.* (glowing redness of the face or else great paleness) *Bryo.*, *Hyos.*, *Opi.* (dark red swollen face) *Sepia, Sulph.* (yellow face, blackish strip across the nose resembling a saddle), *Lyco.*, *Phos.* (circumscribed redness of cheeks) *China, Ars.*, *Verat.* (pale face, sunken eyes with blue margins) *Cina* (blotted pale face with blueness around the mouth, face cold with cold perspiration) *Colocynth* (dark redness of the face, neuralgia of left side which extend to ear and head) *Ferrum* (pale face and lips with great debility, least emotion or exertion produces a red flushed face) *Nit. acid, Dig.* (black pores on the face) *Nit. acid* (small pimples on the face) *Acon.*, *Cham.* (redness and heat of one check and paleness of the other) *Ars.*, *Carb veg.*, *Phos.*, *Verat.* (pale sickly complexion, death like countenance) *Cal c.*, *Sulph.* (circumscribed redness of the face).

Facial neuralgia: *Aconite* (pain severe so wants that something be done for him/her, great fear and anxiety) *Arsenic album* (burning, stinging pain and great prostration) *Belladona* (darting pain in cheek bones and jerking in the facial muscles, intolerance to noise or light) *Causticum* (drawing pains on the right side from check bone to temple, involuntary urination when coughing) *Chamomilla* (pain causes hot perspiration about the head, very impatient) *Chin.a* (periodical attacks, darting pain aggravates by least contact) *Colocynth* (neuralgia of left side of the face, pain aggravates by touch or motion) *Gelseminum* (throbbing pain in the brain) *Pulsatilla* (disposition to weep and complain) *Staphysagria* (drawing, tearing pains in the check bones) *Stromonium* (feels too tall).

Fainting (swooning): *Acon.*, *Colo.*, *Opi.* (if it arises from fright) *Arnica* (if from a fall or blow) *China* (if from loss of blood or other debilating cause) *Ignitia* or *Chamomilla* (from sudden mental emotions) *Acon.*, *Cocculus* or *Chamo-*

milla (caused by violent pain) *Heper*. (slightest pain causes fainting) *Chamomilla* or *Heper*. (when preceded by giddiness).

Fainting (tendency to) *Iod*. (from constitutional causes) *China* (from loss of fluid) *Ars*. (due to debility) *Vert. alb*. (coldness and blueness of the skin with cold sweat), *Mosch*. (wakes up with dry mouth) *Cham*., *Cocc*., *Ign*. (Hysterical).

False pains: *Belladona* (backaches as if it would break, pains appear suddenly and goes suddenly) *Coffea* (pains are violent, patient weeps and lament fearfully, very wakeful in the night) *Nux vom*. (every pain produces desire to go to stool, habitual constipation).

Fatigue/Debility: *Alfalfa* (general mental exhaustion and buoyancy all blues dissipated) *Arnica* (physical and mental exhaustion, sleepless when tired) *Calc. carb*. (mental or physical due to over work loaded state) *Carbo veg*. (fatigue even from short walk) *China* (excessive loss of blood, mucus or any fluid from the body) *Nat. mur*. (weakness, emaciation, nervous prostration) *Nux vom*. (due to over use of drugs/medicine) *Phosphorus* (nervous exhaustion mental debility first then physical) *Ruta* (after close work like sewing, reading, typing etc.), *Selenium* (after suffering from exhaustive disease wants to be down and sleep, legs weak when begins to walk) *Psorinum* (sweat on slightest movement, wants to give up and be down) *Phosphoric acid* (from night sweat), *Flouric acid* (nervous and mental from vicious practice, secret vice) *Natrum carb*. (from heat of the summer, causing recurrent headache).

Fauces (sallow): *Merc*., *China*, *Bryo*., *Podo*., *Ars*.

Fauces (swelling of): *Bell*. (with bright redness) *Cham*. (due to toothache) *Apis*. (with puffy swelling).

Fauces: *Bryo*. (very large), *Merc*. (pale and costwe) *Nux vom*., *Collin*. (hard and large expelled only after great efforts in case of spasm of the splinter) *Sulph*. (knotty), *Plumb*. (dark, hard, small balls) *Opi*. (dark and knotty), *Alum*. (soft but difficult), *Dig*. (white, Graph. (hard and knotty) *Ars*., *China*, *Ferr*. (containing undigested food in case of Ars. watery), *Vert. alb*. (watery) *Sec*., *Phos*., *Acid Phos*. (passed involuntarily) *Puls*., *Cham*., *Caps*., *Merc*. (with mucous), *Lept*. (black).

Fear develops ailments: *Aco*., *Ignitia*, *Lyco*., *Nat. mur*., *Opium*, *Phoric acid*, *Phos*., *Puls*., *Silicea*. (as per symptoms)

Fear from crowd: *Ferrum*, *Kali ars*. and *Kali bicrom*., *Kali phos*., *Nat. carb*., *Nux vom*., *Phosphorus*, *Plumbum* and *Stanun*.

Fear from darkness: *Carbo animalis*, *Causticum*, *Stromonium*, *Strontia*.

Fear from dogs: *Bella*., *China*.

Fear from fire: *Cuprum*.

Fear from rattling sound of electricity or typhoon: *Phos*.

Fear from the company of males: *Lyco*., *Nat. carb*., *Hyoseymus*, *Rhus tox*.

Fear of becoming mad: *Actea race*., *Cal. carb*., *Sanicula*, *Canabis indica*, *Puls*.

Fear of becoming poor: *Bryonia*.

Fear of being alone: *Lyco*.

Fear of being poisoned: *Hyosmus*.

Fear of coming bad days: *China Sulph*., *Psoranium*.

Fear of dacoits: *Argn. nit*., *Lach*., *Natrum*., *Arsenic*, *Conium*, *Ignatia*, *Ferrum Phos*.

Fear of death: *Acon*., *Bryo*., *Rhus t*. (great anguish, extreme restlessness) *Aco*., *Ars*., *Cal. carb*., *Cimicifuga*, *Gels*., *Lac. can*., *Nitric acid*., *Phos*., *Platina*.

Fear of ghost: *Calc.*, *Chinium sulph.*, *Psoranium.*

Fear of suffocation: *Phosphorus*, *Stromon ium.*

Fear of unusual happenings: *Arsenic*, *Calcarea carb.*, *Causticum*, *Kali ars.* and *Phosphorus.*

Fear with excitement: *Aco.*, *Anacardium*, *Ars alb.*, *Causticum*, *Ignitia.*

Fears in children: *Opium* (effects last longer) *Hydrophobinum* (from water) *Natrum mur.*, *Naja* (from water) *Crotalus.* (in general or death) Silicea (of being alone) *Aconite* (of crowd, death, of crossing the road) *Sepia* (of evils) *Anacardium* (of examination) *Helonias* (of fits) *Aconite* (of future career) *Ranuncutus* (of ghost) *Phytolacca* (of going to sleep) *Canabis sat.* (of insanity) *Daphne ind.* (of lack of sleep) *Agaricus* (of loss of movement) *Arg. nit.* (of lungs trouble) *Belladona* (of persecution) *Platina* (of stomach trouble) *Hyoscyamus* (of being poisoned) *Calcarea carb.* (from being alone) *Climatis* (from loneliness) *Borax* (of falling down or from downward motion) *Iodium* (of people) *Gelsemium* (of ceasing heart instantly it does not move) *Arg. nit.* (on looking high building) *Stramonium* (from darkness) *Digitalis* (of stoppage of heart if makes movement).

Febricula: *Acon.*, *Camph.* (sudden chilliness), *Bella.* (headache) *Ars.* (with prostration).

Feeling that somebody is following: *Cal. carb.*, *Petrolium*, *Silicea.*

Feeling as if the head is enlarged to greater size: *Corallium*, *Argent. nit.*, *Bella.*, *Bovista*, *Nux vom.ica*, *Rananculus.*

Feeling as if very cold air is passing from the air passage: *Corallium*, *Bromium*, *Carbo veg.*, *Cocenela.*

Feeling of coldness, in the abdomen: *Ambra.*, *Cal. carb.*

Feeling of hard stone in the stomach, better by eructation: *Bryonia*, *Nux.*, *Puls.*

Feeling of opaque curtain before eyes: *Baryta carb.*, *Cal. carb.*, *Phos.*, *Silicea*, *Baryta iod.*

Feeling of spider web on the face tries to remove it: *Baryta carb.*, *Borax.*, *Bromium*, *Graphites.*

Feeling of suffocation: *Phos.*, *Strom.*

Feelings that the ailment will never cure: *Cimicifuga*, *Aurum.*, *Cal. carb.*, *Lachesis*, *Lac. can.*

Feelings: *Variolium* (crazy as if throat is closed) *Thuja oc.* (of alive animal in the stomach) *Phos.phorus* (of coldness always) *Anacaridium* (of emptiness in the stomach) *Aloe* (of heaviness in rectum) *Valeriana* (as if floating in the air) *Thuja* (as if somebody is standing nearby) *Thuja* (as if legs are very long) *Alumina* (as if walking on the cushion) *Ammonium mur.* (of cold in between the shoulders) *Cistus* (of coldness in different parts) *Stannum* (of emptiness in chest) *Alumina* (of pin pricking in the body) *Lycopodium* (of satiety) *Lachnantes* (of ice piece in between the shoulders) *Alumina* (of time is passing slowly) *Thuja* (of soul and body are separated) *Pyrogen* (of as if bed is hard) *Picric acid* (better in the night and worse in the day) *Phosphorus* (of hunger immediately after eating, feels better after eating) *Ambra grasia* (of nervousness among unknown persons) *Baptisia* (of being oppressed after wakening) *Phytolacca* (of soreness all over the body) *Pulsatilla* (of uneasiness in closed room) *Nat. carb.* (worse in the morning after awakening) *Pulsatilla* (worse in the morning after awakening from cold air) *Staphysagaria* (that all limbs are sore and no strength in them) *Ruta* (as if all parts of the body on which one lies are painful and as if bruised) *Arnica* (as if bruised) *Valeriana* (as if floating in the air) *Baptisia* (as if lying on hard board so changes position) *China* (of soreness all over the joints and tearing in spine, sacrum, knees and thighs) *Rhus tox.* (of soreness in every muscle relieved by physical exertion, stiffness and soreness in the beginning to move) *Lachesis* (of uneasiness on awakening).

Feels sleepy but cannot sleep: *Bella., Chamo., Opium.*

Feet (aching) *Arn.* (from overwalking) *Argent. met.* (in general).

Feet (burning in) *Sulph.* (hot and moist must keep them out of the rag in the night) *Canth.* (in hysteric females) *Calc carb., Graph., Phos., Acid phos., Led., Apis., Secale, Chamomilla.*

Feet (coldness of): *Sulph.* (hot hands and face) *Calc. carb.* (as if cold stocking are on) *Ars. alb.* (cold and clamy), *Ferr., Silicea, Nat. mur., Sep., Puls., Graph.*

Feet (Gout in): *Rhus tox., Led. pal., Rhodo., Sulph., Sabina, Arn., Lyco.*

Feet (pain in): *Bryo., Led pal.* (Rheumatic or goaty) *Rhod* (neuralgic), *Rhus., Apis.*

Feet (swelling of): *Ars.* (with emaciation) *China* (with debility) *Ferr.* (with anaemia), *Sil., Apis., Phos., Puls., Caust., Sulph.*

Feet (weakness of): *China, Sulph., Helon., Sil., Acid carbolic.*

Feet rough due to excessive sweating: *Cal. carb., Graphites, Sanicula.*

Felon (whitlow): *Apis mel.* (burning stinging pain, cold water application relieves the pain) *Arsenic* (burns like fire, becomes black, restlessness and prostration) *Belladona* (parts are very red, throbbing headache) *Heper Sulph.* (violent throbbing pain, accelerate suppuration) *Silicea* (suppuration is imminent, discharge fetid, thin and watery: opening slow to heal).

Fester (tendency to): *Petrol., Heper Sulph., Acid nit.*

Fever (General): *Acon.* (restlessness and fearfulness) *Bryo.* (quite patient with constipation) *Bella.* (cerebral erythrism, violence in delirium) *Rhus tox.* (restless, usually Diarrhoea in the beginning).

Fever (intermittent) *China* (great thirst, headache and weakness, violent thirst before and after chill, desires to wrap himself for warmth but that does not give relief, paroxysm follows in regular succession) *Chinium sulph.* (the chill is attended with thirst, pale face, pain in dorsal vertebrae, desire to uncover, cold stage may be long, perspiration does not succeed the heat) *Ars. alb.* (time of aggravation is usually midday or midnight, chill is regular, ameliorated by heat, great restlessness, insatiable thirst at hot stage, drinks often but little at a time) *Capsicum* (there is chill in the back with thirst, better when heat is applied to the back or wrapping up) *Eup. per.* (chill in the morning at 9 AM, chill is preceded by thirst but drinking makes him chilly, better by vomiting, nausea predominant with gastric symptoms).

Fever (simple): *Acon.* (quick pulse, pain in limbs) *Ver. vir.* (associated with gastric and brain problems), *Bell.* (red face, throbbing tamples with moderate pulse) *Gels.* (with perspiration) *Bryo.* (headache, shooting pain limbs), *Ars.* (of long duration) *Bapt. Ars., Acid mur.* (low fever).

Fever in, always cover himself: *Nux.*

Fever of children: *Aconite* (exposure to dry cold air) *Arsenic alb.* (with prostration and restlessness) *Belladona* (with intense headache) *Bryonia* (muscular pain worse on least movement and thirst for large quantity of water) *Cantharis* (due to urinary infection, burning pain before, during and after urination) *Gelsemium* (body pain, no thirst) *Natrum mur.* (periodic fevers) *Nux vom.* (due to constipation, chilly but wants to uncover).

Fever typhoid: *Baptisia* (muscular soreness and prostration, afternoon rise in temperature, restlessness, delirium accompanied with delusion discharges offensive) *Gels.* (muscular aching less afternoon rise of temperature) *Rhus tox.* (restlessness, red triangular tip of the tongue muttering delirium, discharges not offensive).

Fever: *Bell., Bryo., Hyos., Strom* (Pulse hard full frequent), *Ars.., Carbo v., Phos., ac., Verat* (small, contracted weak pulse) *Acon.,* (sensation of coldness in the blood) *Ars., Dig., Merc.* (pulse very irregular) *Ant. crud.* (intermittent fever with great sadness, desire to sleep and no thirst) *Apis mel..* (intermittent chill about 4 PM worse in a warm room or near the stove) *Baptisia* (intermittent fever, chill in the morning, drawing pains in the bones before the fever, typhoid fever with the greatest indifference, putrid breath while speaking forgets the words, fall asleep in the middle of the sentence) *China, Nux vom., Verat. album* (during fever chilliness particularly after drinking) *Arnica, Calc. c.* (during fever chills intermingled with heat or internal coldness and external heat) *Cham., Ign.. Nit. acid.* (external coldness and internal heat) *Bryo., Rhus tox.* (burning heat as from hot water coursing through the veins) *Baptesia* (typhoid fever in head feels as if scattered about tries to get the pieces together) *Baptesia* (scarlet fever of a typhoid nature ulcerated sore throat, fetid breath, dry, sore tongue and vomiting) *Bell.* (scarlet fever with smooth, shining redness skin) *Bell.* (typhoid fever with prominent cerebral symptoms) *Bryonia* (intermittent fever, chill predominant, thirst during the cold and hot stages, dry cough with stitches in the chest) *Carbo veg.* (intermittent fever with thirst only during the chill, followed by burning heat, then night sweats) *Cham., Acon., Nux.* (in fever heat with occasional chills, one hot red check the other pale *China, Ars. alb.* (chilliness over whole body, worse from drinking, thirst before and after the chill) *China* (during the chilly stage headache, nausea, absence of thirst during the hot stage, dryness of the mouth and lips with burning, red face and headache) *China, Phos. acid, Silicea* (in fever exhausting night sweats) *Puls.* (intermittent fever after abuse of quinine with congestion of head, vomiting of food and swelling of spleen, profuse and long continued perspiration, fever without thirst) *Heper Sulph.* (intermittent fever first chill 8 PM then thirst and an hour later fever with interrupted sleep, itching, stinging nettle rash before and during chill) *Igntia* (itching, stinging nettle rash during the fever) *Hyoscyamus* (typhoid fever with low muttering delirium, subsultus tendinum, picking at the red clothes, involuntary discharges of faucets and urine desires to escapes) *Hyoscyamus* (after a correct answer relapses into delirium and unconsciousness) *Ipecacuanha* (intermittent where the gastric symptoms predominant sudden attack of fever at 4 PM with heat no thirst, backache, short chill long fever with thirst, external coldness and internal heat) *Lachesis* (in fever chill at night and flushes of heat in day) *Lachesis* (intermittent fever returns every spring) *Lachesis* (typhoid fever with stupor muttering, dropping of lower jaw, dry red or black tongue, cracked on the tip and trembles when protruded) *Sepia* (in fever great coldness of the hands the fingers feel as if dead) *Merc., Bell., Puls.* (accelerated pulse at a time slow and trembling, chilly especially in the evening) *Nat. mur.* (the chill occurs about 10 AM, commencing mostly at feet) *Nitric acid* (afternoon fever with heat and chilliness) *Nux vom.* (coldness of the whole body with blue skin and finger nails) *Opium* (typhoid fever with spoor, snoring with mouth open twisting of the limbs and perspiration on the hot body part) *Phos., Bella., Nux vom.* (pulse free and quick, chilliness generally in the evening not relieved by heat) *Ars., Bell., Phos., Pulsa., Rhus tox.* (continuous internal chilliness even in the warm, increased) *Rhus tox.* (in fever, great restlessness after mid night, has to move often to get relief) *Calc., Heper., Phos., Silicca, Sulphur* (Hectic fever particularly during a long suppuration) *Silicea* (warm fever) *Staph.* (ravenous hunger before and after the paroxysm of ague) *Veratrum album* (typhoid fever with great prostration, cold sweating coma, vomiting and watery Diarrhea and bluish face).

Fibro-adenoma (of the breast): *Calcarea flour.* (hard, stony knots in the breast), *Chimaphilla* (painful tumor of the mamme in women with large breast) *Conium* (pressing the breast hard gives relief) *Phytolacca* (mamme hard, sore and sensitive).

Fibroid tumor in uterus: *Kali iod.* (womb packed with fibroid tumors, tired, hot burning feets) *Pulsatilla* (fibroid tumors in uterine wall near cervix).

Fissure (anal): *Barberis vulgaris* (internal blind fissures accompanied by thick yellow discharge of pus and burning sensation in the anus) *Graphites* (oozing eczema around anus) *Nat. mur.* (rectum torn, bleeding, constipation, stool dry crumbling) *Nitric acid* (sensaton of splinter or stick piercing into the anus, burning and soreness after stool) *Ratanhia* (rectum aches as if it is full of broken glasses, burns for hours after passing stool, feeling of constriction).

Fistula (anal): *Calendula Q* (for local external application) *Myristica* (stops pus formation, heals when pus has already formed) *Nitric acid* (rectum feels torn, bowels constipated, violent cutting pain after stool lasts for hours) *Silicea* (pus formation, painful, difficulty in passing stool, receding stool).

Fistula of anus: *Sil., Cal carb. Ac. flour., Caust., Aur., Bellis per. Thuja, Hamam., Sulph., Phyto., Lyco.*

Fistula of the lachrymal duet: *Cal. carb* (watering worse in open air and early in the morning) *Fluoric acid* (sensation as if wind blowing through eyes, inner aCanthi itching violently, swelling in the bone above the nose and between the eyes).

Fits in children: *Camphor Q* (with unconsciousness) *Acon.ite* (fever and restlessness) *Belladona* (red face staring eyes) *Chamomilla* (during teething period) *Cina* (due to worms causing indigestion, weakness and fits) *Agaricus* (twisting of muscles) *Veratrum virdis* (convulsions flow each other rapidly) *Ipecac.* (nausea and vomiting) *Nux vom.* (constipation leading to fits) *Opium* (red swollen, hot face) Pulsatilla (intake of fatty food results to fits).

Flabby body: *Cal. carb., Sulph., Graphites, Heper.*

Flatulence in stomach, which does not become better even by eructation or passing the wind: *China.*9

Flatulence in upper part of stomach: *Lyco.*

Flatulence in whole stomach: *China.*

Flatulence: *Carb. v., China, Lyco.* **(incarcerated flatulence).**

Flatulence: *Nux vom., Carbo veg., Puls.* **(of stomach)** *Asaf., China, Lyco.* **(of abdomen)** *Tereb., Collin., Arg. nit. Cal. iod.*

Flooding after delivery: *Belladona* **(flooding with pressure downwards, hemorrhage hot)** *Chamomilla* **(discharge is dark and coagulated, patient irritable)** *China* **(blood discharge in dark clots, debility after loss of blood)** *Ipecac.* **(constant flow of bright red blood, nausea with great prostration, desires to be fanned)** *Pulsatilla* **(the pains are too weak and there is alternating hemorrhage).**

Flushing of heat: *Nux vom.* **(on the face after meal),** *Acon., Bella* **(from excitement),** *Cimici., Sepia, Apis.,* **Lach. (flushes at the climatic period)** *Carbo ani., Glonine.*

Food not digested properly: *Cal. carb., Baryta carb., Silicea.*

Food poisoning: *Arsenic alb.* **(poisoning from decayed food, meat or fruits left in open).**

Foot cold, the other foot is warm: *China, Digitalis, Ipecac., Lyco.*

Foreign bodies in the vitreous: *Aconite, Arn., Calendula, Ham.,* **or** *Rhus.* **(as per symptoms of the remedy).**

Foreign body in the eye: *Arnica* **(injury consequent upon pain pus formation)**

Forgetful people for: *Baryta carb., Carbo. Sulph., Colchicum., Lyco., Merc., Petro., Phos. acid., Platina, Anacard., Lac. can., Glonine., Cannabis ind.*

Forgets letters: *Baryta carb., Plumbum.*

Fractures (to promote adhesion in) *Ruta., Symph., Cal carb., Silicea.*

Freckles: *Phos., Graph., Sulph., Acid nit., Sepia, Nat. mur., Canth.*

Fright (after the fright the fear still remains): *Belladona* **(rush of blood to the head with red face)** *Coffea* **(fright from sudden pleasant surprise, extreme wakeful)** *Gelseminum* **(Diarrhoea sets in due to fright patient feels as intoxicated)** *Opium* **(from fright involuntary evacuations).**

Fright (effects of): *Acon.* **(palpitation or quickened circulation)** *Coff.* **(extreme nervous irritability)** *Opi.* **(stupour),** *Hyos., Bella* **(brain disturbance especially children)** *Ignatia* **(convulsive movement)** *Gels.* **(affecting bowels or bladder),** *Anac., Cham., Nux vom., Puls.*

Frighten easily: *Argent. nit., Ars., Baryta carb., Borax, Graph., Lyco., Nat. carb., Sepia, Stromon.*

From perspiration the ailment subsides: *Ars. alb., Nat. mur., Psoranium.*

Frontier open, unification of head bone delayed: *Apis, Apo., Cal. Phos.., Silicea, Sulphur, Zinc. met.*

G

Gall bladder: *Podo., Bapt., Phyto.* (constant dull pain in the region of gall bladder).

Gall stones: *China, Cal carb. Podophyllum, Merc. Nux vom., Chelsidonium* (to expel and prevents) *Berb. vul.. Aco.. Opi.* (during their passage) *Sulph.* (to prevent the formation).

Ganglion: *Ruta., Arn., Sil., Cal. carb., Acid benzoic, Heper Sulph.*

Gangrene: *Arsenic album* (gangrenous inflammation, gangrene in internal organs, burning like fire, ulcers with blue black base) *Carbo veg.* (senile gangrene beginning on toes or margins, blue, cold skin, bleeds easily) *Kreosote* (of lungs in old age) *Secale cor.* (dry gangrene develops slowly, numbness, burning sensation old people with shrivelid skin) *Lachesis, China, Acid carbolic, Tarentula, Anthraxacnum.*

Gastric trouble caused by anger: *Staph.* (colic pain following fits of anger) *Bryo.* (gastric symptoms are associated with chilliness whitish tongue) *Cham.* (gastric symptoms associated with heart, yellow coating on tongue), *Colocynth* (vomiting, Diarrhoea and colicky pain better bending double).

Gastritis (inflammation of the stomach): *Arnica* (belching with taste of putrid eggs) *Arsenicum* (heat or burning in the stomach, vomiting of things eaten, during vomiting violent pain in the stomach, rapid prostration of strength) *Bryonia* (stomach sensitive, cannot bear least pressure on it, hard and dry stool) *Cantharis* (severe burning in the stomach sometimes extending down into the bowels) *Ipecac.* (diarrhea with grass green stools and cutting colic) *Nux vomica* (burning pain in the stomach which is tender to touch hard difficult stool, worse in the morning) *Veratrum album* (intense thirst for cold drinks, extreme prostration, pulse imperceptible, exhausting Diarrhoea).

Gastrodynia and Gastralgia: *Ars., Bismith., Nux vom.*

Gastroenteritis: *Argentum nit.* (incessent vomiting of food, diarrhea immediately after food or drink, better from eructation, in fresh air) *Arsenic album* (nausea, retching after eating or drinking, throws up acrid and bitter substances, blood, bile and green mucus, icy coldness, great exhaustion and restlessness, unquenchable thirst, drinks little quantity of water at a time) *Veratrum album* (violent vomiting, shooting colic radiating from stomach upwards and both sides, diarrhea rice water colour, thin and copious stool, cold sweat, coldness of extremities).

Gastrolgia (cramps in the stomach): *Carbo veg.* (cramps in the stomach, with continual sour eructation) *Colocynth* (spasmodic pain in the stomach, pain is relieved by bending double and by hard pressure) *Nux vomica* (cramp like pain in the stomach with pressure downwards, the pain is relieved by bending forward and rubbing the parts).

Gathered breasts (mammary abscess): *Belladona* (red streaks runs like radii from a central point with burning pain) *Bryonia* (breast is swollen, hard and feels heavy) *Heper Sulph.* (suppuration takes place which causes throbbing pain and chills) *Silicea* (discharge becomes fetid, thin and watery comes from several openings).

Glandula swellings (chronic): *Merc. iod., Iod., Calc. carb., Arum triphy., Cal. phos., Kali iod., Sulph., Baryta carb., Coni., Cistus. can., Phytolacca* (hard swelling).

Glandular swellings (acute): *Bayrata carb., Bella., Rhus.* (hard stony feeling), *Heper Sulph., Merc., Silicea* (when suppuration to threatened).

Glaucoma: *Gelsemium* (a medicine of importance which has proved its value clinically) *Bryomia* (in general where there is serious inflammation eye feels as if pressed out, sharp shooting pain through the eye and head. The eyes feel sore to touch and on moving them in any direction halo around the light, heavy pain over the eye worse at night) *Aconite* (much heat, redness and burning pain in the eye and fever) *Ocmium* (sudden severe pain in and around the eye, darkness of vision, objects seen in fog. Halo of various colours around the light) *Phos.phorus* (fundus hyper anaemic and hazy, halo around the light of various colours, specially red before the eye sensation as if something has been pulled tightly over the eyes, vision impaired better in the twilight) *Belladona* (throbbing pain, headache and flashed face eyes are infected, pupils dilated, pain in and around the eye, pain worse in the afternoon and evening, eyes hot and dry, sensitiveness to light, photophobia) *Asafoetida* (severe burning pain over the eye and around it) *Cendron* (pain severe and shooting along the course of the supra orbital nerve) *Colocynth* (pain severe, burning, aching, sticking or cutting in the eye and around, relieved by firm pressure and by walking in a warm room, aggravates from rest in the night and upon stooping) *Nux vom.* (glaucoma resulting from atrophy of the optic nerve, aggravation in the morning is a marked symptom) *Prunus spin.* (pain severe, crushing in the eyes as if the eye were pressed as under or sharp shooting through the eye and corresponding side of the head, aqueous and vitreous hazy) *Rhododendron* (glucoma pain is always worse just before a storm, ameliorated after the storm) Spigelia (pains sharp and stabbing through the eye and head worse on motion and at night) *Kali iod.* (congestion and inflammation of choroids) *Merc.* (hepatic, uterine and haemmoridal complaints) *Nux vom. Spig., Bryo. Colch.* (rheumatic or arthritic complaints), *Bell., Spig., Merc. Cham. Ruta* (cillarly neuralgia).

Gleet: *Cinnabar, Cann. sat, Canth., Ferrum, Puls., Nux vom., Petrolium, Petrosel., China, Sulph., Thuja, Acid nit.*

Goitre (exopthalmic): *Bella., Thyroidin, Ferrum* (anaemia) *Ars. China, Acid Phos., Spigilea.*

Goitre: *Spong. Cal. Carb. Merc cod., Iod., Brom., Thyrodinum, Sulph., Lapis alb., Merc. bin. iod.*

Gout (acute): *Acon., Bryo., Colch, Dig., Lyco., Verat. vir., Arnica mon., Urtica urens., Q. Acon., Led pal., Acid acet.*

Gout (Arthritis): *Arnica* (a sensation as if resting upon something hard, great fear of being struck or touched) *Bryonia* (stitching tearing pains, aggravated by motion and relieved by rest, dry hard stool) *Colchicum* (paroxysm of tearing, stitching jerking pains particularly in the finger joints, urine dark and scanty, pain aggravates at night) *Nux vomica* (pain jerking, pain from motion and slight contact, but strong pressure relieves modesties of joints) *Phos.phorus* (affections of wrist and finger joints, long narrow hard stools, sensation of weakness and emptiness in the abdomen) *Pulsatilla* (erratic pains, shifts rapidly from one joint to another, aggravation in the evening or at night, craves fresh cool air) *Rhus tox.* (joints red, shining and swollen, stiffness and lameness of the affects parts, aggravation on first movement or during rest, relieved by motion).

Gout (chronic): *Puls., Sulph., Led., Nux vom., Bryo., Rhod.* (of upper extremities) *Rhus., Kali iod., Staph., Podophyllum.*

Gravels: *Lyco., Sarsa., Acid Phos., Bryo., Nux vom., Eup pur., Berb. v., Acid oxalic.*

Great desire for sexual act but cannot perform because of looseness of penis: *Caladium, Lyco., Selenium.*

Gum boils: *Belladona* (red hard and painful) *Heper.* (after the abuse of mercury) *Mercurius* (profuse saliva from the mouth) *Silicea* (fistulus opening) *Acon., Bella.* (first symptoms), *Merc. v., Sil., Heper Sulph.* (suppurative stage).

Gum rash: *Cham. Ant. crud., Puls., Cal. carb.*

Gums: *Ant. crud., Ars., Merc., Nit. acid., Phos.* (profuse bleeding of the gums) *Merc. v.* (ulcerated gums, recede from the teeth, bleed when touched) *Nit. acid* (gums swollen, white putrid, bleeding) *Phos. acid.* (gums stand off from the teeth, sore and bleed when rubbed).

H

Haematesis (bleeding from stomach) *Acon.* (flushed face, full pulse and in ptethoric person) *Ipecac.* (bright red blood with much sickness), *Ham.* (venous blood) *Arn.* (from injury dark blood) *Acid nit.*, *Acalpha ind.*

Haematesis (vomiting of blood): *Aconite* (blood bright red, in persons of full habit and young people) *Arnica* (caused by mechanical injuries, blood be dark and coagulated, sore bruised feeling in the stomach) *Arsenic.* (vomit of blackish bile and blood, sudden prostration of strengh) *Ipecac.* (sudden attacks, blood dark, constant and continual nausea).

Haematuria (passing blood with the urine): *Ipecac.* (profuse bleeding with deadly paleness, sickness of the stomach) *Cantheris* (constant desire to urinate, discharge of blood in drops) *Ipecac.* (cutting in the abdomen and in the urethra, profuse bleeding, sickness of the stomach) *Nitric acid* (active haemorrhage, urine offensive, suitable after the abuse of mercury) *Nux vom.* (suppression of piles and menstrual disorder) *Secale. cor.* (passive haemorrhage, coldness of body and great weakness).

Haemoptysis (bleeding from lungs): *Ferr. acet.*, *Ferr. phos.*, *Ipecac.*, *Phos.*, *Galic acid.*, *Ham.* (venous) *Millifol.* (arterial) *Acalpha ind.*, *Apocy.*, *Acon.* (plethoric patient) *Arn.* (from injury) *China* (debility morning and night sweat) *Dulcamara* (expectoration of bright red blood) *Ferr.um* (haemorrhage with pain between the shoulder) *Hyoscyamus* (things seems to large) *Phos.phorus* (tight feeling in the chest with a dry tight cough, tuberclular diathesis).

Haemorrhage (from bowels): *Tereb.*, *Ham.*, *Ipecac.*, *Ars. alb.*, *Ferr. phos.*, *Erig. c.*

Haemorrhage (from uterus): *Croc.* (dark) *Sabi.* (bright red), *Secale*, *Ham.*, *Caul.*, *Ipecac.*, *Plat.*, *Trill.*, *Acid nit.*

Haemorrhages from eyes due to injury and eyes become red: *Nux.*, *Arnica*, *Led. pal.*

Haemorrhages from uterus after delivery: *Ipecac.* (profuse bright red blood flow, face becomes white before discharge, causes weakness, nausea and unconsciousness) *Millifolium* (profuse continuous flow of bright red blood day and night) *Phosphorus* (bright red blood flow associated with thirst of cold water) *Aconite* (flow of bright red blood associated with fear of death) *Hamametis* (blood of blackish colour sometimes with clots) *Secale cor.* (flow of blackish blood, patient does not want to be covered).

Haemorrhages of eyes: *Bothrops* (conjunctive Haemorrhages into retina, causing day blindness) *Crotalus h.* (retinal non inflammatory, sub-conjunctiva Haemorrhages, celery neuralgia, sensitive to light).

Haemorrhages: *China* (blackish blood, clotted excessive blood, desires for fanning) *Belladona* (red blood which clots immediately, orifice of blood becomes hot) *Phos.phorus* (excesive bleeding even from small wounds, blood stops for short while and again starts bleeding) *Carbo veg* (continuous bleeding of black blood, the body becomes cold, bluishness develops, desires for fanning) *Hacmamelis* (bleeding of black colour blood associated with pain) *Milifolium* (bright red blood without pain) *Sabina* (red blood clotting bleeding aggravates from motion, pain in legs, body becomes extremely cold but does not like to be covered) *Erige ron* (red clotted blood, pain in urethra and anus) *Acalypha indica* (after dry cough bleeding, from pulmonary artery).

Haemorrhoids (bleeding): *Ham.*, *Trill.*, *Sulph.* (dark blood) *Acon.*, *Aloe.* (excessive bright blood, with much pain) *Collin.* (severe constipation) *Caps.* (with burning).

Haemorrhoids (chronic): *Ars.* (with emaciation) *Ferr.*, *Helon.*, *Hydras.* (Cachetic individual) *Acid nit.*, *Sulph.* (Great burning after passing the stool) *Caust.*, *Hep. Sulph.*

Haemorrhoids (Piles): *Nux vom.* (Haemorrhoids greatly itch which awakes the patient in the night, bleeding in nature), *Aesculus h.* (rectum is full of small sticks, piles are burning better by warmth, stool generally contain jelly like mucus, lumbar sacral pain, rarely bleeding) *Aloe* (piles protrude like bunch of grapes and blue, great burning relieved by cold water) *Muriatic acid* (piles are swollen and blue, sensation that even touch of cloth is intolerable) *Cal. Phos.* (protruding and painful) *Carboneum Sulph.* (sore with inflammation) *Ars. alb* (bleeding, itching, burning piercing pain in all position) *Hypericum* (bleeding and excessively painful) *Hamamelis Q* (bleeding blood blackish clotted, severe backache, purplish in colour) *Cimex* (bleeding constipation stool dry and hard) *Collinsonia Q* (feeling of splinter in the rectum, bleeding blood red shining, severe constipation).

Haemorrhoids: *Arsenic* (blind piles which burn like fire particularly at night, hindering the sleep) *Carbo veg.* (swollen bleeding protruding piles, acrid corroding humor oozing from the rectum, emitting a fetid smell, stools foul with bloody mucus, much flatulence) *Graphites* (prolapsus of rectum without straining, chronic constipation of hard difficult knotty stools) *Nitric acid* (sharp cutting pain in the rectum, lashing for hours after evacuation and is worse after a loose stool, fissures of the anus) *Nux vom.* (habitual constipation with frequent urging to stool) *Pulsatilla* (mostly blind piles, itching in the rectum and soreness of anus, obstinate constipation, disposition to weep and complain, aggravation all worse towards evening) *Sepia* (mostly bleeding piles with protrusion of tumors and rectum during stool, sense of weight of or of a ball in the anus) *Sulphur* (blind or bleeding piles, stinging burning and soreness in and about the anus) *Nux vom.* (great itching of the rectum with ineffectual desire to stool, bleeding piles are very painful) *Aesculus* (feeling of dryness in rectum; small sticks or splinters are piercing the folds of mucous membrane), *Hamam.* (blood dirty red, great soreness of the affected parts) *Aloe* (Haemorrhoids protrude like bunch of grapes, greatly relieved by cold water application) *Sulphur* (great itching and burning in the anus and rectum, piles blind or bleeding) *Ars.* (great burning better by hot water application). *Nux vom.* (for persons of sedentary habit with occasional doses of Sulph.) *Sulph. Aesculus.* (fleshy piles), *Collin.* (constipation with uterine difficulties), *Acon.*, *Ars.*, *Carbo veg.* (when inflamed) *Aloe.*, *Collin. or Nux vom.* (during pregnancy) *Graphites* (with skin ailments) *Aloe* (better by cold washing).

Hairs (falling off) *Canth.* (with kidney trouble) *Acid Phos.* (after illness or from general debility) *Aloe., Acid flour. Iod., Ars., Cal carb., Sepia* or *Silicea Sulph.* (with chronic headache).

Hairs of head entangled with each other, scab or lice on the head: *Baryta carb., Psoranium, Sarsa, Tuberculinium.*

Hallucination: *Absinthium* (frightful visions, loss of memory of recent events) *Anacardium* (impaired memory, senile dementia, thinks he is possessed by two persons) *Belladona* (visual fantastic illusions, lives in a world of his own, acuteness of all senses).

Hands (chaffed): *Petrolium, Acid sulph., Cal. carb., Graphites.*

Hands (coldness of): *Acon., Sepia, Bary carb., Puls., Nat. mur. Sulph.*

Hands (dryness and burning of): *Phos., Sili., Sangu., Lyco., Trillum.*

Hands (pain in): *Colch., Led., Caul.* (rheumatic and gouty) *Rhod* (neuralgic), *Arn.* (from overuse), *Ruta., Puls.*

Hands (Psoriasis, roughness and redness of): *Merc., Petrol., Phyto., Bella., Heper Sulph., Graphites, Baryta carb., Ars., Alum., Selan.* (of palms).

Hands (swelling of): *Bella* (with much redness), *Apis* (acute oedema) *Ars., Iod., China, Ferrum.* (from debility).

Hands (trembling and weakness of) *Phos., Sulph., Anac., Opi., Merc., Nux vom., Sil., Arg. nit., Bella., Acid nit., Agar.* (Q).

Hangover: *Nux vom.* (heavy head in the morning, fast life, excess of stimulants with little exercise, indigestion).

Has to loosen neck color again and again: *Lach., Amyl nitrate.*

Hay-Asthma: *Sabad., Ipec., Acid hydrocy., Kali bich., Euphorsia, Gels., Sangu.* (profuse Lachrymation) *Ars.* (great debility) *Kali iod.* (Propnhylactics) *Sabad., Ars., Kali bich., Psoranium.*

Head and face become red, due to more blood circulation: *Amyl nitrate, Glonine, Bella., Melelotus.*

Head wets, by perspiration during sleep: *Cal. carb., Silicea, Sanicula.*

Head: *Bell., Bryo.* (congestion of the head with great heat and redness of the face), *Bell.,* Bryo., *Merc.* (fullness and heaviness in the forehead as if the brain would start out of the eyes) *Cocc., Ign., Opi.* (sensation of emptiness in the head) *Arnica, Bryo., Hyos.* (heat in the head, while the body is cool) *Bell.* (cold limbs with hot head) *Bell., Sepia* (throbbing in the head with inclination to vomit) *Bapt., Cal. c., Phos. acid., Sulph.* (head feels to heavy) *Stram.* (lightness of the head) *Apis., Hyos.* (with sudden shrill cries, boring of head into pillow) *Calc. c., Nat m., Phos. acid., Rhus., Sulph.* (heaviness and fullness in the forehead) *Graph., Nat. mur., Sulph.* (constant heat on the top of the head) *Sepia, Verat.* (constant coldness on the top of the head).

Headache (billous): *Cham.* (from cold or worry particularly in females) *Iris.* much vomiting of biles) *Bryo.* (worse from movement and vomiting of bitter fluid): *Gels.* (with blind headache) *Glon.* (from the sun heat, brusting headache) *Sangu.* (mostly on right eye) *Nux vom.* (nervous and sick with constipation) *Ipecac.* (with much retching), *retching Ver. alb.* (pain in eyeball, coldness of the skin and prostration) *Acon.* (from cold), *Sulph., Cimi., Lach.* (at the critical age) *Cocc., Merc., Puls., Sepia, Staun.* (attains climax and than decreases).

Headache (catarrhal): *Acon.* (chill alternates with fluses of heat, throbbing at temples) *Euph., Gels.* (with lachrymation) *Bryo.*, *Merc. sol.* (in rheumatic patients) *Merc.*, *Nux vom.*, *Cimicifuga.*

Headache (chronic and obstinate) *Arg. nit.*, *Cal. carb.*, *Phos.*, *Plat.*, *Plumbum.*, *Sil.*, *Stann*, *Zinc.*

Headache (congestive): *Bella.* (redness of face, throbbing of arteries, sensitiveness to light, noise etc.) *Bryo.* (frontal with giddiness, inclination to vomit and bowels irregular) *Acon.*, *Ver. vir.* (with plethora), *Nux vom.* (pain at the back of the head with irregular action of the bowels) *Hell.* (at night, in occiput and nape of the neck) *Sulph.*, *China* (periodical); *Glon.* (more in the morning with excessive throbbing) *Gels.*, *Cact.* (aching in eye balls and giddiness) *Phell.*, *Laptendra.*

Headache (from heart disease) *Cact.*, *Lilium*, *Acon.*, *Bell.*, *Dig.*, *Gels.*

Headache (mental stress, excessive study, anxiety etc): *Nux vom.*, *Aur.*, *Phos.*, *Acid Phos.*, *Anacardium*, *Cimi.*, *Gels.*, *Ign.*, *Sili.*, *Cal. carb.*

Headache (nervous): *Ign.* (monthly or at fortnightly, weight at the back of the head, sense as if nail were dreiven into the skull) *Nux vom.* (in persons of sedentary habits and sensitiveness to noise, light etc) *Coff.* (with sleeplessness) *Gels.* (with giddiness) *Sulph.*, *China.* (periodic), *Ars.* (periodic in forehead and or bile) *Hell.* (stunning, stupefying pain in nape of the neck) *China*, *Acid Phos.*, *Ferr.* (from debiliting loss) *Cham.*, *Spig.*, *Coloc.*, *Sepia*, *Cimici.*, *Kali carb.* (runs for short or longer periods).

Headache (rheumatic): *Acon.*, *Bryo.*, *Cimi.*, *Acid nit.*, *Rhus*, *Spigelia*, *Phyto.*

Headache (sick): *Arsenic alb* (great weight in the head, particularly in forehead, cold application relieves the pain) *Belladona* (sick headache, head feels as if it will burst, nausea and vomiting bile, mucus or food, in women menstruation too frequent and profuse) *Calcarea carb.* (stupefying headache from early morning until after noon, aggravation by mental exertion) *Nux vomica* (headache excited by overeating, alcoholic liquors, mental exertion, nausea and vomiting of sour or bitter substance etc.) *Ipecac.* (nausea and vomiting are the most prominent feature of associated headache) *Sepia* (painful beating in the top of the head, headache as if the head would burst, feted urine) *Veratrum album* (paroxysms of pain in various parts of the brain, as if bruised, cold sweat on the forehead).

Headache aggravates from hot and better by cold application: *Aloes.*, *Ars. alb.*

Headache associated with heavines on eye brows: *Baryta carb.*, *Carbo veg.*, *Carbo ani.*

Headache better by eating: *Lyco.*, *Psoranium.*

Headache in children: *Arnica* (with fever on injury) *Belladona* (throbbing pain in temple) *Gelsemium* (due to cold) *Glonine* (sudden fainting hot headache) *Iris vers.* (with bilious vomiting) *Nux vom.* (due to indigestion) *Pulsatilla* (due to taking fatty food).

Headache is relieved by tightening head with cloth: *Argent. nit.*, *Apis*, *Puls.*, *Lac defloratum.*

Headache with hand and feet icy cold: *Cal. carb.*, *Menyanthus*, *Sepia.*, *Puls.* (from bathing) *Acon.*, *Ant. crud.*, *Ign.* (from the use of tobacco) *Ant. crud.*, *Puls.* (stupefying headache with nausea, worse in the evening after eating or drinking) *Ars. alb.* (periodical nervous, better from application of cold water) *Baptisia*, *Con.*, *Dul.*, *Gels.* (dull stupefying headache) *Bell.*, *Nat. mur*, *Puls.* (beating pulsating headache) *Strom* (beating headache particularly on top) *Sulph.* (beating and periodical headache).

Headache, due to dyspepsia or nervous disturbance particularly in those who have continuous sitting work: *Anacard.*, *Argent. nit.*, *Bryo.*, *Nux vom.*

Headache, soon after awakening in the morning: *Bryo.*, *Lac. defloratus.*

Headache: *Arnica* (headache, principally over the eyes) *Arsenic* (great weight in the head particularly in the forehead, bursting pain in the forehead with inclination of vomiting) *Belladona* (nausea and vomiting of bile, mucous or food) *Bryonia* (headache sets after awakening the headaches as it will burst) *Chamomilla* (headache from cold or drinking coffea, over sensitive to pain) *Cocculus* (violent headache aggravated by talking, laughing, noise or a bright light) *Coffea* (headache as if a nail were driven into the brain head feels too small) *Lachesis* (headache aggravates after sleeping, pain in the left ovarian region in the night) *Nux vomica* (pressing boring pain, stupefying headache especially in the morning, aggravated by mental exertion, person of sedentary habits or troubled with piles) *Pulsatilla* (tearing, drawing or stitching pains, worse toward evening) *Sepia* (beating, stitching pains mostly in the forehead or temple) *Sulphur* (pressing, throbbing or tearing pains, constant heat on head) *Veratrum alb.* (nervous headache, great thirst for cold drinks) *Gelsminum*, *Floric acid*, *Lac defloratum.* (are related with urine problem as in Gels. the headache is relieved by passing the urine, in Floric acid urine should pass in full quantity and in lac defloratum. as headache increases the quantity of urine is increased but there is nausea and vomiting) *Sangunaria* and *Iris vers.* (have nausea and vomiting in headache, in Sangunaria the headache is usually on right side, in Iris the headache is associated with burning in the alimentary canal).

Hearing (morbidly sensitive): *Ign.*, *Nux vom.*, *Cann. ind.*, *Cup. met.*, *Coff.*, *Bella.*, *Aurum*, *China.*, *Cham.*

Heart (congestion of): *Acon.*, *Cact.*, *Ver. vir.*, *Asaf.*, *Opi.*, *Puls.*, *Sulph.*

Heart (disease of): *Dig.* (slow or quickened and feeble, irregular and intermittent pulse, dilation) *Cact.* (sesation as if the heart was grasped firmly), *Acon.* (violent palpitation), *Lilium* (with uterine disorder), *Spong.* (stabbing pain) *Ver. vir.* (cardic debility with Diarrhoea, faintness and collapse) *Arn.* (induce by over exertion), *Collin.* (with dyspepsia or portal congestion), *Phos.*, *Acid Ph+os.*, *Cal. carb.* (fatty degeneration dropsy etc), *Apis.* (threatened dropsy), *Camp.*, *Mosch.* (from various paroxysmal sufferings).

Heart (inflammation and its membranes) *Acon.*, *Spig.*, *Cimic.* (violent action of the heart, rheumatic, peri or endo cardites), *Bryo.*, *Aselep.*, *Tuber.*, *Acon.* (pesicardites) *Bryo.* (in rheumatic patient and when serious effusion is threatened) *Colch.*, *Apis.* (gouty patients) *Ars.*, *Lach.*, *Naja* (great debility).

Heart (palpitation of): *Acon.*, (from excitement and organic disease) *Mosch.*, *Camp.* (simple nervous) *Ign.* (from grief) *Coff.* (from joy and wakefulness *Cham.* (from worry or anger in females), *Ver. vir.* (from fright with fluttering dysponea), *Bell.* (pulsation extending to head), *China*, *Acid phos.*, *Ver. vir.*, *Ferrum.* (from debility), *Nux vom.*,

Gels. (from spinal irritation), *Cact.*, *Spig.*, *Gels.*, *Dig.*, *Lachesis*, *Naja*, *Puls.*, *Iod.*, *Heper.*, *Ambra grasea*, *Baryta carb.*

Heart burn (water brash): *Nux vom.* (heart burn with sour eructation, regurgitation of food while eating, habitual constipation) *Phophorus* (sour regurgitation of food, water brash particularly after taking acids) *Pulsatilla* (putrid taste particularly on rising in the morning) *Sepia* (water brash in the afternoon, vomiting milky water or milky mucus) *Sulphur* (putrid taste in the morning, flushes of heat) *Puls.*, *Bismith* (3 X), *Iris.*, *Bryo.*, *Lyco.*, *Caps.* (Q) *Nux vom.*, *Carbo veg.*, *Cal. carb*, *Robina* (with chronic acidity).

Heart trouble: *Iodine* (sensation as if heart was squeezed together) *Cactus* (sensation as if an iron band has prevented its function) *Lilium tig.* (as if heart is grasped and released alternatively) *Lachas's* (constriction of heart which is also not found in chest, bladder, rectum, uterus vagina etc.).

Heart: *Acon.*, *Dig.* (palpitation of the heart and great anguish) *Ars. alb.*, *Dig.* (palpitation of the heart especially at night and when laying on the back) *Bell.* (palpitation of heart, reverberating in the neck and head) *Cal. carb.* (palpitation of the heart at night or after eating with anguish) *Cocc.* (palpitation of the heart) *Dig.* (the least movement produces violent palpitation of the heart), *Gels.* (sensation as if the heart would stop beating if ceased walking) *Graph.*, *Dig.*, *Bell.*, *Con.* (violent throbbing about the heart) *Heper* (palpitation of the heart) *Nat mur.*, *Dig.* (palpitation of the heart with slightest motion) *Nux v. Dig.* (palpitation of the heart with inclination to vomit and heaviness in the chest) *Sulph.* (palpitation of heart, anxious, visible, heart feels too large).

Heat stroke: *Glonine* (confusion with giddiness, head heavy and cannot lay it on pillow, throbbing, congestive headache) *Lachesis* (vertigo, flickering, dim vision, pale face) *Natrum carb.* (great debility caused by summer heat, exhaustion, headache from slightest mental work, vertigo from exposure to sun) *Sangunaria* (sun headache, worse right side, pain begins in occipital spreads upwards and settles over the bone of right eye) *Veratrum album* (head full, throbbing arteries, cold sweat on forehead, nausea, vomiting, watery stool).

Hectic fever: *China*, *Acid phos.*, *Gels.*, *Phos.*, *Ars. alb.*, *Haper sulph.*, *Silicea*, *Sulph.*

Helminthiasis (worm) *Cina* (Q), *Sant.* (3x), *Merc.*, *Teuc.*, *Ign.* (Q) *China* (Q) *Ferrum*, *Ant. crud.*, *Spigilea.*

Hemianopia (Nyctalopia, night blindness): *Lycopidium* (most commonly needed for this disorder) *China*, *Hyos.* and *Ranunclus bul.* (as per symptoms of the remedy).

Hemicrania: *Bell.*, *Nux vom.*, *Ign.*, *Coff.*, *Puls.*, *Aur.*, *Ars.*, *Chelsid.*, *Cal. carb.*

Hemiplegea: *Baryta. carb.*, *Nux vom.*, *Lyco.* (of right) *Arn.*, *Cocc.*

Hepatitis: *Arsenic* (vomiting of brownish or blackish substances, rapid prostration of strength) *Belladona* (starting and jumping during sleep) *Mercurius* (green bilious or frothy stool with frequent urging and tanesmus cannot sleep before 3 AM) *Pulsatilla* (yellow coated tongue, green slimy Diarrhoea usually at night, chilliness even in the warm room, weeps and complains).

Hernia (acute pain from) *Acon.*, *Nux vom.*, *Bell.*, *Silicea* (in children).

Hernia femoral: *Plumbum met.* (strangulated femoral hernia, common in women).

Hernia inguinal: *Calcarea carb.* (inguinal swelling) *Lycopodium* (of right side, distension of abdomen, rumbling sound) *Nux vom* (of left side).

Hernia of left side: *Nux.*

Hernia umbilical: *Calcarea carb.* (to be tried first) *Aurum met* (of babies) *Nux vom* (of infants).

Hernia, of right side: *Lyco.*

Hernia: *Nux v.* (umbilical hernia of infants) *Nux* (incarcerated hernia).

Herpes (circinnatus): *Tellu., Iris., Sepia, Acid nit.*

Herpes zoster: *Mercurius viv.* (the eruptions extends from the back around the abdomen like a girdle, pustules burn when touched) *Pulsatilla* (due to gastric derangement, eruptions itches at night in the bed, mild tearful disposition) *Rhus., Ran bulb., Cist., Ars., Canth.*

Herpes: *Acon.* (fever, neuralgia) *Rhus* (general), *Ars., Merc., Iris., Graph.* (ulcerating) *Phos.* (in phthisiscal. constitutions), *Ran. bulb.* (Pleurodynia) *Graph., Nux vom., Juglans* (chronic).

Hiccups (singultus) in children: *Belladona* (face flushed with moaning when hiccough) *Hyoscymus* (frequent hiccough and jerking of the limbs) *Ign.itia* (hiccough especially after eating or drinking frequent sighing) *Nux vom.* (hiccough from overeating, gulping up the food, constipation with frequent colic).

Hiccups: *Nux vom.* Simple spasm and in hard drinkers). *Acid Sulph., Rob.* (acid eructations) *Acon., Ars., Bella., Ver. vir., Gels., Hyos.* (in brain affections).

Hip disease (Coxalgia): *Ars.enic* (pale death like colour of the face, Diarrhea worse in mid night, wants to drink often) *Cal.carea carb.* (scrofulous habit, great emaciation with swollen abdomen and good appetite, sweat on head during sleep, feet cold) *Mercurius* (glandular abscesses, suppuration is about to take place or has taken place) *Phos.phorus* (hectic fever with dry hacking cough, thirst for very cold drinks, suitable for tall slender persons) *Rhus tox.* (disease with pain joint, pain in the knee predominant, better by motion) *Silicea* (where suppuration has taken place and there is a profuse discharge from fistulas opening around the joint, caries with discharges of pieces of decayed bone, hectic fever, constipation stool recedes back after partially expelled) *Sulphur* (white swelling of the knee, early morning Diarrhoea, frequent weak faints spells).

Hip joint disease: *Acon.* (with fever) *Coloc., Rhus., Bella., Merc. sol.* (pain) *Sil., Cal. phos., Cal. carb., Ferrum iod., Heper sulph., Acid phos., China, Kali carb.*

Hoarseness of throat: *Arnia*(from overuse) *Belladona* (sudden violent hoarseness, voice changes, choking sensation, dry cough, sudden loss of voice) *Bryonia* (due to taking cold drinks or taking oily or fried food followed by cold drinks) *Wyethia* (of public speaker, singers, throat dry, itching in posterior nacres, throat and swollen, dry hacking cough).

Hoarseness of the chest: *Causticum* (hoarseness and roughness) *Mercurius* (voice hoarse and rough with burning and tickling in the throat) *Chamomilla* (catarrhal hoarseness, patient irritable) *Nux vom.* (scarping in throat, constipation) *Phos.phorus* (loss of voice, chronic hoarseness).

House maid's knee: *Apis., Sil., Puls., Lyco., Arn., Rhus tox.*

Hunger: *Lyco., Cina, Merc.* (excessive hunger soon after eating) *Rhus., China, Hep., Merc., Puls* (complete loss of appetite for any kind of food) *Bryo., Nux., Rhus., Verat.* (excessive hunger).

Hydrocele: *Calcarea flour.* (with indurations of testicles) *Digitales* (scrotum enlarged like bladder) *Merc. sol.* (testicles swollen, hard shining) *Pulsatilla* (testicles retraced, enlarged, dark red and very sensitive to touch) *Silicea* (testicle swollen on account of hydrocele).

Hydrocephalus (acute), associated with continuous movement of left leg or hand: *Apocynum, Bryo.*

Hydrocephalus in children: *Apis mel.* (bulging of head, soft spots on the skull) *Merc. sol.* (after measles or scarlet fever) *Helleborus* (head enlarges fast, convulsion, bore head into pillow) *Cal.carea carb.* (soft spots on the skin do not join) *Apocynum Q* (drinks lot of water but perspiration and urine scanty).

Hydrocephalus: *Aconite* (intolerance to light and noise, great fear and anxiety, the child is sleepless and restless and cries much) *Apis mel.* (boring the head deep into pillow, grinding of the teeth, profuse perspiration on head) *Belladona* (great intolerance of light or noise) *Bryonia* (manifist sign of effusion) *Stromonium* (black fluid stool).

Hydrophobia: *Bell., Stram., Lach., Hydropho., Scutel.*

Hydrothorax (dropsy of the chest): *Apis mel.* (following scarlet fever, urine scanty) *Arsenicum* (violent palpitation of the heart, rapid prostration) *Bryonia* (stitching pain in the chest, wants to remain perfectly quiet) *Lycopidium* (red sandy sediment in the urine).

Hyper acidity: *Heper., Rheums, Argent. nit., Cal. carb., Carbo veg., Nat. carb., Nitric acid, Nat. Phos., Nux vom., Puls., Robinia, Sulphur, Sulphuric acid.*

Hyper aesthesia retinal: *Belladona* (due to anomaly of refraction or irritation, eyes sensitive to light sometime causes headache which is aggravated in the afternoon and evening) *Conium* (oversensitiveness of retina to light, during reading letters runs together, photophobia every thing looks white) *Natrum mur* (photophobia is excessive in the morning and better as day advances) *Ign.itia* (in hysterical patient who dreads of light) *Lactic acid* (aching pain in and behind the eye ball) *Macroton.* (celery neuralgia marked) *Merc. sol* (sensitive to artificial light in the evening).

Hyper anaemia of disc: *Belladona, Doboisea, Phos.phorus* and *Pulsatilla* (as per symptoms of the remedy).

Hypochondriacal anxiety: *Arn., Nux., Puls* (with peevishness).

Hypochondriasis: *Aur., Nux vom., Ana.* (chiefly in males) *Cimic., Ing., Sepia., Petrol., Plat.* (chiefly in uterine derangements i.e. at the change of life).

Hysteria during menses period: *Actea racemosa, Cal. lactica., Puls.*

Hysteria: *Asafoetida* (flatulence in stomach, gas goes upward which create difficulty in respiration) *Hyoscymus* (fear of getting poisoned a strong symptom, envies others) *Platina* (proudly short tempered, considers other low people) *Moschous* (works according to their will, obstinate nature, cries suddenly and says I am dying, lips turn blue from weeping, stares continuously and ultimately becomes unconscious) *Valereana* (headache from little exertion and becomes unconscious, sensation of a thread in throat) *Ignitia* (changeable temperament, flatulence with little eating, mouth dry in spite of it no thirst) *Mosch.* (with tendency to fainting, headache, constriction of the chest and general chillness) *Ign.*, *Puls.*, *Gels.*, *Cimi.*, *Plat.*, *Cocc.*, *Asaf.*, *Caulo.*, *Zinc. val.*, *Hyos*,. *Bell.*, *Nux mosch.*

Hysteric and nervous women for: *Ignitia*, *Puls.*, *Valariena.*

Hysteric convulsions: *Camp.* or *Mosch.* (by olfaction) *Acon.*, *Opi.* (if caused by fright).

Hysteric patient, who sometimes cry or becomes silent: *Crocus*, *Ign.itia*, *Puls.* *Ignitea* (suppressed grief with a feeling of emptiness in the stomach to everything) *Phos.phoric acid* (indifferent to the affairs of life, not disposed to talk) *Cocculus* (headache and nervousness following grief) *Lachesis* (unhappy and distressed after sleeping, cannot bear anything tight around the neck) *Pulsatilla* (mild, tearful disposition with weeping sadness) *Ignitia* (single parts seems to be convulsed or single muscles here and there, spasms return every day or every other day about the same hour) *Stromonium* (awakens with a shrinking look as if afraid of the first object seen).

I

Impetigo of children: *Arsenic alb* (oozing of corrosive discharge) *Heper Sulph.* (on pus formation) *Mezerium* (red spots turn into blisters which cracks down) *Viola tricolor* (due to eczema).

Impetigo: *Voila tric., Ant. tar., Hep. sulph., Ant. crud., Kali bich., Clem., Ars. alb., Acid carbol.*

Impotence: *Phos., Coni., Dig., China, Acid Phos., Hyper., Selen., Nux vom., Ferr., Baryta carb., Agnus, Nuph., Sulph., Iod.* (atrophy of the testicles) *Cal.adium* (with coldness of the organs) *Arnica* (from an injury).

Impotency (complete), no desire for coitus: *Agnus cast., Caladium, Selenium.*

Impotency caused from gonorrhoea: *Thuja, Caladium.*

Impotency: *Agnus castus* (suffer from gonorrhoea or excessive indulgence of sex causes looseness in penis) *Selinium* (with physical weakness great desire for sex but no erection, nightly emission) *Caladium* (penis erect, tight and painful during sleep but becomes loose after sleep, perspiration sticky) *Picric acid* (with slightest provocation even seeing the girls the semen discharges at the act of coition erection lost).

Impotency: when a desire for coition, the penis becomes loosen: *Agnus cast., Argent. nit., Caladium, Selenium.*

Imprint of teethes on the tongue: *Merc., Ars., Rhus tox., Podo., Chel.idonium, Stromonium.*

Indigestion: *Antim crud.* (indigestion from overeating from intake of fatty food) *Argentum nit* (hyper acidity, ulcerative pain in stomach radiating in all direction, perforating ulcer in stomach) *Arsenic album* (colic, burning pain in the stomach, in abdomen) *Carbo veg.* (acidity, simplest food disagrees), *China* (abdomen bloated, colic due to flatulence, no relief from belching or passing the wind) *Lycopodium* (flatulence as a result of taking food which ferments inside, distention of stomach) *Ipecac.* (nausea most prominent in any form of indigestion) *Nux vomica* (indigestion from irregular eating habits, late nights, heavy consumption of liquor, pain) *Pulsatilla* (indigestion due to liking for butter, pastries, cakes, fruits, creamy food).

Indisposed: *Con., Acid nit., Phos.* (to work), *Mag. carb., Dig., Phos. acid.* (to speak or talk).

Inflammation (glandular): *Anantherum* (glandular inflammation, painful swelling in various parts, leading to pus formation) *Asterias rubens* (glands of armpit swollen, hard and knotted, very painful) *Bacillinum* (glands of neck enlarged) *Belladona* (glands swollen, tender red, localized inflammation, painful with intense heat) *Carbo ani.* (glands indurated, swollen, painful on neck, armpits, mammae groin etc., hard, feeling of piercing sticks).

Inflammation of eyelids: *Belladona* (eyelids stick together and bleed when opened, great intolerance to light) *Heper Sulph.* (the eyes ache from bright-light of the day when moving) *Mercurius v.* (the lids turn outward the edges ulcerated and scabby) *Sulphur* (ulceration of the margins, purulent mucus in the eyes, intolerance to sunlight).

Inflammation of eyes: *Aconite* (sudden bright red inflammation on exposure to dry cold wind, lids swollen, feeling of foreIgn. body in the eye) *Apis* (suppurating inflammation, burning, stinging pain, better by cold water application) *Argentum nit* (severe inflammation and suppuration, purulent discharge) *Belladona* (inflammation in the optic nerve and in retina, eyes red protruding, pain throbbing, worse motion, light and cold air exposure) *Heper Sulph.* (pus in the anterior chamber, iritic copious discharge, eyes and lids red and inflamed shooting pain in upper lids, sensitive to touch and air) *Merc. sol.* (due to exposure to glare of fire, burning pain, black floats, excoriating burning flow) *Petroleum* (inflammation of eye lids, marginal blepharitis, acanthi fissured) *Pulsatilla* (profuse green or yellow bland discharge) *Syphilinum* (recurrent inflammation of cornea succession of abscesses copious discharge, lid swollen, intense photophobia, pain at night) *Zincum met.* (inflammation of inner acanthi, itching severe, discharge excoriating) *Iris.* (eye painful with redness and excessive flow of water) *Heper Sulph.* (pus in anterior chamber, shooting pain, eye red and inflamed, worse on touch) *Merc. cor.* (inflammation of the iris and thick, muddy in colour, thick iris do not contract or dilate, pain bearing, shooting and burning in iris, worse at night).

Inflammation of male genital: *Pulsatilla* (orchitis inflammation of testicles from catching cold or from mumps) *Sulphur* (inflammatory phimosis, constriction of the orifice of fore skin) *Thuja* (in-

flammation of fore skin of glans penis).

Inflammation of the eyes (ophthalmia): *Aconite* (intense reduces and swelling of the affected part, great intolerance to light) *Apis mel.* (burning and stinging pain in the eyes) *Ars.enic album* (dark redness and congestion of the vessels, great anguish and restlessness) *Belladona* (acute opthalmia with very great intolerance to light or noise) *Cal.carea carb.* (swelling and redness of the eyelids, desires to keep the eyes in darkness) *Graphites* (purulent secretion and agglutination, sticky glutinous fluid watery) *Dulcamara*, *Mercurius vivus* (gonorrheal or scrofulous opthalmia). *Pulsatilla* (after suppressed gonorrheal discharge evening aggravation) *Sulphur* (feeling as if sand is in the eyes).

Inflammation of tongue: *Aconite* (great nervous excitability, constant tossing about) *Apis mel.* (burning and stinging pain) *Arsenic alb.* (threatened mortification, intense thirst but drink little) *Belladona* (the tongue is dark red, face flashed and eyes red) *Mercurius vivus* (constant flow of saliva from the mouth, the tongue feels as if burnt) *Urtica urens* (inflammation caused by burn or a scald).

Influenza: *Bapt.*, *Acon.*, *Gels.* (in sequence in general case) *Ars.*, *Kali iod* (second and later stages) *Eup. per.* (in bone pain), *Phyto.* (with throat problem) *Sang.*, *Kali bich.*, *Scilla.* (troublesome chest symptoms), *Rhus.*, *Caust.*

Injuries, bruises, cut wounds, surgery sprains etc.: *Arnica* (bruised sore feeling all over, every thing on which he lies feel hard, continuously changes position) *Calendula Q* (in bruises for external application) *Ledum.* (on tetanus formation with shooting pain), *Hypericum* (wound from nails, splinters, pins or animals bite) *Nitric acid* (wounds which do not heal) *Ruta g.* (bruises of bone, cartilage, tendon, periosteun etc.) *Rhus tox.* (strains of muscles and tendon) *Cal.carea carb.* (injuries to tendon and muscles with extreme weakness) *Staphysagaria* (for surgical cuts, burning and stinging pain, limbs sore and strengthless) *Symphytum* (injury to eye), *Srontia.* (surgical operation with much cutting, great debility, coldness in the body), *Carbo veg.* (surgical. shock which develops collapse, fear of death, blue face and skin) *Veratrum alb.* (surgical shock, skin blue, face pale prostration, cold sweat and cramps) *Calcarea phos.*, (injuries to bone, promotes union of bones) *Calcarea sulph.* (cuts, wounds bruises do not heal easily) *Cimex lectularis* (bruised and sprain with feeling of contraction of tendon, cannot stretch the body) *Eupatorium perfolatum* (bruised feeling as if body is broken, all bones ache) *Sulphuric acid* (bruises from injury, hard skin profuse sweat) *Manganum* (bruises remain sore for a long time) *Hamamelis Q* (apply when skin rapture from bruises) *Ammonium mur.* (sprain chronic) *Rhus tox.* (sprain of ankle with edema) *Nat. carb.* (sprain and easy dislocation of ankle) *Carbo animalis* (frequently suffer from sprain) *Bryonia* (sprain pain aggravates from least motion) *Kali mur.* (sprain with swelling of joints, pain worse from motion) *Cimex* (wounds at anus) *Echinacea Q* (apply on inflamed wound) *Ammonium carb* (wound turns into ulcer) *Alumina* (wound on the mouth of uterus) *Ledum pal* (punctured wounds) *Heckla lava* (unhealthy wound) *Gun powder* (wounds on legs, do not heel due to blood poisoning and discharge) *Lachesis* (wound of postmortem room, becomes poisonous) *Sulphur* (wounds turn into weeping pus).

Insanity: *Aconite* (fear and anxiety of mind with great excitability) *Belladona* (pupil dilated, tears his clothes and try to injure himself or around him) *Hyoscyamus* (throws off her clothes and wants to remain naked) *Nux vom.* (very irritable and wishes to be alone, desires to kill even his best friends, constipation) *Opium* (rage with fixed ideas, full and slow pulse, constipation, stool hard black balls) *Pulsatilla* (desire caused due to uterus problem, patient mild tearful disposition).

Insert head into the pillows: *Apis.*, *Bella*; *Hellaborus*, *Podo*.

Insomnia: *Aconite* (of the aged) *Ambra grisea* (cannot sleep from worries) *Arnica* (when over tired with restlessness) *Camphor* (insomnia with cold limbs) *Cannabis indica* (obstinate and intractable insomnia, wants to sleep but cannot sleep) *Chamomilla* (due to unbearable pain at night in bed) *China* (due to copious menstruation in women, no sleep night after night) *Coffea* (sleeplessness on account of mental activity and flow of ideas) *Nux vom* (cannot sleep after 3.00 AM until towards morning) *Raphanus* (insomnia due to excessive desire in women, copious and long lasting menstruation).

Intermittent fever: *Aconite* (cough during the fever, great fear and anxiety of mind) *Antim. crud.* (chilliness predominates, great sadness and woeful mood, white coated tongue) *Arsenic* (during fever restlessness and anguish, after paroxysm great prostration, urgent thirst but drinks little) *Belladona* (slight chill with much fever or vice versa, heat and red face) *Ferrum* (great loss of muscular power, least exertion or emotion produces redface) *Gelsemium* (chill mostly in the evening commencing in the hand and feet) *Ignitia* (thirst only during chill, the chill is relieved by external heat, during the fever, nettle rash over whole body) *Ipecac.* (nausea and vomiting predominate, the a pyrexia is marked by gastric disturbance) *Nux vomica* (long lasting hard chill, great heat even then wants to be covered, during the chill pain in the sacrum, during the fever, headache vertigo pain in the chest and vomiting) *Pulsatilla* (chill and heat simultaneous, no thirst during entire paroxysm, thickly coated tongue and bad taste in the morning, much gastric disturbance) *Sepia* (great coldness of the hands with sensation as if the fingers are dead, perfect absence of thirst).

Internal haemorrhage: *Arsenic alb.* (vomit of blood, bile, green mucus, brown black mixed with blood) *Cantharis* (discharge of blood with urine, from kidney of bladder) *Carbo veg* (loss of resistance to disease). *Cinnamonum* (bleeding from nose) *Crocus* (black and stringy haemorrhage, clotted blood) *Crotalus* (when blood does not clot) *Hamamelis* (of dark, clotted and venous blood) *Millefolium* (bleeding from nose as a result of injury or otherwise) *Nitric acid* (bright and profuse blood from bowels) *Phosphoric acid* (haemorrhage in typhoid) *Trillium* (Hamorrhage with faintness and dizziness) *Lachesis* (every cut and scratch bleed) *Phosphorus* (even small wounds bleed often and much) *China* (debility flow of blood from any part internal or external, faintness, weakening vision, ringing in ears.) *Ipecac.* (nausea and bleeding blood bright red active and copious).

Intertrigo in children: *Aethusa* (excoriation of thighs on wilting perspire easily) *Causticum* (soreness in folds of skin of ears. between thigh) *Graphites* (rawness in bends of limbs, groin neck etc.).

Intestine: *Kali bich.*, *Merc.* (chronic intestinal ulceration).

Intolerance of noise, light and music: *Nux vom.*, *Nux moch.*, *Cal.adium*, *Agaricus*, *Tarentula*.

Intolerance to touch: *Bella.*

Intoxication in, as if: *Bapt.*, *Carboneum Sulph.*, *Carbo veg.*, *Glonine*, *Nux mosh.*

Iris (bilious motions and colic by pains): *Cup. met.*, *Ver. alb.*

Iritis (traumatic): *Bryo. Gels.*, *Merc. cor.*, *Ars.*, *Kali bich.*, *Bella.*, *Acon.* (rheumatic), *Cinnab*, *Merc.*, *Clem*, *Merc. iod.*, *Kali iod.*, *Aur* (syphilitic).

Irritable and short-tempered: *Graphite*, *Sulphur*, *Manganum*.

Irritable children: *Antim. crud.* (seeing by the unknown the child becomes angry and if touched starts weeping) *Chamomilla* (irritable child but becomes quite when roamed in the laps) *Cina* (child becomes irritable due to worms in the stomach, at piece fingers in the nose frequently) *Iodium* (child feels always hungry, cry for food, but in spite of it he is weak) *Sanicula* (irritable but becomes joyful if he is loved, while weeping gets perspiration on head and neck) *Silicea* (perspiration on head only whereas old nature, head and abdomen enlarged).

Irritable: *Bryo.*, *Cham.*, *Hep.*, *Lyco.* (exceedingly irritable, everything makes him angry).

Irritates easily: *Nux vom.*, *Cham.*, *Ign.atia*, *Staph.*, *Bryo.*.

Itching excessive in vulva, which develops sexual excitement and compel to go for masturbation (generally in girls): *Caladium, Origanum, Zinc.*

Itching of eyes: *Ambrosia* **(lachrymation, smarting and burning with watery coryza, sneezing, wheezing and coughing)** *Zincum met.* **(eye sore and inflamed, itching severe inner angle of the eye, eye lids sore excoriating discharge)** *Cadmium Sulph.* **(of cornea, night blindness)** *Calcarea carb.* **(dilation of pupils, foggy, duet closed on exposure to cold, spots and ulcer on cornea, worse in morning and open air)** *Naphthaline* **(detachment of retina soft cataract).**

Itching of the skin: *Arsenic* **(dry skin with burning and itching)** *Mercurius* **(itching worse at night from warmth of the bed, dry rashes eruption readily bleeds when scratched)** *Sulphur* **(worse from the heat of the bed).** *Acon.* **(great itching with feverishness)** *Sulph., Aur., Petrol., Rhus., Rad. brom.* **(with dry hars.h skin worse in bed or by warmth)** *Ign.* **(fine pricking itching),** *Rumex* **(worse on undressing)** *Rhus, Crot. tig., Nux vom., Arg. nit., Mez., Merc. iod., Led., Dolichos.*

J

Jaundice (acute): *Acon., Merc., China, Merc sol., Nux vom., Cham.*

Jaundice (chronic): *Phos., Lept.* (stool black), *Chelsid* (pain in right shoulder blade), *Podophyllum* (with Diarrhoea), *Hydrastis* (under garments turn yellow) alternate with *Nux vom. Dig., Ars., China.* (in children), *Heper Sulph., Acid nit., Merc.*

Jaundice (Malignant) *Phos., Ars.*

Jaundice in children: *Chels.idonium* (skin has jaundiced look) *Chionanthus* (lever sore enlarged) *China* (great debility due to outflow of liquids from body) *Thyroidinum* (in infants with vomiting and diarrhoea) *Antimonium tart* (with enlarged and swollen liver).

Jaundice of infants: *China* (yellow skin, stools white) *Mercurius* (skin very yellow, grayish white stools).

Jaundice-uterus: *China* (yellow colour of the skin, white stools, aggravation every other day) *Digitalis* (frequent and painful emission of scanty brown urine, irregular or intermittent pulse) *Mercurius* (painfulness of the region of liver, skin very yellow a bad smell from mouth) *Nux vom.* (swelling and hardness of the liver, constipation with unsuccessful urging to stool) *Pulsatilla* (chilliness with vertigo on rising from a sitting posture, green slimy diarrhoea thirstless). *Bryonia* (pin pricking pain, pain in right scapula, bitter taste, white coating on the tongue, enlarged liver, constipaton, passing of stool painful, feeling of coldness) *Chelidonium* (pin pricking pain, pain in right scapula, bitter taste, stool chalk coloured, diarrhoea of yellowish stool in large quantity) *Chamomilla* (ailment caused due to anger, feeling of warmth, tongue coating yellowish colour, one cheek is red and hot the other cheek is white and cold) *Nux vomica* (ailment is caused from taking undigestable food or from alcoholic drinks, poor digestion, ineffectual desire for stool).

Jaw (caries of) *Phos., Sil., Acid phos., Aur mur., Plumbum.*

Jaw (pain in) *Acon., Merc., Cimic., Bella* (with rigidity), *Spigelia* (neuralgic or rheumatic), *Petrol* (as though dislocated).

Joint (dropsy of) *Iod., Bryo., Kali iod., Canth.*

Joints (aching and stiffness): *Arn* (from exertion or old injury), *Rhus.* (from a strain), *Bryo., Thuja., Phyto.* (rheumatism), *Ruta, Caust, Nux vom., Macrot.*

Joints (inflammation of synovitis): *Bryo.* (rheumatic patient), *Led.* (with constant chilliness), *Merc. prot. iod.* (chronic and painful), *Puls* (female and children), *Sil., Heper sulph.* (chances of suppuration); *Merc.* (chronic case), *Phyto.* (with throat problem), Kali iod. (syphilitic); *Berb.* (related with kidney problem), *Acid benzoic* (urine smells offensively).

Joints (swelling of): *Sil. Cal. phos.* (white swelling) *Merc., Heper sulph., Puls., Bella acid phos., Sulph., Cal. carb.* (as constitutional remedies).

Joints (weakness in) *Cal. carb., Ruta., Caust., Kali carb., Merc., Lyco., Sulph.*

Joy (effects of) *Coff., Puls.* (excessiveness).

Keeps enemy relations with others: *Artimisia vulgaris.*

K

Kidney (congestion of): *Terebenth.*

Kidney (inflammation): *Acon., Gels., Bella., Hellob.* (with fever), *Terebenth* (suppressed or scanty, smoky, foetid, or even bloody urine) *Erigeron.* (with copious albuminous discharge), *Canth., Ars.* (disquamative), *Plumb* (granular degeneration), *Ars., Apocy., Apis., Heper sulph.* (post scarlatinal nephritis, with scanty, albuminous or suppressed urine, debility, dropsy) *Canna. sat., Apis., Cheli., Ferrum., Nux vom., Puls., Acid benzoic, Zinc* (pain in the kidneys).

Knees (enlargement of): *Silicate of lime.*

Knees (inflammation of): *Acon.* alt with *Puls., Rhus., Bryo., Acid benzoic.*

L

Labour after (constipation): *Collin., Bryo., Opi., Lyco., Plumbum, Alumina, Verat alb.*

Labour after (diarrhoea): *Puls., China, Hyos.*

Labour after (Lochia): *Acon.* (too profuse and bright red), *Bella., Cimici* (scanty) *Vert. vir* (scantly with headache) *Kreos., Carbo ani., Secale* (offensive), *Kreos.* (intermittent), *Sabi., Cimic.* (continuing too long and red) *Caulo., China., Cal. carb.* (too prolonged), *Acon.* (suppressed), *Hydras.* (offensive with suppressed or scanty urine).

Labour after (puerperal fever): *Acon., Bella., Verat. vir.* (brain symptoms), *Bryo.* or *Merc.* (peritonitis) *Pyrogen, Coloc., Terebenth.* (much tympanites), *Hyos., Bapt., Arn., Lach.* (bad cases).

Labour after (retention of placenta): *Arn., Puls., Secale, Ign.*

Labour after (retention of urine): *Acon., Bell., Canth., Hysoc., Rhus.*

Labour after or during haemorrhage: *Secale, Sabi., Ipecac., Eryng., Arn., Puls., Ign., Cimi., China, Ferrum* (for consequent debiity).

Labour after pains: *Arn., Caulo., Cimici., Gels., Ign., Secale, Collin., Cham., Coffea, Puls., Bella.*

Labour pain (abnormal conditions of): *Gels., Bell., Caulo.* (rigidity of the O.S. Uteri) *China* (intermittent pains): *Croc., Puls.* (irregular), *Cham. Gels., Coff.* (excessive) *Ign., Bell., Hyos.* (convulsion and delirium), *Cocc., Nux vom.* (spasms etc.), *Puls., Secale, Cimic., Caulo.* (pain casuing too much weakness), Labour pains: *Caulophyllum* (intermittent pains of uterus and in bladder, rigid OS) *Secale cor.* (contractions are continuous, everything seems loose and open), *Pulsatilla* (pains are deficient, irregular and spasmodic, suffocating and fainting spell, wants to open the doors and windows) *Gels.* (pains are insufficient or none at all, OS widely open and there is complete agony).

Labour pain (to promote): *Cimic., Caulo., Puls.*

Lactation (abnormal condition of): *Acon., Agnus., Asaf., Puls., Coni., Cal. carb.* (absent or scantly late), *Cal. carb., Sulph., Sil., Merc.* (deteriorated), *Cham.*, (from anger), *Cal. carb., Kali iod., Bryo., Phos., Silicea, Iod.* (excessive or too long continued flow), *Cimifuga* (mental dullness and melancholy), *Cal. Carb., Iod., Sulph., Acid phos.* (menses occurring during lactation.

Lactation (fever) *Acon., Bell., Bryo.*

Laryngitis (acute): *Acon., Spong., Hep. Sulph., Kali bich., Apid* (oedema of the glottis).

Laryngitis (inflammation of the larynx) *Aconite* (febrite symptoms predominate, tenderness of the throat, parts burn) *Belladona* (larynx very painful and loss of voice, barking cough) *Heper sulph.* (cough when any part of the body is uncovered) *Lachesis* (cannot bear anything to touch the throat, it excites cough and a sense of suffocation) *Spongia* (dry hollow or whistling cough, resembles like croup).

Laryngitis *Chronic* (throat consumption) *Calcarea carb.* (painless hoarseness, takes cold easily, cold damp feet) *Carbo veg.* (throat consumption, expectoration of pieces green mucus) *Causticum* (short and backing great dryness in larynx) *Lachesis* (hoarseness with feeble voices worse after sleeping) *Mercurius* (burning and teckling in the larynx) *Nitric acid* (dry barking cough) *Sulphur* (complete loss of voice, ulcerative phthesis). Croup: *Aconite* (first stage, high fever, great restlessness, loud breathing during expiration, but not during inspiration) *Belladona* (face flushed and eyes red, sleepiness but cannot sleep) *Calcarea* (a pallied flabby state of body), *Chamommila* (much hoarseness, wheezing and rattling of mucus in the trachea) *Heper sulph.* (loose, rattling of mucus in the trachea) *Heper sulph.* (loose, rattling, choking cough) *Kali bich.* (true membranous croup sound as if passing through a metallic tube) *Lachesis* (distressing aggravation after sleeping) *Spongia* (non membranous croup, crowing, barking cough, slow, loud wheezing and saving respiration, sound is heard during inspiration, cough dry) *Antim. tar.* (cough sounds as if much mucus is lodged, chest expands with great difficulty, anxiety and prostration).

Laryx: *Arsenic alb.* (dirty looking growth on larynageal membrane, velvety projection) *Conium* (malignancy with continuous hacking and dry cough) *Kali bich.* (benign tumor of larynx with thick ropy discharge inwards) Phytolacca (malignancy, throat hot, pain at the root of tongue extending to ears.) *Thuja* (benign tumour of the larynx with chronic laryngitis).

Lead colic: *Plat., Opi., Alum., Bell., Ac. sulph.*

Legs (weakness of): *Rhus., Rad., Arg. nit., Nux vom., Phos., Sulph., Bell* (trembling), *Electricity.*

Legs cramp in: *Ver. Vir., Nux vom., Cup met., Cham., Cal. carb., Arn., Colch.*

Legs paralysis of: *Cocc., Rhus., Gels., Arg. nit., Coni., Phos., Bell., Nux vom., Acid. oxalic, Electricity.*

Legs ulcer on: *Bella.* (erysipeleous) *Kali bich.* (chronic), *Merc. sol.* (exzematous) *Phos.* (debilaterd patients), *Ham., Puls., Sil., Acid nit., Acid flour* (varicose).

Leprosy: *Ars., Ant crud., Merc., Kali iod., Hydrocotyle asiatica.*

Leucoma (white spot on the cornea): *Bella., Cann sat., Cal. carb., Euphorbia, Puls., Phos., Coni., Kali iod.*

Leucorrhoea discharge only in the night: *Ambra., Causticum, Merc., Nitric acid.*

Leucorrhoea in little girls: *Caulophyllum, Cal. carb., Cina, Puls., Sepia.*

Leucorrhoea of childern: *Calcarea carb.* (scrofulous habit, the feet are cold and damp) *Graphites* (discharge is very profuse in healthy skin) *Nux vomica* (discharge fetid, tingling the linen yellow habitual constipation) *Pulsatilla* (milky leucorrhoea, swelling of external parts) *Sulphur* (discharge is acrid making the part sore).

Leucorrhoea two weeks after menses: *Baryta carb., Bovista, Conium, Mag. mur.*

Leucorrhoea: *Cal. carb., Graph., Puls.* (leucorrhoea like milk with burning and itching in the parts) *Carb v., Ars., Con* (morning leucorrhoea very acrid, excoriating the parts) *Caust.* (leucorrhoea at night) *China* (leucorrhoea before the menses with pressure towards the groin, bloody leucorrhoea) *Cocculus* (leucorrhoea in place of menses) *Con. Puls.* (leucorrhoea of white, acrid mucus burning and smarting) *Graph.* (profuse leucorrhoea, discharge white, thin and often excoriating with great weakness in the back) *Kali bich.* (ropy yellow leucorrhoea with itching, burning in the parts) *Lyco.* (profuse leucorrhoea with cutting pains across the right side to the left, bloody) *Lyco.*, *Calc.*, *Puls.* (milky leucorrhoea) *Nat. mur.* (leucorrhoea, greenish especially when walking) *Sulph.* (burning painful leucorrhoea making the parts sore) *Calcarea carb.* (milk like discharge during micturitation, sensitive to cold) *China* (bloody leucorrhoea before menses) *Conium* (leucorrhoea smarting and excoriating indurations on ulceration of OS uteri) *Pulsatilla* (milky leucorrhoea with swelling of vulva, vertigo while rising, mild tearful women) *Sulphur* (burning in vagina frequent weak spill during day, burning of soles and feet) *Puls.*, *Helon.*, *Sepia*, *Acid nit.* (corrosive or excoriative) *Iod.*, *Senec.*, *China*, *Sepia.* (yellow white), *Ferr.*, *Merc.*, *Collin.*, *Aloes*, *Xantho.*, *Hydrast.*, *Caul.*, alternate with *Cimi.*, *Kreos.*, *Cal. carb.*, *Iod.* (in tubercular women and children) *Sepia* (leucorrhoea with itching in vagina, discharge yellowish or watery) *Sepia* (leucorrhoea like milk only in the day time) *Sepia* (profuse, watery offensive leucorrhoea) *Podophyllum* (leucorrhoea discharge thick, transparent mucus with bearing down in the genitals and constipation).

Libia inflammation with itching but less redness: *Rhus tox.*, *Kali bich.*

Lichen: *Sulph.*, *Ant. crud.*, *Petrol.*, *Ars.*, *Nux.*, *Juglans*, *Apis*, *Led.* (prickly heat).

Lienteria: *China*, *Ferrum.*, *Phos.*, *Acid phos.*, *Puls.*

Light not tolerated: *Aco.*, *Bella.*, *Conium*, *Lachesis*, *Graphites*, *Nux vom.*, *Phos.*

Likes cold wet weather: *Nux.*, *Causticum*, *Heper.*, *Mendorrihnum.*

Liking for cold food: *Phos.*, *Silicea.*

Liking for eating ice: *Cal. carb.*, *Phos.*

Liking for saltiest items: *Cal. carb.*, *Nat. mur.*, *Meddorihnum*, *Causticum.*

Liking for sour items: *Antim. crud.*, *Antim. tart.*, *Ars. alb.*, *Heper.*, *Mag. sulph.*

Lips (cracked sore, etc): *Merc.*, *Graph.*, *Sulph.*, *Acid sulph.*, *Hydras.*, *Bryo.* (dryness) *Nat. mur.* (cracked in the centre) *Acon.*, *Ars.*, *Bryo.* (lips dry and black) *Ars. alb.* (lips dark, dry and parched which he constantly licks) *China* (blackened) *Aurum.*, *Ars.* (discolouration bluish, pale coppery eruptions) *Condorango* (reached to ulcerative stage) *Conium* (hard tumor of the lips) *Hydrastis Q* (apply externally) *Bryo.* (lips parched, dry and cracked).

Liver (abscess of): *Acon.*, *Merc.*, *Hep. sulph.*

Liver (congestion and chronic enlargement or its complaints) : *Merc.*, *Lept.*, *Merc. iod.*, *Phos.*, *Acid nit.*, *Agar.*, *Nux vom.*, *Sulph.*, *Podophy.*, *Chels.*, *Carbo veg.*, *Lyco.*, *Ars.*, *China* (consequent on ague).

Liver (inflammation of): *Acon.*, *Bryo.*, *Merc cor.*, *Heper Sulph.* (threaten abscess).

Liver problems: *Cal. carb.*, *Lyco.*, *Phos.*, *Sulphur*, *Acon.* (pressure in the region of the liver, liver inflammation, bowels inflammation with sharp shooting pains in the whole abdomen which is tender to touch) *Chlolesterinum* (obstinate hepatic engorgement) *Podophyllum*, *Acon.* (belching of hot flatus, very sour, gagging or empty retching, fullness and pain in the region of liver) *Podo.*, *Merc.* (burning pain in the region of liver).

Liver spots: *Sulph.*, *Sepia.*, *Bor.*, *Lyco.*

Lochia: *Bryo.* (suppressed lochia, with splitting headache) *Dulc.* (lochia suppressed by cold or dampness) *Rhus tox.*, *Bryonia.* (vitiated and diminished lochia with shorting upward virgina with bursting sensation in head) *Bryonia.* (suppression of Lochia with headache fullness and heaviness of the head, worse by motion) *Calcarea carb.* (Lochia last long and profuse suitable to pallid, flabby state of body) *Pulsatilla* (suppression of lucid discharge, no thirst, sudden disappearance of milk, mild tearful) *Rhus tox.* (black watery and offensive last long, sharp pain shooting through the head) *Secale cor.* (thin offensive lucid suitable to thin screwy women).

Lock Jaw (Tetanus): *Aconite* (pulse hard, full frequent, fear and anxiety of mind, face alternately red and pale) *Arnica* (arising from external injury, especially from a bruise and where lockjaw is threatened, feeling of soreness all over the body) *Belladona* (sensation of constriction in the throat, clenching of the jaws, foaming and distortion of the mouth, painful stiffness of the back) *Hyoscymus* (furious look and foams from the mouth, constriction of throat, inability to swallow especially liquids) *Ignitia* (constant inclination to yawning yet unable to open the mouth suppressed grief, worse when touched or handle) *Nux vomica* (throat feels constricted, cramp like pain in the stomach, obstinate constipation).

Locomotor ataxia: *Bell.*, *Zinc.*, *Arg nit.*, *Mag. phos.*, *Kali iod.*, *Secale*, *Phos*, *Alumnia*, *Lythyrus.*, *Sulph.*

Looses neck color again and again: *Lach.*, *Amyl nitrate.*

Loss of appetite: *China* (aversion to all kind of food, everything tastes bitter) *Heper Sulph.* (after the abuse of mercury or quinine) *Mercurius* (putrid taste, when sitting the food weight like a stone in the stomach) *Nux vomica* (bitter taste, bitter belching, bitter vomiting, all kinds of food are tasteless) *Pulsatilla* (putrid bitter taste, aversion to fatty food, eructation after meal).

Loss of sleep after lying on bed: *Phosphorus*, *Phosphoric acid.*

Loss of speech even then no pain in thraot: *Cal. carb.*, *Caust.*, *Phos.*

Loss of voice: *Causticum* (loss of voice especially in the morning) *Mercurius* (loss of voice with constant hoarseness, short dry cough) *Phosphorus* (complete loss of voice, roughness of the larynx and wind pipe) *Sulphur* (creeping sensation in larynx, constant heat on top of the head).

Lumbago: *Acon.*, (recent) *Rhus.*, *Rad.* (pains worse during rest and at night from cold), *Arn* (from severe exertion) *Ant. tar.*, *Acon.*, *Dulc.*, *Colch.*, *Berb.*, *Arn.*, *Belladona* (feeling in the back as if it would break, hindering motion, red face and hot head) *Bryonia* (severe aching or darting pain in the back, aggravated by slightest motion) *Mercurius vivus* (symptoms all worse at night and in damp rainy weather, perspire freely without relief) *Nux vomica* (pain as if bruised worse from turning in bed, intemperate habits) *Rhus tox.* (pain as if bruised or sprained, pain relieved on lying on hard, worse at night).

Lungs (congestion of): *Phos.*, *Acon.*, *Kali bich.*, *Ver. vir.* (from chill) *Ars.* (cardic complication), *Bell.*, *Ant. tar.*, *Ver. vir.* (from cold) *Ars.*, *Iod.*

Lungs (gangrene of): *Ars.*, *China*, *Lach.*

Lungs (haemorrhage from): *Acon.*, *Ham.*, *Kreos.*, *Phos.*, *Ipecac.*, *Ferr.*, *Mill.*, *Arn.* (from injury).

Lungs (inflammation of): *Acon.*, *Phos.*, or *Bryo.*, *Ant. tar.*, (broncho-pneumonia and in children) *Sulph.*, *Chelid.*

Lungs (paralysis of): *Phos.*, *Opi.*, *Ant. tar.*, *Baryta carb.*

Lungs: *Ferr.* (Haemorrhages from the lungs with pain between the shoulders, emptiness of the lungs) *Millefolium* (coughing up of pure blood) *Phosphorus* (streaks of blood in mucus from the lungs, sputa rusty blood colour or full of mucus)

Lupus: *Ars.*, *Phyto.*, *Sulph.*, *Hydrast.*

Lymphatic glands (enlarged): *Acon.*, *Cistus.*, *Merc iod.*, *Baryta carb.*, *Dulc.*, *Bella.*, *Auram mur.*, *Coni.*, *Rhus.* (indurated) *Sulph.*, *Sil.*, *Cal. carb.*, *Iod.* (constitutional remedies).

M

Madness after delivery of a child: *Arum., Bella., Cimicifuga, Cuprum., Hyos., Lyco., Platina, Puls., Stromonium, Veratrum album.*

Malaria during trembling in one foot and cough in cold stage: *Rhus tox.*

Malaria of children: *Natrum* (with pneumonia) *China mur* (chill comes at 10.30 AM, extremities turn blue) *China* (chill generally in forenoon, fever with all stages well define) *Arsenic alb.* (fever with marked periodicity at which chill will come) *Eupatorium perf.* (with unbearable pain in the body) *Natrum sulph.* (associated with colic and vomiting of green bile) *Natrum mur.* (chill comes 10 or 11 AM) *Chininuim ars.* (periodical attacks with prostration, liver and spleen enlarged) *Ipecac.* (with persistent nausea and vomiting) *Pulsatilla* (absence of thirst in all stages of fever, sweating on one side).

Malaria strict to timing: *Eupat. perf., Ipecac., Nat. mur., Ars. alb.*

Malaria: *China* (thirst before the shivering, thirst lost with the onset of shivering, thirst before onset of fever, thirst lost with the rise of fever) *Chin. sulph.* (thirst with shivering, backache, fever lost for short period, after fever perspiration starts, but as soon as perspiration starts the fever comes with shivering) *Eupatorium* (shivering at 9.00 AM, do not drink water even when there is thirst, because by drinking water the shivering starts) *Arsenic alb.* (great thirst but soon after drinking water there is vomiting, so avoid drinking water) *Capsicum* (cold starts from back, cold starts with thirst from drinking water shivering starts, great pain in the body) *Cyclamen* (ailment aggravates with drinking water).

Male genitals: *Arsenic alb.* (restlessness due to pain of genital) *Conium* (Pain of penis or of testis) *Crotalush.* (prostate with haemuturia).

Marasmus (Atrophy) of children: *Arsenic* (general emaciation with dry parchment like skin, feverish heat, prostration and coldness of extremities) *Cal.carera carb.* (large head with open fontanels, general emaciation with a good appetite, cold damp feet, much perspiration abut the head) *Nux vomica* (obstinate constipation, hunger with aversion to food, cannot sleep after 3 AM) *Staphysagria* (canine hunger, even when the stomach is full of food).

Mariners disease: *Carbo sulph.* (defective hearing with buzzing and ringing noise) *Chenopodium* (sensitive to high pitched sound, sudden giddiness, aural vertigo, buzzing in ears) *Silicea* (roaring in ears, loud pistol like report, caries of mastoid, fetid discharge).

Measles (false roseola): *Acon.* internally and externally *Rhus tox., Bella.*

Measles (mobille): *Aconite* (at the beginning when there is dry hot skin, full quick pulse and much thirst) *Apis mel.* (cough and soreness in the chest diarrhoea in the morning) *Arsenic* (burning and great dryness and itching of the skin, bloated ness of the face and dry parched lips, constant craving of cold water, rapid prostration) *Belladona* (red and hot face, starting and jumping during sleep) *Bryonia* (congestion of chest, dyspnoea and quick breathing, sitting up in the bed causes nausea and faintness) *Ipecac.* (constant tickling cough, rattling of phlegm in the chest, nausea and vomitting, suppression of the eruption) *Phos.phorus* (exhausting cough and rust coloured sputa, hoarseness with loss of voice) *Pulsatilla* (dryness of mouth, without thirst, the eruptions are tardy in coming out, craves for cool, fresh, worse in a warm room).

Measles (prophylactic): *Puls.*, *Bella.*

Measles in children: *Bryonia* (abort disease, painful cough, worse motion) *Aconite* (fever, headache, rapid pulse) *Euphrasia* (eyes and nose inflamed) *Belladona* (restlessness, flushed face, thirst-lessens) *Gels.iminum* (puffed and flushed face, drowsy, no thirsts) *Kali bich.* (with decline of fever laryngitis develops, thin ropy green mucus) *Pulsatilla* (coryza with profuse flow of green mucus from nose) *Sulphur* (when eruptions are slow in coming out) *Squilla* (after cough) *Arsenic alb.* (curative and preventive).

Measles: *Acon.* (fever) *Puls.*, *Euphr.*, (Lachrymation and coryza), *Kali bich.* (Laryngeal cough), *Gels..*, *Bryo.* (when eruptions does not come out well), *Bella.* (sore throat and brain symptoms), *Verat. vir.* (congestion of lungs, nausea) *Merc. iod.* (glandular swellings), *Phos.* (chest symptoms), *Ammon. carb.* (Malignant), *Sulph.* (deficient eruptions, intense headache and tendency towards coma also during convalescence to prevent sequel) others are *Rhus tox.* (restlessness), *Camph* (chilliness) *Opi.* (problem of constipation) *Meddorihnum*, *Puls.*, *Sulph.*

Memory (weakness or loss of): *Acid Phos.*, *Anacard.*, *Zinc.*, *Alum.*, *Aur.*, *Ign.*, *Verat.*, *Bary carb.*

Meningitis (simple): *Acon.*, *Bell.*, *Bryo.*, *Apis.*

Meningitis (syphilitic) *Merc.*, *Kali iod.*

Meningitis (traumatic): *Acon.*, *Arn.*

Meningitis (tubercular) *Bell.*, *Bacill.*, *Hell.*, *Cal. phos.*, (when effusion has taken place) *Cal. carb.*, *Sulph.*, *Apis.*

Menopause (cessation of the menses): *Bryonia* (congestive headaches, as if forehead would spilt open, exceedingly irritable) *Cocculus* (leucorrhoea in place of menses) *Lachesis* (heaviness of head with burning and beating on the top, chills at night and flushes of heat in the day, worse after sleep) *Pulsatilla* (one sided headache, dizziness when looking up) *Sepia* (great sadness weeps frequently, prolapsis uteri) *Sulphur* (constant heat on the top of the head, painful sensitiveness of the abdomen, burning painful leucorrhoea).

Menopause during there is fast supply of blood to the face so face becomes red: *Amyl nitrate*, *Glonine*, *Bella dona*, *Meli lotus.*

Menorrhagia (Menses too copious): *Belladona* (early and profuse red imparting a sense of heat, throbbing headache and pain in small of the back) *Calcarea carb.* (menses too soon and profuse, very sensitive to the least cold air) *Phosphorus* (menses too soon, too copious and lasting too long, sensation of weakness and emptiness in stomach, belching up large quantities of wind after eating, long slim hard stool) *Sabina* (very profuse and depilating menses, labour like pain) *Sepia* (menses early and profuse, emptiness at the pit of the stomach, fetid urine, yellow spots on the face prolepsis uteri).

Menses delayed: *Bryonia* (frequent bleeding of nose, constipation, hard dry stools) *Pulsatilla* (pain in the abdomen across the back, hysterical symptoms, better in open air, worse towards evening).

Menses during hot feeling: *Amyl nit.*, *Cimici.*, *Glonine*, *Ignitia*, *Lach.*, *Manganum*, *Sangunaria*, *Sepia*, *Sulph.*, *Sambul.*

Menses flows more during sleep in hysterical patients: *Cimicifuga*, *Caulo.*, *Mag. mur.*

Menses stops, from wetting the feet: *Puls.*, *Graphites.*

Menses: *Acon.*, *Bell.*, *Cal.*, *Puls.* (menses too profuse and protracted especially in young and plethoric women) *Acon.*, *Lyco.* (suppression of menses from fright) *Dulc.*, *Podo.*, *Puls.*, *Sulph.* (suppression of menses from cold) *Bell.*, *Calc.*, *Cimi.*, *Canth.*, *Puls.*, *Dulcamara* (menses too early and profuse) *Con.*, *Dulcamara*, *Phos.*, *Sulph* (menses too late and scanty) *Cham* (during menses, tearing pains in the legs), *Cal. carb.* (least excitement causes to return, during menses vertigo, rush of blood, to the head, toothache and cold damp feet) *Canth.*, *Puls.* (menses too early and too profuse, black discharge) *Carb veg.* (menses to early, too profuse, blood thick corrosive and of acrid smell) *Cham.*, *Cimi.* (painful menstruation with labour like pains, discharge dark and clotted with tearing pains in the legs) *Cimici.* (painful menstruation, especially in rheumatic subjects, accompanied by great mental and nervous irritability) *Cocculus* (menstrual colic, the pains are spasmodic and irregular) *Crocus sat.* (painful menstruation with dark stringy blood) *Dulcamara.*, *Puls.* (suppression of menses after taking cold or getting the feet wet) *Carb v.*, *Graph.* (before or during menses fatiguing cough) *Ferrum* (earlier to discharge of long pieces of mucus from the uterus) *Con*, *Nat mur.*, *Sil.* (menses too early and scanty) *Graph.*, *Heper.*, *Puls.* (menses too late and scanty) *Bell.*, *Cal. c.*, *Nit acid*, *Sabina.* (too early and too profuse) *Phos.*, *Con.*, *Puls.* (profuse smarting with corrosive leucorrhoea) *Phos. acid.* (too early and too long continued menstruation with pain in the liver) *Phyto.* (painful menstruation in barren females) *Phyto.* (menses too often, too profuse with increase of tears. saliva, bile and urine) *Podo Puls* (suppression of menses in young girls) *Puls.*, *Con.*, *Dulcamara*, *Phos*, *Sulphur* (menses too late and too scanty and too short duration with cramps in abdomen) *Puls.*, *Bell.*, *Cal. carb.* (too early and too profuse) *Graph.*, *Puls.*, *Sulph.* (menses too late pale and scanty) *Graph.* (during the menses severe tearing pain in the stomach) *Ign.*, *Puls.* (menses scanty, black of a putrid odor) *Kali bich.* (menses too soon with vertigo, nauseas and headache) *Lach.*, *Puls.*, *Sepia.* (at the cessation of menses frequent uterine Haemorrhages) *Lach.* (menses at regular time but too short and feeble) *Lyco.*, *Cal. carb.*, *Bell.*, *Bryonia* (menses too soon and too profuse) *Mag. carb.* (during menses great debility chilliness, headache, pale face and pain in the small of the back) *Mag carb.*, *Nux v.* (menstrual blood thick dark, like pitch) *Nat. mur.*, *Puls.* (menses delay which become more and more scanty) *Nat mur.*, *Bell.*, *Nit. acid.* (very sad and gloomy during the menses, palpitation of heart, morning headache pressing and bearing down in the genitals as if every thing will come out of vagina) *Puls.*, *Con.*, *Nat. mur.*, *Phos.*, *Silicea* (too early and too scanty), *Puls.*, *Caust.* (too late and too profuse) *Puls.*, *Ars.*, *Phos.* (vicarious menstruation splitting of blood) *Puls.*, *Kali bich.*, *Nat. mur.*, *Sulph.* (delayed and difficult first menstruation) *Sabina* (suppression of the menses followed by a thin fetid leucorrhoea) *Sabina* (painful menstruation with violent pain extending from back to the pubes) *Silicea* (increased menses with ice coldness of whole body).

Menstrual flow: *Carbo anamalis* (the flow weakens the patient), *Chamomilla* (menstrual flow is dark with peculiar mental symptoms) *Puls.* (flow is scanty comes in fits and start with puls temperament).

Menstruation (delay in first) *Puls.*, *Ferr.*, *Sepia*, *Cycl.*, *Sulph.*, *Phos.*, *Acon.* (disturbed circulation).

Menstruation (excessive): *Secale. cor.* (dark clotted discharge, severe pain before expulsion) *Croc. sat.* (dark and clotted, clots long and tenecions) *Sabin.* (bright red with pain chiefly at first discharge) *Cal. carb.* (too early and too profuse in patients who have cold clammy feet) *Acon.*, *Bell.* (in plethoric patients) *Ham.* (profuse venous) *Ipecac.* (simple, bright red discharge with or without nausea) *Hyos.* (nervous and hysteric patients) *Phos.* (mental and sexual excitement, sensitiveness) *China* (after excessive discharges); *Senec.*, *Ferr.*, *Iod.*, *Borax*, *Aloes*, *Mag. carb.*, *Ambra gra.*, *Aut. nit.*, *Trill.*

Menstruation (irregular or infrequent) *China* (when profuse and consisting of dark lumps), *Puls.*, *Cycl.* (scanty) *Iod.* or *Phos.* (gradually diminishes), *Sepia*, *Nux vom.*, *Bella.*, *Sulph.*, *Sence.*

Menstruation (membranous) *Borax* (profuse discharge at one time and scanty at another, with severe labour like pains in the back, hips and hypogastric region).

Menstruation (painful or dyememorrhoea): *Secale* (forcing pain of expulsive nature with dark coagulated or scanty discharge) *Collin.* (piles, constipation etc.) *Sence* (scanty or profuse flow) *Gels.*, *Caulo.* (spasmodic pains) *Cimic.* (rheumatic patient) *Cham.* *Coff.*, *Xantho.* (neuralgic pains) *Cocc.* (colicky pain) *Hama* (ovarian irritation) *Bella* *Acon.*, *Ign.*, *Plat.*, *Sabin.*, *Viburnum op.*, *Macrot.*, *Cimic.* (habitually painful).

Menstruation (scanty): *Puls.*, (simple cases) *Ferr.*, *Helon* (with anaemia), *Bella.*, *Acon.* (in full blooded patient) Merc. (sallow complexion, liver derangement etc) *Arg. nit.* (watery discharge) *Graph.* (constipation and unhealthy skin); *Sepia* (chlorotic appearance, leucorrhoea etc) *Phos.* (constitutional delicacy, chronic Diarrhea, tendency to chest diseases) *Kali carb.*, *Dulc.*, *Sulph.*, *Cycl.*, *Plat.*, *Nat. mur.*, *Baryta carb.*

Menstruation (suppressed): *Acon.*, *Opi.*, *Verat. alb.* (fright) *Coni.*, *Senec.*, *Sepia* (chronic).

Menstruation (too early and long lasting): *Cal. carb.*, *Cal. phos.*, (profuse), *Sec.*, *Sabi.* (painful) *Iod.* (with emaciation) *Trill.*, *Plat.* (every two weeks) *Nux vom.*, *Ferr.*, *Ign.*, *China*.

Menstruation (Vicarious) *Sabina*, *Bry.*, *Ham.*, *Ferr.*, *Senec.*

Menstruation (cessation of at critical. age): *China*, *Ferr.* (pressure and burning on the top of the head; profuse discharges) *Lach.* (headache, sleeplessness also flushes); *Glon.* (rush of blood to the head, with throbbing and noises in the head or ears., giddiness) *Cimic.*, *Acid hydrocy.* (sinking at the stomach), *Sulph.* (flushes of heat, mental depression etc.) *Amyl. nit.*, *Sangu.*, *Acid sulph.* (flushes) *Ambra. gr.* (numbness and stinging in the arms); *Sep., Plat., Gels., Cocc., Apo., Ign., Kali carb.*

Mental weakness: *Ambra., Anacardium, Baryta mur., Bufo., Conium, Hyosym., Lach., Lyco., Nux mosh., Nux vom., Opium, Phosphoric acid, Picric acid, Silicea, Sulphur, Stromonium, Veratrum alb. Sulph., Kali brom., Acid phos., Anac., Gels., Ign., Plum., Zinc.*

Metallic taste with anorexia: *Lac. can., Merc.*

Metatarsalgia: *Aloe* (pain in sole while walking) *Antim crud.* (feet tender pain in heels) *Cannabis sativa* (pain in the ball of the foot and under the toes).

Metrorrhagia: *Ipecac.* (blood bright red clotted oppressed breathing).

Migraine: *Nux vom.* (one sided neck and occipital pain, pain above eye brow generally left-sided, pain starts from sun rise to sunset, associated with acidity symptom) *Sanguinaria* (right sided pain) *Glonine* (pain aggravates from sun rays, specially left sided migraine) *Belladona* (face becomes red during pain).

Miliaria (milary fever): *Acon., Bry., Merc., Joborandi.*

Milk crust: *Iris., Rhus., Merc., Sepia, Phytolacca, Clem., Cal. carb., Silicia.* (chronic) *Croton.*

Milk fever after delivery: *Aconite* (dry and hot skin, few doses of this are sufficient in the beginning) *Calcarea* (deficiency in secretion of milk sensitive to cold air) *Pulsatilla* (feverish and fretful mild fearful subject).

Milk intolerable: *Aestha., Antim. tart., Cal. carb., Carbo veg., China, Mag. carb., Nitric acid., Sepia, Silicea.*

Milk leg after delivery: *Arnica* (after severe and protected labour or where mechanical means have been resorted to in the delivery) *Bryonia* (Lucia suppressed with headache as if head would burst) *Rhus tox.* (red strikes running up the course of the veins of the legs).

Miscarriage (threatened): *Sabi.* (free discharge of blood) *Caulo., Sec.* (severe expulsive pains) *Cham.* (if caused by anger, fright etc), *Arn.* (if from a fall or some mechanical injury), *Acon., Puls., Cedr.*

Miscarriage (to prevent): *Caulo., Sabi., Sepia, Helon, Sec., Nux vom.* (associated with constipation whch causes straining) *Cal. carb., Sulph.* (for tubercular patients).

Morning sickness: *Arsenic* (vomiting fluid as soon as taken) *Ipecac.* (continual nausea all the time, vomiting of large quantity of mucus) *Phosphorus* (vomiting soon as they get warm in the stomach, very sleepy after meals).

Mouth (inflammation of) *Merc., Ars., Acid mur., Acid nit., Carbo veg.*

Mouth (ulcers) *Merc. Ars., Bapt* (with Hydras lotion as a mouth wash).

Mouth dry, but no thirst: *Nux mosh., Puls.*

Mouth very much dry: *Apis., Lachesis, Nux mosch., Puls.*

Mouth: *Acon., Ars., Bryo.* (great dryness of mouth and tongue with thirst) *Bell., Lyco.* (great dryness of mouth and tongue without thirst) *Bell* (soreness of the inner cheeks) *Canth.* (vesicles in mouth) *China* (optimism from abuse of mercury) *Bella.* (foam from mouth during sleep) *Ignitia* (increased secretion of saliva) *Kali bich.* (discharge from the mouth and throat tough and stringy) *Lachesis* (burning in the mouth as from pepper great dryness) *Lyco.* (dryness of the mouth and tongue without thirst) *Nat mur., Nit acid, Rhus.* (dryness of the mouth and tongue with much thirst) *Merc., Ars., Hyos., Nux.* (bloody saliva) *Nit acid* (fetid ulcers in mouth and fauces) *Phos.* (nursing sore mouth).

Movement of mouth unconsciously, as if grinding something: *Bryo.*, *Bella.*, *Helloborus*, *Stromonium*, *Aco.*

Mucus: *Aloe* (mucus in large quantity in stool) *Ipecac.* (mucus in amoebic dysentery, green grass stool, griping pain) *Merc. cor.* (shreds of mucus membrane in stool, blood and mucus in dysentery) *Merc. sol.* (mcus dysentery, worse at night) *Sulphur* (mucus with blood in stool).

Mumps in children: *Aconite* (pain and fever) *Belladona* (restlessness with flushed face) *Apis.* (soft swelling, puffy, rosy and tender) *Bryonia* (hard swelling, thirst for cold water) *Pulsatilla* (when disease spreads to testicles or mammae) *Merc. sol.* (with saliva in mouth, thirst for large quantity of water) *Parotidinum* (curative and preventive).

Mumps: *Acon.* (with fever) *Merc. iod.*, *Merc. sol.*, *Carbo veg.* (swelling of the glands), *Bell* (brain implication), *Puls.* (implication of the testicles or breast) *Belladona* (bright red swelling of glands especially on the right side, dark red swelling of glands on the left side) *Rux tox.* (sudden disappearance of the swelling with throbbing, headache and delirium, sleepiness but cannot sleep) *Hyoscymus* (twisting and jerking of the limbs) *Merc. vivus.* (hard swelling of them glands, stools with severe tens us) *Pulsatilla* (metastasis to the female mammal and to the testis in male pain up to spermatic chord, vertigo, thickly coated tongue).

Muscae volitantes (singular shaped bodies floating about in the vitreous humour and their position with every movement of eyes, chiefly caused by overuse of the eyes), *Merc.*, *Acid nit.* (from liver disorder), *Dig.* (weak slow beating of heart), *Verat. alb.* (weak, irregular or quick action of heart) *Phos.*, *Tereb.* (kidney trouble), *Mosch*, *Agar.* (nervousness) *Phos.*, *Acid phos.* (sexual excesses) *Phos.* (general debility), *Kali iod.*, *Nux vom.* (Obstinate cases).

Myalgia (pain in the muscles): *Ver. vir.* (prostration of the muscular system and muscular rheumatism) *Gels.* (with feverishness) *Arn.* (from over exertion), *Bryo.*, *Gels.*, *Rhus tox.* (with inflammation) *Cimic.*, *Ammon. mur.*, *Caust.*, *Bryo.*, *Dulca.*, *Valer.*

Myasthenia gravis: *Ferrum met.* (weakness of muscles with anemia, worse after any active effort, weakness from mere speaking or walking though looking strong).

Myelitis: *Rhus tox.*(inflammation, pain and stiffness in the small of the back, stiffness of the nape of the neck, better motion, lying on hard bed).

Myocarditis: *Arsenic iod.* (chronic weakness of the heart muscle, irregular fluttering with a tendency to faint, difficulty in breathing on going upstairs, severe pain in cardiac region going to back) *Digitalis* (weakness and dilation of muscle of heart, pulse weak and irregular and slow quickened by least movement, sensation that heart would stop if not moved, incomplete contraction of heart, heavy breathing worse by lying.

Myopia (near sightedness) *Bell.*, *Spig.*, *Macrot.*, *Acon.* (brutability, congestion or inflammation).

N

Nails (disease of ingrowing toe nails) *Merc., Graph., Sil., Ant crud, Alumina, Ars. alb., Mag net austral.* (in high potency).

Nasal catarrh (chronic): *Calcarea carb.* (ulcerated nostrils, gnawing pain at the root of the nose, scrofulous subject) *Kali bichrom* (discharge of tough green masses from the nose) *Lachesis* (the nose inside is sore and scurfy) *Silicea* (stoppage of the nose from harden mucus).

Nasal catarrh (for dry coryza): *Bryonia, Dulcamara, Nux vom., Sepia.* (when there is stoppage of nose) *Arsenic, Chammomilla, Merc., Pulsatilla, Sulph.* (fluent coryza with mucus or watery discharges) *Arsenic* (frequent sneezing with fluent coryza, intense thirst, restlessness and prostration) *Belladona* (throbbing headache, children cry with coughing, sleepy) *Bryonia* (lips parched, constipation, wants to keep quite) *Chamomilla* (fluent acrid discharge from nose, dry cough, irritable) *Heper Sulph.* (take cold easily stitches in throat, hoarse croupy cough) *Lachesis* (fluent coryza, dryness of the mouth with burning as if from pepper) *Mercurius* (headache frequent sneezing ulcerated tonsils) *Nux vomica* (fluent coryza during day; dry at night, worse in the morning) *Pulsatilla* (craves fresh, cool air, worse towards evening) *Sepia* (nose swollen and inflamed, violent coryza, sense of emptiness in the stomach).

Nasal polypus: *Calcarea carb.* (flabby bloated patient, frequent sneezing, feeling cold damp feet) *Phosphorus* (nose bled easily, lean slender patient) *Sepia* (obstruction of the nose-frequent sneezing suitable for females feted urine) *Silicea* (worse at every new moon) *Staphysagrea* (stoppage of the nose with frequent sneezing without catarrh; teeth turn black).

Nature changeable: *Puls.*

Nausea from the smell and looking towards food: *Ars. alb., Colchicum, Sepia.*

Nausea/vomitting: *Ipecac.* (intense nausea and vomiting) *Antim tar* (except lying on right there is vomiting, after vomit sleepiness) *Arsenic album* (from eating ice cream, drinking cold water or from alcoholic drinks) *Asarum* (tongue clean, after taking food or during pregnancy the symptoms are aggravated) *Bismith* (vomiting soon after drinking, symptoms develops after abdomen operation, vomiting is associated with Diarrhoea, stool foul) *Carbolic acid* (vomit of greenish colour) *Cocoolus ind.* (vomiting during journey by car, boat or by train) *Colchicum* (vomiting from smell of the food) *Ferrum met.* (vomiting after eating, after it again starts eating) *Kali bich.* (vomiting from ulcer in stomach, vomit stringy) *Kali carb.* (vomiting along with spasmodic cough, feeling as if something is present in abdomen) *Lac defloratum* (taking journey during pregnancy) *Lobelia* (nausea and vomiting associated with perspiration on head and weakness) *Tabacum* (vomiting from movement, cold perspiration on whole body) *Veratrum album* (vomiting with diarrhoea, cold perspiration on the forehead.

Nausea: *Ant. crud.* (violent nausea) *Graph.* (morning sickness during menstruation) *Ars., Bryo., Puls., Nux.* (nausea after a meal) Nausea: *Ipecac., Nux vom., Kreos., Ant. tar., Ant crud., Cocc. Lobel., Iris., Tabac., Apomorphia.*

Neck (stiffness of) *Ant. tar. Acon.* (from draught) *Dul.* (from damp), *Bryo., Cimic., Bell., Phyto., Rhus tox.*

Nephritis: *Lycopodium* (renal colic, the pain is felt along the urethra into bladder, red sandy sediment in the urine, terrific pain in the back previous to every urination with relief as soon as the urine begins to flow) *Mercurius* (urine scanty and red with strong smell, much perspiration without relief) *Pulsatilla* (pale watery urine with jelly like sediment, bad taste in the morning vertigo when rising) *Sepia* (fetid urine deposit of clay coloured sediments, sense of great weight in the anus) *Sulphur* (burning and drawing pain in small of the back, very fetid urine, constant heat on the top of the head).

Nervousness (great) fears from slights of noise: *Asaram, Borax, Caladium, Nux vom., Terentula his.*

Nervousness: *Coff.* (with sleeplessness) *Cham.* (restlessness, irritability and senstiveness) *Ign.* (extreme senstiveness, pains in various parts, hemicrania, sensation as if ball is in throat), *Hyos.* (perverted brain function, restless, dreamful sleep or sleeplessness) *Agar.* (pains as from icycold points, twitchings, tremors etc.) *Bor.* (noises intolerable) *Acon., Nux vom.* (from anxiety, night watching etc. with palpitation, indigestion etc.) *Puls., Bell., Ars. alb., Acid phos., Gels., Scutell., Cimici., Cyprip., Kali brom., Znic., Valeriana, Ambra.*

Nettle rash: *Acon.* (feverishness), *Rhus., Apis., Pulsa.* (from food which disagrees) *Ars.* (when caused by an irritable stomach), *Dulc.* (from chlli and wetting), *Ant crud., Copavia, Hydras., Bryo.* (sudden restracession).

Neuralgia (in the bones) *Zinc.*

Neuralgia (in the face and head): *Bella.* (redness of the affected parts, senstiveness to noise, light etc. and confusion), *Ars. alb.* (burning and tearing pains intermittent or periodic, worse in the night or during rest with extreme restlessness and anguish in weak person) *Verat. vir.* (from cold) *Acon.* (facial neuralgia from cold, anxiety with palpitation, full pulse especially in plethoric persons) *Spig.* (head, face, eyes and orbits are involved aggravated by stooping and movement), *Coloc.* (sudden violent lancinations extending from the point of origin to a distance chiefly on the left side) *Cham., Merc. sol.* (extreme senstiveness and irritability especially in children and females) *Coff.* (nerve pains with restlessness and sleeplessness), *China, Sulph.* (from malaria loss of animal fluids etc.) *Chelid* (with live derangement pain over right eye) *Cimic., Gels., Sticta., Strych. nit., Nux vom., Staph., Coni., Bella., Cedron., Argent. nit., Kali iod., Puls., Phos.,*

Neuralgia (intercostals): *cimic* (infra mammary pain especially in females) *Ran. bulb., Rhod., Arn., Bell.*

Neuralgia (of the extremities) *Rhod., Ars.*

Neuralgia cillary: *Thuja* (cold sensation in the eyes as if cold air blows on it, pain in the eye ball upward) *Mezerium* (cold sensation in the eyes as if cold air blows on it, pain in the eye ball shoots downward) *Spigelia* (the pain extends to the back of the head, feeling of as if the eye ball will be pressed out of from orbit) *Cendron* (the pain appears exactly at fixed time every day).

Nevus (moles): *Thuja 30* (internally) *Thuja Q* (externally be applied) *Phos.*, *Lyco.*, *Arn.*, *Acid carbolic.*

Nictitato (constant blinking of eyes: due to reflex, from worms, decayed teeth remove the cause and then give Agaricus which will complete the cure).

Night sweats: *Acid Phos.*, *Cal. carb.*, *China*, *Ars.*, *Hep. sulph.*, *Samb.*, *Sulph.*, *Ipecac.*, *Merc.* (profuse, sour perspiration) Bryo, Gels. (sweat of phthisis).

Night terrors in children: *Aconite* (anxious dreams, restlessness, tossing about) *Belladona* (scream out in sleep, mumbles) *Phosphorus* (easily frighten, afraid of being alone, cannot stay in dark).

Nightmare: *Nux vom.* (from indigestion) *China* (with oppression) *Sulph.* (with palpitation) *Acon.*, *Puls.*

Nipple sore: *Sulph.*, *Cham.*, *Sil.*, *Phell.* (pain after each suckling) *Crot. tig.* (shooting pain from nipple to shoulder blade).

No satisfaction from urination in spite of passing of urine frequently: *Apis.*, *Canth.*, *Squilla.*

Nodes: *Sil.*, *Kali bich.* (soft nodes on the scalp) *Kali iod.*, *Phyto.* (syphilitic nodes with nightly pain) *Aur.*

Noise (sensitiveness to): *Bella.*, *Cham.*, *Coff.*, *Ign.*, *Cann. ind.*, *Nux vom.*, *Borax.* (extreme cases).

Nose from, irritating and biting discharge: *Allium cepa*, *Ars.*, *Ars. iod.*, *Arum triphyllum*, *Lac can.*

Nose (bleeding from) *Ipecac.*, *Acid sulph.*, *Arn.* (from a blow) *Acon.* (full pulse and in the plethoric) *Bella.* (flowing freely with congestion) *Croc.* (dark stringy blood), *Bryo.* (preceded or accompanied by severe headache) *Hamm.* (dark fluid frequent) *Milli folium*, *China.* (frequent recurrence) *Phos.*, *Nux vom.*, *Ferr.*, *Phos.*

Nose (catarrh of) *Merc. Ars.*, *Nux vom.*, *Puls.*

Nose (fetid from): *Iod.* (putrid ulceration of the lining membrane in tubercular patient) *Elaps.*, *Merc. iod.*, *Aur.*, *Kali bich.*, *Formica rufa.*

Nose (inflammation of) *Bella.*, *Acon.* (acute) *Sulph* (chronic).

Nose (fetid of): *Ars.*, *Merc.*, *Graph.*, *Sulph.*, *Aur.*

Nose affections: *Arnica* (inflammation of the nose caused by a blow, contusion or mechanical injury) *Calcarea carb.* (inflammation with nostril ulcerated) *Mercurious vivus* (red shining, scurfy nostrils) *Heper sulph.* (when caused by the abuse of mercury).

Nose bleeding of children: *Aconite* (from excitement) *Arnica* (due to injury) *Hamamelis* (blood oozes in drops, blood dark red) *Millifolium* (bleeding of red blood) *Kali carb.* (when washing the face in morning) *Ammonium carb.* (on blowing the nose and coughing).

Nose blocked so has to respire from mouth: *Lyco.*, *Ammon. carb.*, *Heper.*, *Sambucus.*

Nose: *Acon.*, *Bell.*, *Con.*, *Hep.* (acuteness of smell), *Anit. crud.* (bleeding of nose after headache) *Ant. crud.* (coldness of the nose when inspiring, sore cracked and crusty nostrils) *Arnica mont* (swelling of nose) *Ars. alb.* (profuse fluent coryza with discharge of burning, excoriating water) *Acon., Bell., Puls.* (bleeding of nose, when the menses should appear) *Bryo.* (dry coryza fluent during day) *Cina, Phos. acid.* (constantly picking and rubbing the nose) *Kali bich., Graphites, Nit. acid.* (great dryness of the nose) *Kali bich., Graph, Merc., Puls., Rhus* (Green fetid discharge from the nose) *Cal. c., Merc., Nit acid.* (caries of the bones of the nose, fetid smell from nose) *Ars., Lach, Merc.* (fluent coryza) *Nit acid., Nux., Sepia.* (dry coryza) *Lyco.* (fan like motion of the nostrils) *Puls.* (fetid yellow discharge from nose) *Graph., Kali bich., Merc.* (green fetid discharge) *Ars., Merc.* (violet fluent coryza) *Dulc., Nux vom., Sepia.* (dry coryza) *Nux vom., Merc.* (fluent coryza during the day and dry coryza at night) *Nux vom.* (first stage of ordinary catarrh with oppressive dullness in the head) *Phos.* (frequent bleeding from the nose, in the morning) *Bryo.* (frequent bleeding from nose at night, during stool or from bodily exertion) *Puls.* (cold in head with loss of taste and smell) *Bryo., Nit. acid., Nux vom., Phos.* (dry coryza with obstruction of nose) *Sepia* (discharge of yellow green plugs from the nose) *Kali bich., Sepia, Sulph., Silicea.* (loss of smell) *Euphrasia* (profuse fluent coryza), *Condorango Q* (vomiting of food, constant burning pain, behind sternum, stricture of oesophagus food seems to stick) *Cadmium Sulph.* (acidity, nausea, black vomit, burning and cutting pains, violent thirst, cold sweat) *Kreosotum* (sour and acrid vomiting, worse from warm food and better by cold food) *Nux vom.* (with spasm and in gouty person) *Lyco.* (with gavels) *Ac. benzoic, Nux., Allium cepa.*

O

Obesity: *Ars., Cal. carb., Ferr., Kali iod., Sulph.*

Oedema after bleeding or suppression of malaria: *Carbo veg., China, Ferrum met.*

Oedema, due to suppression of boils: *Apis., Hellaborus, Zinc. met.*

Oedema: *Apis.* (oedema due to kidney or heart ailments, scanty urine with albumen and casts, swelling below the lower lid of the eyes and feet, difficulty in respiration in sitting position, thirst lost) *Apocynum* (intense thirst, abdomen painful, physical weakness) *Arsenic* (edema due to liver, heart or kidney problems, urine thick, swelling on face and feet, intense thirst, vomiting after eating or drinking, respiration difficulty on lying) *Helleborus* (acute problem, scanty urine with albumen and casts, respiration difficulty better on lying) *Lycopodium* (from heart, liver or kidney problems, scanty urine, swelling on lower extremities, respiration difficulty on lying by back side) *Kali carb.* (swelling on upper eyelid of the eyes, worse lying on the left side and in the morning around 3 AM, better while moving around).

Oesophagus: *Millifolium* (coughing up of pure blood) *Phosphorus* (streaks of blood in mucus from the lungs; sputa rusty) *Silicea* (thick yellow, lumpy mucus). *Arsenic alb.* (oesophagus feels chocked blocked everything swolled seems to lodge in it, nothing seems to pass).

Offence breath: *Nux vom., Silicea* (breath is bad only in the morning) *Pulsatilla* (when it occurs only in the morning and at night) *Cham., Sulph.* (when it occurs after dinner only) *Carb. veg., Hep., Lach., Sulph.* (it arises from the abuse of mercury).

Ophthalmia (catarrhal) *Acon., Bell., Euph., Merc.*

Ophthalmia (neo natorum): *Arg. nit., Acon.* and *later Merc., Heper sulph.*

Ophthalmia (purulent): *Heper sulph., Acid nit., Arg. nit., Cal. carb., Iod., Clem., Sulph.*

Ophthalmia (tubercular) *Merc. cor., Bell., Ant. tar., Euphr.* (acute) *Cal. carb., Clem., Heper sulph., Ars., Sulph.* (chronic).

Ophthalmia syphilitic: *Merc., Acid nit., Aur.*

Opi (bloated, dusky red face, stupor and stetor), *Phos., Cocculus, Rhus, Lyc., Arnica.* (after effects).

Opthalmia of infants: *Belladona* (inflammation of the eye and red, cannot bear the light) *Calcarea carb.* (swelling and redness of the eye lids with nightly gluing) *Mercurius viv* (the eye lids are very much swollen and contain underneath them purulent matter, scrofulous opthalmia) *Sulphur* (the corners of the eyes appear raw with itching).

Os uteri: *Bell., Con., Gels., Acon.* (rigidity of the Os uteri).

Osteomyelitis: *Aconite* (high fever with cold sweats and face sensation as if cold waves pass through body, numbness, shooting pain in limbs, joints with red swelling and shining red streaks radiate) *Bryonia* (joints red swollen, stitching tearing pain, fever with full hard pulse, worse on motion, warmth, touch) *Natrum mur.* (fever with chill, violent thirst, arms and legs weak, pain in back) *Silicea* (frequent discharges from the abscesses between the skin and the bone, broken bone pieces in the pus, slow healing).

Otitis (inflammation of the ear): *Aconite* (great sensitiveness to noise) *Belladona* (throbbing tearing pain, face flashed, eyes red) *Mercurius vivus* (the pains are much worse at night, profuse sweating about the head) *Pulsatilla* (darting, tearing pains, discharge of pus from the ear, chilly and easily vexed persons).

Ovaries (inflammation of): *Acon., Bell., Merc iod., Puls., Ham., Coni. Plat* (with induration) *Merc sol.* (3 x) or *Bryonia* (1 x) (when pain extends towards hip or upwards) *Phos.*, (when pain extends downward along the inner side of the thigh), *Cimic., Puls.*

Ovaries (neuralgia of): *Zinc., Val., Hamm. Caulo., Colocy.*

Ovaritis (inflammation of ovary): *Aconite* (after exposure to dry cold winds) *Rhus tox.* (from wet weather) *Apis mel.* (ovaritis of right side) *Belladona* (stitching throbbing pain in the right ovary, cannot bear the least jar) *Bryonia* (stitching in the ovaries suppressed menses) *Cantharis* (constant desire to urinate, bearing down towards the genital) *Lachesis* (ovaritis of left side).

Ovary: *Apis mel.* (inflammation, indurations, swelling and dropsy of the right ovary with sharp cutting pain) *Graph.* (aches left ovary swelling with pressing and stitching pain) *Bell.* (ovaritis of right side with great tenderness) *Bell., Lach.* (left ovary swelling with pressing, stitching pain) *Podophyllum, Lach.* (numbness, aching pain in left ovary).

Ozaena: *Aur., Kali iod., Kali bich., Hydras., Ars., Merc iod., Sang., Acid nit., Zinc., Cad. sulph.*

P

Pain acute and unbearable: *Aconite* **(pain associated with fever)** *Chamomilla* **(pain with irritation better by movement)** *Coffea* **(severe sensation of unbearable pain)** *Ignitia* **(hysterical women, severe pain due to deep sorrow).**

Pain aggravates by bending downward: *Bella., Kalmia, Nux vom.*

Pain aggravation at 4 PM evevening: *Lyco.*

Pain aggravation at 6 AM morning: *Colch., Oxalic acid.*

Pain aggravation at menses: *Lachasis, Nat. mur., Sulphur.*

Pain associated with numbness: *Aconite* **(acute and severe pain which alternates with numbness)** *Rhus tox.* **(slow and low pain alternates with numbness)** *Chamomilla* **(acute pain which alternates with numbness)** *Platina* **(pain gradually increased and reaches to peak which alternates with numbness).**

Pain changeable: *Pulsatilla* **(intense pain associated with intense cold)** *Chamomilla* **(pain associated with perispiration)** *Heper.* **(pain associated with unconsciousness)** *Thuja* **(pain associated with urination)** *Veratrum alb* **(pain associated with agony)** *Magnum* **(crosswise pain in organs)** *Lac can.* **(roaming pain from one side to other side).**

Pain develops slowly and goes off suddenly: *Sulphuric acid.*

Pain develops slowly and reaches peak and then goes off slowly: *Stanum.*

Pain in eyes: *Apis mel.* **(piercing pain, burning and stinging grandular lids, trachoma)** *Arnica* **(after close work, tired after sight seeing, or movie, result of injury to the eye)** *Belladona* **(throbbing pain deep in lying down, pupil dilated sudden and protruding conjunctiva red, dry and burning, eyes staining lid swollen)** *Chels.idonium* **(pain right eye associated with right cheek and ear, excessive lachrymation preceded by pain in the liver, better by pressure)** *Cimicifuga* **(intense pain in the eye ball, shooting pain from eye to head, dislike for artificial light, better by warmth of worse during morning cold and menses)** *Cinnabaris* **(pain from lachrymal duct around eye to the temple, celery neuron, redness of the whole eyes, granulated lids)** *Gelsemium* **(orbital neuron with constriction and twitching of muscles)** *Heper sulph.* **(piercing pain in upper bones of the orbit, purulent conjunctivitis)** *Kali bich.* **(supra orbital neuron, pain deep in the orbits, infected sinus)** *Lycopus virg.* **(supra orbital pain with aching in testicles)** *Merc. cor.* **(severe aching pain beyond the eye balls, the eyes being forced out)** *Nat. mur.* **(pain in eyes when looking down)** *Plantago* **(reflex neutron of the eyes on account of toothache or inflammation of the middle ear, eye ball tender to touch)** *Ruta* **(eye strain due to fine work followed by headache particularly in students, teachers, doctors etc.)** *Spigelia* **(pain on**

turning the eyes, feeler of being too large for the sockets, severe pain which extends deep into the socket) *Allium cepa* (sensitive to light, eyes burnt smart) *Arsenic alb* (extensive burning sensation, swelling) *Aurum met.* (extreme photophobia, uper half of object invisible) *Belladona* (intense photophobia and pain) *Cimicifuga* (dislike of artificial light).

Pain in nipple: *Croton* (Pain from nipple goes through the back to scapula) *Phytolacca* (pain goes from nipple to uterus) *Silicea* (with pain there will be vaginal bleeding or when child takes the breast).

Pain in the small spot on the right knee and its back side: *Chel., Kali carb., Merc.*

Pain in throat canot swallow solid or even liquid: *Medorhinum, Merc.*

Pain increases every time with movement: *Lac. can., Merc., Phyto.*

Pain intensive, drives the patient for constant walking: Chamomilla, Rhus tox., Ferrum *met., Veratrum alb.*

Pain reduces by walking (movement): *Rhus tox., Cobalt, Znic. met., Puls., Ferrum met., Sambucus; Mag. Phos.*

Pain remains from night till morning: *Merc., Phyto., Syphlinum.*

Pain roaming, goes one part to another part of the body: *Mangnum acetic, Lac can., Kali bich., Kalmia.*

Pain which does not allow to lie down so compel to go for movement: *Rhus tox., Chamomilla.* (as per symptoms)

Painful side becomes more painful from touch but by pressing the side pain goes off: *Bella.*

Pains after delivery: *Arnica* (sore feeling all through the patient as if a bruise) *Chamamilla* (the pains are very distressing, impatient and furious).

Pains: *Kali bich.* (pains appear and disappear suddenly, pain does not stay long in a place) *Puls.* (pain stay long at a place) *Manganum* (pains shift crosswise from joint to joint) *Lac can.* (pain alternates sides i.e. worse on one side one day, worse on other side next day) *Bell., Kali sulph.* (have wandering pains).

Palpitation of heart: *Aconite* (the beating of heart is very violent and attended with great agitation, thinks he will die). *Arsenic* (violent palpitation of the heart, fear of death, rapid prostration, *Belladona* (palpitation with intermitting pulse, great anguish about the heart throbbing headache) *Phosphorus* (tightness across the chest, palpitation worse after eating) *Veratrum alb* (anxious palpitation cold sweat on the forehead, exhausting diarrhoea.).

Pancreas: *Calcarea ars.* (burning pain).

Pancreases (acute): *Belladona* (bleeding pancreases, rise in temperature) *Iris versicolor* (burning, distress in the region of pancreas, diarrhoea containing undigested food).

Pancreatitis: *Iod., Merc., Iris., Kali iod., Merc., Rhus., Acid nit., Nux vom.*

Paralysis (due to third nerve): *Causticum* (resulting from exposure to cold) *Gelsemium* (from diphtheria or muscles of throat) *Rhus tox.* (resulting from rheumatism or exposure to cold or getting the feet wet) *Aconite* (exposure to a draught of cold air) *Kali iod.* (paralysis of the muscles of syphilitic organ) *Euphrasia* (catarrhal symptoms, blurring of eyes, relieved by winking) *Senega* (diplopia is relieved by bending the head backward) *Arnica* (due to injury) *Chelsidonium* (distant object blurred looking steadily two are seen, pain in the eyes on looking up) *Nux vom.* (worse by the use of stimulant or tobacco) *Paris quad.* (pain drawing from eye to head or pain as if the eyes were pulled into the head) *Phosphorus* (due to sexual abuse) *Spigellia* (sharp stabbing through the eye and head, strabimus or squintness: inability to bring the visual axis of both eyes to meet at a certain point) *Cicuta vir.* (caused from convulsion to which child is subject) *Jaborandi* (resulting from spasm of internal recta or squintness after operation) Strabismus *due to helminthiasis Cina, Cyclamen or spigellia.* Strabismus *due to spasm, convulsion or any intra-cranial disorder, Agar., Bell., Gels., Hyos., Stram* (Oscillation of the eye ball) *Agaricus* (associated with spasm of the lids on chorea, twitching of lids or eye balls, spasmodic movements are absent during sleep but return on waking) *Belladona* (if accompanied by headache and hyper aesthesia of the senses) *Hyoscyamus* (spasmodic action of eye balls) *Ignatia* (incitation and spasmodic affections in nervous hysterical women - Asthenopia: various tired and strained sensation in eyes) *Ruta graveolens* (aching in and over the eyes, eyes feel hot like ball of fire, run water in the evening after working all day) *Onosmodium* (heaviness and dullness of the eyes, pain in the left side of the head, prostration and tired feeling over entire body) *Gelsemium* (soreness of eyeballs, diplopia) *Senega* (dullness of the head with pressure and weakness of the eyes; aggravation upon using the eyes) *Natrum mur.* (the muscles feel stiff and drawn and ache on moving the eye in any direction, pain in the eye upon looking down) *Sepia* (aggravation of symptoms morning and evening) *Argentum nit.* (letters blur and sight vanishes on reading or writing) *Cinnabar* (pain in the inner acanthus extending above or around the eye) *Aconite* (eyes feel very hot and drying after use, relieve by cold water application temporarily) *Agaricus* (sudden jerks of the ball, twitching of the lids) *Calcarea* (pain burning and cutting worse in damp weather and warmth, dim vision after fine work) *Conium* (great dread of light) *Kalmia* (stiff and drawing sensation on moving the eyes) *Lachesis* (especially in left eye; worse upon thinking and walking in the morning) *Lilium tig.* (burning, smarting and heat in eyes after reading, relieved in open air, photophobia) *Mercurius perennis* (dryness of eyes and heaviness in lids, mist before the eyes in the morning, burning pain in the eyes in the evening) *Phosphorus* (moistness and vanishing of vision with pain and stiffness in eye ball better in twilight) *Rhododendron* (always worst before the storm) *Spigellia* (sharp stabbing pain through the eyes extending to the head).

Paralysis (from cold): *Rhus tox.* (worse in damp weather, restlessness in the night) *Phos.* (aphonia and nervous prostration hoarseness worse in the evening) *Caust.* (aphonia and nervous prostration hoarseness worse in the morning, cough better by drinking cold water), *Aco., Dul., Acid phos.*

Paralysis agitans (shaking palsy), *Merc., Rhus., Acid nit., Nux vom.*

Paralysis diphtheritic: *Gels., Caust., Ign., Coni., Electricity.*

Paralysis facial: *Caust., Acon., Ign.*

Paralysis general: *Phos., Coni., Gels., Coca., Baryta carb., Ant. crud., Ars. alb., Teucrium.*

Paralysis glasso laryngeal: *Bell., Hyos., Caust.*

Paralysis hysterical: *Ign.*

Paralysis infantile: *Gels., Bell., Sec., Plumb.*

Paralysis of extremeties: *Arsenic album* (paralysis of lower limbs with atrophy) *Aurum sulph.* (paralysis agitans, constant nodding of head) *Cannabis indica* (paralysis of lower extremities) *Carbo sulph.* (paralysis of knees, congestion of nerve centres) *Causticum* (gradually appearing paralysis) *Conium* (of lower extremities spreading upwards, severe pain in coxae) *Crotalus* (right sided paralysis) *Lachesis* (paralysis of right side of the body) *Mag. phos.* (paralysis agitans, ceaseless involuntary, jerking of hands, of limbs, of knees, finger tips stiff and numb) *Phosphorus* (ascending paralysis from the ends of fingers or of toes, great difficulty in holding any thing, numbness of arms and hands) *Rhus tox.* (caused by exposure the body to cold) *Strychinia phos.* (paralysis weak spine, spinal cord anaemia, worse motion).

Paralysis of lower extremities: *Phos., Strych., Kali bich., Coni., Arg. nit., Rhus, Caulo., Kali iod., Coca., Ver. vir., Electricity.*

Paralysis of one side: *Barryta carb., Nux vom., Coca, Arn.*

Paralysis painters: *Opi., Iod., Cup. ars., Nux vom., Alumen.*

Paralysis rheumatic: *Acon., Rhus., Arn., Strych., Sulph.*

Paralysis wasting: *Bell., Phos., Plumb.*

Paralysis: *Belladona* (congestion of blood to the head paralysis of the one and spasm of the other side of the body) *Causticum* (paralysis of the face and tongue with giddiness, weakness of the sight) *Cocculus* (paralysis of the face and tongue, weak and nervous subject, swelling of the feet) *Gelsemium* (paralysis of throat following diphtheria or paralysis of the eyelids).

Pemphigus: *Rhus tox., Phos., Ran. bulb.* (infants) *Ars., Merc. cor.*

Penis becomes tight before coition but as soon as inserted in vagina it becomes loose: *Caladium, Conium, Graph., Lyco.*

Pericarditis: *Bryonia* (constrictive pericarditis with tenderness in abdomen and swelling of ankles, shooting pain in chest, strong pulse, better when still, worse with least motion) *Colchicum* (pericarditis in acute rheumatic cases, violent cutting and stinging pain in the chest, difficulty in breathing, tightness in chest, palpitation, vertigo, at times loss of consciousness on sitting upright, pulse imperceptible) *Digitalis* (weakness and dilation of the muscle of the heart, sudden inflmmation of heart muscle, pulse weak slow and irregular, quickened by least motion, sensation as if heart will stop beating if moved, hard breathing worse on lying) *Kalmia lat.* (pain in heart region so sharp as to take away the breath, shooting pain through chest above heart and into shoulder blades, tumultuous action of heart, fast pulse worse bent over, lying left side) *Spigelia* (pericarditis with heart attack, sharp shooting pain through heart to back or radiating from the heart down the arm and spine, worse by sitting down or leaning forward).

Periostitis: *Apis.* (inflammation, pain caused by anything) *Arnica* (when inflammation is caused by an injury) *Kali bich.* (pain stiffness, swelling and cracking of anyparts, pain shifts from place to place) *Merc. sol.* (dropsical swelling of feet and leg, limbs weak, cold sweats on legs at night).

Peritonitis simple: *Acon., Merc. cor., Bella., Bryo., Canth., Merc. dulsis., Colocyn., Colch.*

Perspiration (excessive): *Merc.* (foul smell perspiration, aggravation increases with perspiration) *Tilia* (aggravation with increase of perspiration) *Sambucus* (perspiration starts after sleep) *Kali bich.* (perspires when sitting calmly) *Causticum* (perspires in open place and less in closed room) *Conium* (perspires immediately after closing the eyes but soon stops after sleep) *Hyoscymus, Graphites, Veratrum.* (excessive perspiration during menses).

Perspiration all the time, in the night as soon as closes the eyes: *China, Conium.*

Pharynx: *Phos., Lach., Nat. mur.* (dryness in pharynx and fauces day and night hawking up mucus in the morning) *Sepia, Apis mel., Bell.* (stringing sore throat) *Staph.* (dry and rough with soreness when talking or swallowing) *Verat.* (coldness in throat).

Phimosis circumcision: *Merc. sol., 1x* (wrap the organ in a compress soaked with Hamm. Solution).

Phimosis: *Aconite* (acute inflammatory phimosis) *Apis.* (acute phimosis, great swelling) *Nitric acid* (phimosis with swelling, soreness and burning in glands and beneath prepuce).

Phlegmasia alba dolens (white leg milk leg): *Puls.* (simple case) *Hamm.* (varicose condition) *Phos., Ars., Lach.*

Photophobia (intolerance of light): *Ant. tar., Bell., Kali brom., Euphr., Merc. cor., Nux vom., Coni., Ars., Sulph.*

Phthisis (Tuberclusis): *Aconite* (febrite excitement, stiches in the chest and thirst) *Calcarea carb.* (very sensitive to dold air, great liability to take cold, serofulous habit) *China* (suitable to persons who have had frequent attack of pneumonia, debilated by Haemorrhages) *Ferrum met.* (Haemorrhages from the lungs, with pain between the shoulders, painless diarrhoea) *Lycopodium* (circumscribed redness of the cheeks, red sandy sediments in the urine) *Phosphorus* (hoarseness with loss of voice, constipation, stools long narrow and difficult to expel) *Pulsatilla* (dry cough during night goes off when sets up in women associated with suppression of the menses) *Sulphur* (dry cough also loose cough, expectoration of greenish lump having sweetish taste, cough worse in the morning, dry unhealthy stem).

Phthisis haemoptysis: *Ham., Ipecac., Drosera, Ferrum Sulph., Ferrum acetate, Arn.*

Phthisis indigestion: *Cal. carb., Lyco., Hydras., Merc., Kali bich., Puls., Nux vom.*

Phthisis pulmonalis (for the cachexia): *Sulph., Hydras., Cal. carb., Iod., Ars., Ars. iod., Chelsi, Thuja, Phos., Ferr., Cal.c. iod., Sangunaria, Aur. iod., Crotalus h., Elaps.*

Physical. and mental tiredness due to sleeplessness: *Cuprum, Coccolus, Nux.*

Piles: *Nux vomica* (intense itching at anus ineffectual desire for stool, bleeding piles) *Aesculus* (heaviness in the abdomen, dryness at anus, feeling of sticks inside with piercing pain) *Aloes* (grape like bunches of piles, feels better by washing with cold water, stool passes with flatus) *Hammelis* (excessive black blood comes out with pain) *Collinsonia* (pin pricking pain at anus with constipation) *Sulphur* (bleding piles with burning, hot and itching) *Peonia* (piles of bluish colour, unbearable to walks with open legs touching) *Pulsatilla* (pain continuous, protuding piles with piercing pain, aggravation on lying) *Ammon. carb.* (painful piles better by lying) *Arsenic alb.* (unbearable painful piles with pin piercing pain).

Pimples: *Sulph., Cal. carb., Bella., Heper sulph., Kali bich., Ant. crud., Carbo veg., Kali brom.*

Pityriasis: *Ars.*, *Graph.*, *Lyco.*, *Terebenth.*, *Canth.*

Placenta (retained): *Sabi.*, *Puls.*, *Sec.*

Plethora: Ferr., *Ars.*, *Cal. carb.* (all in high potencies) *Aco.*, *Bella.*

Pleurisy of children: *Aconite* (with fever, dry cough and restlessness) *Bryonia* (difficulty in breathing, worse on movement) *Sulphur* (with convulsion) Veratrum virdis (difficulty in breathing, stitching pain).

Pleurisy/Pneumonia: *Acon.*, *Bryo.*, *Phos.* (pleurisy and pneumonia with great heat, muscle thrust, dry cough and nervous excitement) *Merc. vivus* (pneumonia stitches in the right chest), *Bell.*, *Phos.* (pneumonia left side with sharp stitches in the chest, rust colored sputa, respiration oppressed quick anxious) *Ant. tar.* (pneumonia with impending paralysis of lungs, cough with suffocating attacks, rattling hollow cough worse at night).

Pleurisy: *Aco.*, *Bryo.*, *Canth.*, *Ver. vir.* (acute cases), *Kali iod.*, *Sulph.* (chronic cases) *Bryonia* (stitching pain in the effectd part, head aches as if it would split, nausea and faintness hard stool) *Phosphours* (difficult respiration, tightness across the chest, dry shaking cough) *Rhus tox.* (if disease arises from metastasis of rheumatism, or exposure to wet, pain worse during rest- Pleurodynia: false pleurisy stitches in the side) *Arnica* (pain mostly on left side especially during inspiration, difficulty of breathing) *Bryonia* (pain as if a sharp instrument had penetrated the side) *Nux vom.* (stitching pain in the muscles between the ribs, pain increases by the sensitibility of the external parts) *Pulsatilla* (stitching pain in the side only when lying, pains shift rapidly aggravation towards evening) *Sulphur* (stitch like pain extending to the back, worse when lying down or raising the arms).

Plica polonica: *Vinca minor.*

Pneumonia after constant cough: *Lyco.*

Pneumonia of children: *Aconite* (high temperature, shivering) *Antim tar* (difficulty in taking out phlegm, chest full of phlegm) *Bryonia* (stitching pain in chest, respiration painful) *Phos.phorus* (breathing difficult, pain under the breast bone, rust coloured sputa) *Sulphur* (a complementary medicine).

Pneumonia of right lung associated with liver problem: *Chelsi.*, *Merc.*

Pneumonia: *Aconite* (first stage, piercing and stitching pain in chest, great fear and anxiety of mind) *Arsenicum* (rapid prostration of strength, great fear of death) *Belladona* (flushed face, dyspnoea with pain in lower and middle portion of the chest) *Bryonia* (expectoration of tenacious mucus of a reddish or rusty colour, shooting or stitching pains in the side of chest, lungs feel as if tney would not expand) *Phosphorus* (dry cough and rust coloured sputa, long narrowed hard stool) *Phos.* (simple typhoid like and in children) *Acon.*, *Bryo.*, *Ver. vir.* (early congestive stage) *Ver. vir.*, *Lyco.* (Pleuro-pneumonia); *Ant tar* (broncho-pneumonia), *Sulph.* (tubercular patients) *Chel.* (right sided lower lobe) *Ferr.*, *Phos.*

Poliomyelitis in children: *Aconite* (due to exposure to dry cold) *Belladona* (paralysis with convulsion, flushed face, intolerance to light) *Gels.emum* (fever, cold, convulsion, body pain) *Rhus tox.* (poliomyelitis after fever) *Nux vom.* (lower limbs affected, indigestion, constipation).

Polyps of colon or rectum: *Merc. cor.*(blood and shreds of mucus membrane in stool) *Millefoleum* (bleeding in stool, hemorrhoids, urine bloody simultaneously) *Phosphorus* (with pus and inflammation) *Teucrium* (itching at anus, nightly restlessness).

Polyps (násal): *Cal. carb., Foromica rufa., Teuc., Merc. iod., Kali bich., Thuja, Phos., Sang.*

Porrigo (Capitis): *Cal. Carb., Sulph., Viola., Sil.*

Porrigo (favus): *Sepia., Rhus., Merc cor., Ars. iod.*

Pregnancy (appetite lost) *Cal. carb., China, Nat. mur., Carb veg., Sil.*

Pregnancy (disorder of): *Cham.* (nervous, restlessness, irritability, fidgets): *Acon.* (circulatory disturbance, palpitation) *Coff.* (sleeplessness), *Gels.*

Pregnancy (during cough and difficult breathing) *Bell., Coni, Hyos., Nux vom.*

Pregnancy (during depression of spirits): *Cimi., Ign., Puls., Plat.*

Pregnancy (during diarrhoea): *Puls., Acid phos., Phos.*

Pregnancy (during morning, sickness, nausea etc.) *Nux vom., Ipecae, Sepia, Kali brom., Kreos., Puls., Cocc., Apomorph.*

Pregnancy (false pains): *Cham., Puls., Sec., Caul., Cimi.*

Pregnancy (headache) *Bell., Bryo., Nux vom., Ver. vir., Puls. Cocc.*

Pregnancy (heart burn): *Caps., Puls., Iris, Cal. carb., Nux vom., Robina, Sangu.*

Pregnancy (salivatiòn): *Iod., Merc., Heper sulph., Nat. mur.*

Pregnancy (toothache and neuralgia) *Merc., Bell., Coloc., Cham. Coff.* (during the attack), *Sepia, Cimic., Nux mosh., Nux vom., Canth., Cocc., Puls., Causticum.*

Pregnancy during (constipation) *Nux vom., Sulph., Plumb., Opi., Alum., Collin., Aloe., Sepia, Bryo.*

Pregnancy during (convulsion): *Bell., Ignatia., Ver. vir., Cic., Coff.*

Prickly heat of children: *Chamomilla* (kept too warm, fretful and must be carried all the time) *Dulcamara* (eruption, appears every time the baby is exposed to damp, cold air) *Rhus tox.* (when the vesicles incline to be watery, rubbing the affected parts increases the eruption).

Prolapsus of anus: *Ignitea* (difficult stool causes prolapsus anus, blind piles) *Mercurius* (prolapsus during diarrhea or dysentery where there is much straining) *Nux vom.* (habitual constipation, stools large hard and difficult, persons of intemperate habits, painful hemorrhoid tumors) *Podophyllum* (during and after stool prolapsus anus).

Prolapsus uteri: *Belladona* (sensation of heat and dryness in the vagina, backache) *Calcarea carb.* (the menses are too frequent and profuse vertigo on going up) *Lachesis* (cannot bear the least pressure upon the uterine region, painful swelling in the right groin or ovarian region) *Nux vom.* (prolapsus after straining, constant desire to go to stool) *Sepia* (sensation as if everything will come out of the vagina, the urine deposits clay like sediments, sallow condition of skin) *Sulphur* (frequent weak faint spells, constant heat on top of the head, suits to lean women who walks stooping).

Prostate glands: *Arsenic alb* (restlessness on account of pain) *Conium* (cancer of male genital) *Crotalus h.* (cancer with haematuria).

Prostatitis (inflammation of prostrate): *Puls., Iod.* (acute) *Kali iod.* (chronic), *Thuja, Staph., Acid nit., Sabal serrulata, Bell.*

Prostrate (enlargement): *Sabal serrulata (Q), Solidigo ver., Arg. nit., Ferrum pic., Thuja, Phyto.*

Pruritus (itching of private parts): *Bryonia* (when dryness and heat in the parts) *Carbo veg.* (parts are covered with a whitish curd like substance) *Mercurius* (small red pimples on the labia, itching furiously) *Sepia* (soreness and redness of the parts, violent itching of the pudendum) *Sulphur* (intense itching of the private parts, which are covered with pimples, burning in vagina).

Pruritus (vulvae): *Chlor. hyd., Collin., Sepia., Acid nit., Ambra., Copavia., Bor.* (internal and external), *Cal. carb., Sil., Phos., Ver. vir., Caust., Sulph., Cal. phos.*

Psoriasis (palmasis): *Heper Sulph., Ars., Caust., Graph., Selen.*

Psoriasis: *Merc iod., Acid nit., Phyto., Sulph., Ars., Petrol., Ant. tar., Secale. cor.* (as per symptoms)

Pterygium: *Rhus. tox., Zincum* (pricking pains, itching, soreness in the inner angle, worse at night, pressure across the root of the nose) *Calcarea carb.* (caused from exposure to cold and wet).

Ptosis (drooping of upper lid) *Causticm* (drooping of the lid, resulting exposure to cold, eye is closed involuntarily) *Rhus tox* (related to rheumatic diathesis, working in the wet, getting the feet wet or change in weather) *Alumina* (dryness and burning, absence of lachrymation) *Ledum* (resulting from an injury) *Spigellia* (sharp, stabbing pains through the eye).

Ptosis (paralysis of the eyelids): *Gels., Bell., Caust., Stram., Spig., Ver alb., Sepia.*

Puberty on set at, without pregnancy the milk comes out from the breast: *Puls., Merc., Cyclamen.*

Puerperal convulsion: *Ver. vir., Bella., Chlor hyd., Cupr.*

Puerperal fever: *Acon., Bell., Bapt., Hyos., Stram., Merc., Bryo., Ars.*

Purpura (haemorrhagea): *Ham., Merc., Ars., Phos., Acid sujlph., Tereb., Acid Phos., Lach.*

Pus (with urinary problem): *Asparagus* (pus with cystitis, mucus and tenesmus, burning and pain in urethra) *Berberis vulgaris* (thick mucus with bright red sediments, kidney sore, frequent urination) *Cannabis sativa* (pus and mucus in urethra constriction) *Chimaphilla* (urine scanty with loaded with ropy mucus, purulent sediments, blood mix with mucus) *Hydrangea Q* (heavy deposit of mucus, frequent desire of urination, burning pain in urethra).

Pus formation quick in the slightest injury: *Borax, Calendula, Heper Sulph., Graphites, Lach., Merc., Petrolium, Silicea.*

Pyelitis: *Phyto., Uva., Ferr..*

Pyorrhea: *Calendula* (chronic pyorrhea) *Carbo veg.* (easily bleeding and retracted gums) *Kali carb.* (gums separating from teeth, oozing of pus, worse from hot drinks) *Merç. sol.* (ulceration of mouth and gums, foul smell, pus pockets, spongy and receding of gums, severe itching in gums and roots of the teeth) *Silicea* (boils and gums, abscess in the root of teeth, sensitive to cold wind and water) *Staphysagaria* (spongy gums bleed easily, teeth black and crumbling).

Pyrosis (water brush, Heart burn): *Carbo veg.* (water brash especially at night, sour eructation) *China* (gratefulness after each meal) *Nux vom.* (vomiting after every meal, constipation) *Puls.* (eructation tasting and smelling what he has been eating, mild tearful disposition) *Sepia* (water brush after eating or drinking burning in the stomach) *Phosphorus* (heart burn, very sleepy after dinner) *Carbo veg., Lyco., Acid Sulph., Nux vom., Ars., Bryo. Puls., Acid sulph.* (be given in 20-30 drops in water).

Q

Quinine misuse: *Ipecac.*, *Ars.*, *Nat. mur.*, *Puls.*, *Ferrum*, *Carbo veg.*

Quinsy: *Baryat carb.*, *Hep sulph.*, *Arum triphy.*, *Phyto.*, *Phos.*, *Bell.*, *Merc iod.*, *Ars.*, *Lac.*, *Acon.*, *Baryta carb.* is almost specific.

Quinsy (tonsilites) *Belladona* (swollen, inflamed and of a dark red colour on the right side) Heper sulph. sensation of a lump in the throat) *Lachesis* (tonsilites especially of left side) *Silicea* (indication of forming of abscess).

R

Rachitis: *Acid Phos., Sil., Sulph., Cal., Phos., Asaf., Cal. phos.*

Ranula (a cyst under the tongue of variable size containing albuminous fluid) *Bella., Merc. sol.* **(acute case),** *Cal. carb.* **(chronic)** *Thuja.*

Rectum: *Carduus maranus Q* **(profuse Diarrhoea)** *Ruta* **(stitching pain of rectum, prolapse of anus, every time the bowels move)** *Spigelia* **(unbearable pain),** *Ruta g.* **(tearing and stitching in rectum, difficult faeces, unsuccessful urging to stool).**

Red gums: *Cham., Puls., Cal. carb., Ant. crud.*

Red sand particles in urine: *Lyco., Sarsaparilla, Sanicula, Borax.*

Redness of eyes: *Aconite* **(lids red and swollen due to exposure to dry cold air)** *Agaricus.* **(inner angles and acanthi red)** *Antim. crud.* **(acanthi red, raw and fissured)** *Argent. nit.* **(inner acanthi swollen and red, copious flow of water)** *Arsenic alb.* **(eye lids red, dry, burning, eye lids swolen, eyes protruding)** *Belladona* **(conjunctiva red, dry, burning, eye lids swollen, eyes protruding)** *Dubosia* **(red spots afloat in the field of the vision with conjunctivitis)** *Graphites* **(eye lids red and swollen with or without eczema of the eye lids)** *Merc. cor.* **(lids swollen, red, excoriating, severe burning and soreness of the eyes).**

Relapsing fever: *Bry.* **(associated with constipation),** *Bapt.* **(excretion offensive body pain),** *Gels., Eup. perf., Podophyllum* **(associated with diarrhea).**

Remedies provide coldness: *Ars., Phos., Lyco., Nat. mur, Puls., Sulphur.*

Remedy indicated when stops to act: *Opium* **(when there seems to be no vital reaction, when lack of reaction due to psoric taint)** *Psorinum* **(when psoric obstructions to vital reactions and sulphur fails).**

Remittent fever: *Gels., Camp.* **(incasive stage),** *Acon., Bell.* **(hot stage),** *China* **(during exacerbation)** *Ipecac., Bryo.* **(gastric disturbance)** *Bapt., Ars.* **(typhoid symptoms, Hyos., Bell. (brain symptoms)** *Merc. vivus.* **(during remission)** *China, Sulph.*

Renal colic: *Cantharis* **(violent pains and burning in the bladder, frequent micturation with scanty emission of dark or bloody urine)** *Lachesis* **(sensation as of a ball in the bladder)** *Nux vom.* **(burning and lacerating pain in the neck of the bladder and urethra)** *Phosphorus* **(urine white like curdled milk, soon becomes turbid with brick dust sediment, constipation stools long, narrow, hard and very difficult to expel)** *Pulsatilla* **(scanty red, brown urine with reddish or mucus sediments)** *Sulphur* **(urine fetid, burning in urethra during micturation)** *Nux vom.* **(pains extend into genital organs and down the leg, usually the right kidney is affected)** *Bella.* **(shooting pain which comes suddenly)** *Berberis vul.* **(pains are of shooting character but patient can not make the slightest motion)** *Lyco.* **(pains extend along the**

urethra and end in the bladder, do not descend down the leg, backache relieved by urination) *Cal. carb.* (perisphere during attack of pain and obese).

Repetition of same thought in mind: *Cal. carb., Coffea, Graphites.*

Respiration difficulties ameliorate on lying down: *Eupharasia, Manganum.*

Restless due to it cannot sit at one place: *Ars. alb., Rhus tox.*

Restless during typhoid: *Rhus tox., Tarax., Zincum.*

Restlessness of infants: *Belladona* (sleepy but cannot sleep) *Chamomilla* (the child is very cross, wants to be carried all the time) *Coffea* (child woeful frets and worries in a pitiful manner).

Retention of urine after delivery: *Belladona* (back feels as if it would break)

Retinitis albumin rica: *Mercurius cor.* (pregnancy the exciting cause) *Apis* (drowsiness with little thirst and scanty urine) *Gelsemium* (dimness of the vision appears suddenly, haziness in sight) *Kalmia* (nephritic retinitis).

Retinitis haemorrhages: *Lachesis* (retina swollen, extraversion of blood) *Crotalus* (Haemorrhages accompanied by inflammation) *Belladona* (congestive headaches, suppressed menses, retina and optic nerve inflamed and congested).

Retinitis syphilitica: *Mercurius* (nocturnal aggravation of the symptoms).

Retinitis: *Belladona* (the retinal vessels enlarged and tortuous, optic disc swollen, pains aching and throbbing, congestive headaches, sensitive light, worse in the afternoon.

Rheumatic fever in children: *Aconite* (on the onset of fever) *Bryonia* (heat and swelling of joints) *Rhus tox.* (pain in muscles, tendon and ligaments) *Formic acid* (acute fever, pain) *Cimicifuga* (chorea with muscular rheumatism) *Calcarea Phos.* (chronic enlargement of tonsils), *Cactus* (rheumatism related to heart) *Eupatorium perf.* (aching in bones and prostration) *Variolinum* (with throat pain).

Rheumatic fever, associated with pain in joints and muscles: *Bryo., Salicysic acid.*

Rheumatism (acute) (with rheumatic fever): *Acon., Bryo., Rhus., Bell., Ferr., Phos., Cimici.* (mild cases) *Colch.* (when the smaller joints are affected) *Aconite* (high fever with great agitation of the heart, affected parts sensitive to contact and motion, fear and anxiety of mind) *Bryonia* (redness of the inflamed part, stitching pains, hard dry stool, highly irritable) *Colchicum* (chilly feeling, profuse sour smelling sweats, urine dark and scanty) *Lycopodium* (urine dark and turbid or with sediment of red sand, constant sensation of satiety) *Pulsatilla* (pains shift rapidly, chilly feeling, craves for fresh air, mild nature, bad taste in the mouth in the morning) *Rhus tox.* (pains worse during rest and when first commencing to move, better from continual motion).

Rheumatism (chronic): *Calcarea carb.* (parts swollen and worse every change of weather, cold damp feet) *Causticum* (stiffness with tearing pains, great weakness and lameness of the lower limbs, worse towards evening) *Dulcamara* (worse after every cold change in the weather) *Pytolacca* (dull, heavy aching pain, generally in damp weather, dark red urine) *Rhus tox.* (worse during rest and when first commencing to move) *Sabina* (cannot bear the heated room, feels decidedly better in the cold air and room) *Rhus., Bryo., Ars., Lyco., Sulph., Phos., Cimici., Caust, Merc., Acid nit., Phyto., Iod., Kali bich.*

Rheumatism (gonnorrheal): *Merc bin. iod.*, *Acon.*, *Mer. sol.*, *Thuja*, *Nat. sulph.*, *Dul.*, *Medorr.*

Rheumatism (of joints) *Bryo.*, *Rhus.*, *Ruta.*, *Rhod.*, *Lyco.*, *Colch.*, *Led.*, *Caust.*, *Kali iod.*, *Sangu.* (of right shoulder) *Puls.* (wandering pain) *Sulph.*, *Arn.*, *Phos.*

Rheumatism (osteo arthirits): *Sabi.* (in females with irritation of the uterus, bladder and bowls) *Puls.*, *Acon.*, *Caul.*, *Colche.*, *Macrot.*, *Sepia.*

Rheumatism is caused from slightest cold drift, while not in warmth condition: *Acon.*, *Bryo.*, *Nux mosch.*

Rheumatism of chest: (intercostal muscles): *Bryo.*, *Arn.*, *Rhod.*, *Rhus.*, *Rad. brom.*, *Cimici.*

Rheumatism of shoulder: *Rhus tox.*, *Syphi.*

Rheumatism of the heart: *Aconite* (high fever with great agitation of the heart, great fear and anxiety of mind) *Arsenicum* (palpitation of heart particularly at night and on lying on the back, extreme restlessness and fear of death) *Belladona* (bloated red face with throbbing headache) *Lachesis* (cannot bear nothing to touch the neck, worse after sleep) *Spig.*, *Dig.*, *Acon.*, *Ver. vir.*, *Cimici.*

Rheumatism: *Bryo.* (joints red swelling stiff with stitching pain from slightest motion) *Rhus tox.* (complaint better by movement), *Colch.* (pains are shifting and are stitching like electric shocks, heart complaints are present) *Caulo.* (rheumatism of phalangeal and meta carpet joints) *Bryonia* (mostly muscles are affected, piercing pain located at one point, serum membrane dryness, mostly larger jopints are affected and inflamed) *Rhus tox.* (tissues are affected, local inflammation aggravation from drenching in water during perispiraton) *Colchicum* (pain changes place, piercing pain like *Bryonia* at one place) *Ledum pal* (pain in small joints especially the thumb of leg is affected first, the ailment goes from lower to upper parts) *Caulophyllum* (small joints are affected first and pain changes place quickly).

Rickets in children: *Calcarea carb.* (head and joints enlarged, voracious appetite) Cacarea *phos.* (with diarrhoea and weakness) *Theridion* (pain in bone with feeling as if broken).

Ring worm: *Sepia* (eruptions burn and moist, suitable to females having delicate skin) *Staphysagaria* (eruption is dry and crusty itches violently in the evening, burns after scratched), *Bacillinum* (worse night and early morning).

Rings around the eyes: *Abrotanum* (blue ring around eyes) *Acetic acid* (dark ring around eyes, sunken eyes) *China* (blue rings around eyes in anemic person, face pale and sallow) *Phos.phoric acid* (blue ring around the eyes liking for cold drinks, feeling of sand in the eyes) *Aconite* (acute feeling of sand in the eyes) *Apis mel.* (eyes as swollen, watering with granular lids).

Ringworm (of the scalp): *Sepia*, *Cal. carb.*, *Sulph.*, *Acid sulph.*, *Bacillinum* (200).

Ringworm (verscular): *Iris.*, *Tellu.*, *Rhus.*, *Sulph.*, *Bacillinum.*

Roscola (rose rash) *Acon.*, *Rhus.*, *Bella.*

Rub the head on pillow constantly: *Apis.*, *Bella.*, *Helloborus*, *Podo.*

Rubella (German measles) in children: *Aconite* (fever, flushed face and restlessness) *Belladona* (glands are enlarged with sore throat) *Ferrum phos.* (fever, rosy spots on cheeks, chill, frequent sweating) *Pulsatilla* (weeps, wants company and sympathy, green mucus, better in the open air).

Running of the ear (Otorrhoea): *Calcarea carb.* (suited to scrofulous women and children) *Heper sulph.* (discharge of fetid pus from the ear, whizzing and throbbing in the ears.) *Mercurius v.* (offensive discharge of syphilitic origin, vesicular eruptions) *Pulsatilla* (eArs. feel as if stopped otorrhoea following measles) *Silicea* (stoppage of the ear which sometimes open with loud report, scrofulous individuals).

Rupia (atonic foul ulcer): *Merc.* (simple) *Acid nit.*, *Kali iod.*, *Iod.* (from mercury) *Aur.* (syphilitic).

S

Salivation: *Merc.*, *Kali chlor.* (idiopathic) *Acid nit.*, *Iod.*, *Heper sulph.* (mercurial.)

Sarcitis and degeneration: *Baryta mur.*, *Plumb.*, *Aurum mur.*

Scabies (the itch): *Sulph.*, *Rumex*, *Acid acetate*, *Psorin.*

Scald head: *Viola tri.*, *Heper sulph.*, *Ars.*, *Staph.*, *Cal. carb.*, *Rhus.*, *Lyco.*, Sulph.

Scarlatina (scarlet fever): *Apis mel.* (fever of typhoid character, nose discharges, a thick white fetid or bloody mucus, ulcerated throat) *Arsenic* (pale with rapid prostration, great anguish and thirst but drinks little and often) *Belladona* (eruptions are smooth and scarlet colour, tonsils inflamed and of a dark red colour having stinging and burning pain) *Nitric acid* (putrid smelling breath, mouth full of fetid ulcers) *Rhus tox.* (rashes dark colour and itches violently much fever after mid night, pain in limbs and joints, restlessnes).

Scarlet fever (malignant) *Alianth.* (1 x), *Ars.*, *Bapt.*, *Phyto.*, *Cup. acetate* (with great mental depression) *Apis.*, *Acid carbolic.*, *Acid mur.*

Scarlet fever (simple): *Acon.*, *Bell.*, *Apis.*, *Sulph.* (during decline) *Ars.* (during desquamation).

Scarlet fever (with rheumatic symptoms) *Rhus tox.*, *Bryonia.*

Scarlet fever of children: *Aconite* (fever begin with) *Belladona* (sore throat, dry barking cough) *Bryonia* (frontal headache, cough with little mucus) *Euphrasia* (copious burning, discharge from eyes, swelling of eye lids) *Pulsatilla* (cold, bland green phlegm) *Sulphur* (after eruptions are subsided) *Kali mur.* (as a preventive).

Scarlet fever, after kidney ailments: *Apis.*, *Hellaborus*, *Lachesis*, *Terebintha.*

Scarlet fever: (Anginosa) *Alianth.*, *Apis.*, *EChinacea* (Q) *Canth.*, *Merc.*, *Arum triph.* (ulceration of throat) *Apis.* (much swelling) *Ver. vir.* (cerebral hyperanemia, severe vomiting and high fever).

Sciatica: *Arsenic* (burning, stinging pain, as if pierced with red hot needles, aggravation in the night) *Belladona* (darting or tearing pains dread of noise or light, aggravation in afternoon) *Colocynth* (violent rendering or darting pains, aggravated by motion or touch, screwing pains) *Rhus tox.* (pains aggravated by rest, worse after mid night) *Colocyanth.*, *Acon.* (Q) (recent rheumatic with much pain) *Graph.*, *Iris.*, *Lyco.*, *Lach.*, *Rhus.* (chronic rheumatism) *Ars.* (neuralgia) *Senec.*, *Kali carb* (of right side) *Nux vom*, *Phyto.* (chronic) *Cimici.*, *Ammon. mur.*, *Ruta.*, *Apocy. can.*

Scirrhus: *Coni.*, *Hydras.*, *Ars.*, *Thuja.*, *Phyto.*

Sclero choroiditis: *Belladona* (sclerochoroiditis posterior, face flushed, throbbing congestive headache, opacity in vitreous, eyes sensitive to light) *Prunus spin* (Staphyloma posterior, pain in the ball as if pressed as under, or sharp shooting in and around the eyes) *Spigelia* (sharp shooting pains) *Thuja* (inflammatory condition of sclera especially in strumus or syphilitic subjects).

Sclerosis: *Ferrum met., Ferrum iod., Puls., Cal. carb., Sepia, Nat. mur., Helon., China, Petrol.*

Screams of infants: *Cham., Aco., Ver. vir., Bell., Caps., Kali brom* (night screaming).

Scrofula-King's evil: *Calcarea carb.* (suited to scrofulous children with large head and where openings are slow to close, curvature of spine, voracious appetite, dry and flabby skin) *Heper sulph.* (scrofulous inflammation of the eyes, hip disease where there is suppuration) *Silicea* (large-head with open fontanels caries of bones, constipation with hard, difficult stools, which recede after being partially expelled) *Sulphur* (fistulas ulcers).

Scurry of the mouth (Stomatitis): *Arsenicum* (burning, gums turn black) *Carbo veg.* (from abuse of mercury or excessive salty food, the gums recede and bleed easily) *Mercurius vivus* (constant flow of fetid saliva, worse at night no better from profuse sweating).

Sea sickness (nausea marina): *Arsenicum* (excessive sickness with utter prostration and helplessness) *Cocculus* (sickness associated with giddiness and nausea when rising up in bed or standing erect) *Ipecac.* (constant and continual nausea without prostration) *Petrol, Staph., Cocc., Tabac., Nux vom., Chlor, hyd., Apom.*

Secretion of milk: *Calcarea carb.* (secretion of milk abundant, suitable to pale flabby state of body) *Pulsatilla* (suppression of secretion of milk, inclination to be chilly).

Self abuse: *Nux vom., Con., Acid phos., Acid pic., Cal. phos.*

Seminal discharge with blood: *Canth., Led. pal., Merc., Petro., Srsaparilla.*

Seminal emission (from masturbation): *Calcarea carb.* (apprehensive of some misfortune, cold feet) *China* (very debility, weak digestion, exhausting night sweats) *Nux vom.* (very irritable and wishes to be alone, habitual constipation, stool too long and hard) *Phosphoric acid* (frequent involuntary very debilitating emissions, profuse morning sweat) *Staphysagaria* (worries about the ailment and incline to weep, weakness of the memory).

Sensation as if the skull bones are opening and closing: *Actea racemosa, Cannabis indica.*

Sensation of coldness at different part of the body: *Cal. carb., Kali bich.*

Sensation of emptiness in stomach: *Sepia* (severe constipation, does not go for stool for days together in spite of it great hunger and eats well) *Coccolus ind.* (sensation develops during journey by train or steamer or from loss of sleep), *Ignitia* (nervous women always sigh and sorrowful) *Kali carb.* (feeling goes off after eating, flatulence develops) *Lobelia* (with the symptoms nausea, excessive perspiration are associated) *Petrolium* (symptoms develop after passing the stool) *Phosphorus* (symptoms felt mostly in the night, eats in the night) *Hydrastis* (sensation due to ulcer in abdomen) *Sulphur* (sensation felt at about 11 AM has to eat to control the symptom).

Sensation of prolapsus of uterus: *Agaricus* (after menses is over) *Sepia* (sensation is felt all the time so the lady sits in cross leg position, press the uterus or tight it with bandage, avoids coitus) *Belladona* (no such sensation on standing or sitting upright) *Lilium ting.* (sits with cross leg like Sepia but has intense desire for sexual act) *Sanicula* (hands and feet burns, keep them out of covering during sleep).

Sensation of stone in the stomach: *Bryo.* (very thirsty, drinks large quantity of water at long interval, bitter taste), *Nux vom.* (thirst is less), *Puls.* (no thirst or very little quantity of water, bitter taste).

Sensations: *Sarsaparilla* (as if in a dream) *Secale cor.* (as if fingers become numb) *Staphysagaria* (as if stomach and abdomen are hanging down) *Cactus grandiflora* (of a cord tightly tied around the heart) *Silicea* (of a splinter in throat when swallowing) *Sepia* (of a ball in upper part of the body) *Sulphur* (of burning in whole body or in parts with hot flushes) *Ammonium mur.* (of coldness in between the scapulae) *Lilium tinglum* (of heart with uterine problems) *Staphysagaria* (of crawling of worms over the body) *Thuja oc.* (of crying of animal in the abdomen) *Carboneum sulph.* (of hair in the throat) *Carbolic acid* (of pricking of needles all over the body) *Graphites* (of spider web on the face) *Nitric acid* (of splinter in affected parts in piles, throat etc) *Natrum mur.* (of worm creeping in the nostril) *Labelia inf.* (as if heart will stop beating) *Variolium* (as if a thread is hanging down in the throat) *Alumina* (as if ants are moving on the body) *Cocculus ind.* (as if arms have been swollen) *Lac. can.* (as if breath will stop on lying) *Apis mel.* (as if every breath will be his last breath) *Valeriana* (of a great coldness in the head) *Thuja oc.* (as if limbs are made up of glass and can easily break down) *Secale cor.* (as if mice are creeping on all parts of the body) *Crocus sat.* (movement of something in the stomach, abdomen uterus or chest) *Iodium* (as if heart has been clasped with iron band) *Lobelia inf.* (as if thousand needles are pricking her) *Calcarea carb.* (as if wearing cold damp stockings) *Kali ars.* (as if a ball is rising from the pit of stomach to throat causing suffocation) *Sepia* (as if all pelvic organs will come out) *Abies nigra* (of boiled egg in the stomach) *Natrum mur.* (of coldness about heart) *Calcarea carb.* (of coldness in the single part of the body) *Cistus* (of coldness in whole body) *Argentum nit.* (of electric current passing from top to bottom) *Cistus can.* (of crawling, tingling and running of ants) *Gnaphalium* (of flowing of cold water over the body) *Arsenic alb.* (of hot pin pricking) *Merc. prot. rubber* (of movement of iron rod in the anus) *Agaricus* (of pin pricking in the body) *Bryonia* (of eaten food lying in the upper part of the stomach) *Graphites* or *Borax* (of spider web on the face) *Moschus* (as if somebody is inserting nail in the body).

Sensitiveness: *Ign.*, *Bella.*, *Cham.*

Septic condition in: *Ars. alb.*, *Carbolic acid*, *Lachesis*, *Secale cor.*, *Anthracinum*, *Pyrogenum*.

Sexual organ females: *Puls.* (mal-position of foetus, thin acrid or milky leucorrhoea) *Rhus tox.*, *Dulc.*, *Merc.*, *Podo.*, *Puls.* (derangement of uterine functions from repeated drenching in the rain or taking cold) *Apis.* (great soreness of the parts after labour) *Apis.* (cannot walk erect on account of sore bruised feeling in the uterine region), *Nat. mur.*, *Nit. acid*, *Sepia.* (great pressing towards the genital as if everything would protrude) *Cimici.* (severe pains in the back, down the thigh and through hips) *Coffea* (great, sensitiveness of the private parts) *Croc. sat.* (uterine haemorrhages, the blood dark and stringy worse from least exertion), *Lach.* (cannot bear pressure upon the uterine region) *Puls.*, *Cham.*, *Cimi.*, *Nux.* (menstrual colic violent, so tosses in every direction) *Secale cor.* (copious flow of black, liquid blood, worse from slightest motion in miscarriage) *Secale cor.* (uterine Haemorrhages, every discharge of blood is preceded by violent painful contraction of the womb or by distressing bearing down pain) *Sepia, Merc.* (prolapses uteri and vagina with burning pain in the small of the back) *Sepia, Lach.* (disorders at the change of life) *Verat album* (dysmenorrhea with vomiting and purging or exhausting diarrhoea with cold sweat). *Lyco., Heper., Mag. carb.* (diminished sexual desire, penis small, cold, relaxed) *Canth., Nux v., Phos.* (increased sexual desire) *Merc. vivus.* (chancre ulcers on the prepuce and glans) *Cal. c., Canth., Nux v., Phos.* (irritable desire of an embrace) *Phos. acid., China, Gels., Phos.* (seminal emission, especially after animism) *Silicea, Heper., Lyco., Mag carb.* (weak and almost extinguished sexual desire) *Sulph.* (stitches in penis).

Shiverings: *Camph., Acon., Bryo.* from cold) *Gels., Ign.,* (nervous without coldness) *Ars., Carbo veg.*

Sick headache: *Iris., Bryo., Nux vom., Gels., Vert. album., Ipecac., Puls., Sangu., Sepia.*

Sickness: *Ipecac.* (simple) *Puls., Ant. crud.* (from rich food) *Nux vom.* (from alcohol) *Kreos.* (chronic).

Side (pain in): *Cimici., Puls.* (hysterical or uterine left side), *Bryo.* (right side, rheumatism or from liver problem) *Ran. bulb., Ars.* (left side neuralgic or anaemic) *Ars.* (left side muscular).

Sighing: *Cal. Phos., Cimicifuga, Ignitia.*

Sight (dim): *Sabi., Gels.* (with vertigo and diplopia).

Sight (double): *Stram., Hyos., Nat. mur.;* *Cicuta, Gels., Aurum met.*

Sinking at the stomach: *Acid hydrocyn., Ign., Gels., Lauro., Hydras., Apocyn., Bapt.* (from chronic dyspepsia) *Sepia, Cimici.* (at the critiCal. age) *Murex.* (with prolapsus uteri) *Sulph.*

Skin: *Acon.* (measles, rash of children or small pox) *Ars. alb.* (black blisters burning and painful) *Ars. alb., Carbo veg., Silicea, Sulphur* (putrid ulcers with feted labor) *Ars. alb., Bell., Con., Heper.* (ulcers discharging a thin bloody pus) *Ars. alb., Caust., Merc., Rhus tox, Silicea* (carbuncles which burn like fire) *Bell.* (smooth shining redness of the skin not much swelling *Canth.* (Erysipelas with more burning than itching and exudation of serious fluid, forming blisters) *Bryo., Puls.* (erysipelas particularly of joints) *Cal. carb.* (hard white elevated eruptions, burning itching) *Carbo veg.* (putrid ulcers, readily bleeding ulcers) *Carbo veg.* (dry rash like itch) *Acon., Chamomilla* (rash of infants and nursing female) *Ars., Conium.* (blackish ulcers, with bloody fetid, chorus discharge) *Graphites* (sticky glutinous discharge from ulcer) *Cal. carb., Con., Dulc., Graphites* (humid tatters) *Dulc.* (eruptions oozing out watery fluid) *Cal. carb., Heper., Silicea.* (unhealthy skin; every little injury suppurates) *Ars., Heper.* (ulcers very sensitive to contact, burning stinging easily bleed) *Kali bich.* (postural eruptions resembling small pox) *Lachesis* (carbuncles surrounded by small boils and purple spots) *Mag. c., Rhus tox.* (vesicles and pimples, sometimes itch violently) *Mag. carb.* (small red elevated herpes, scaling off) *Merc., Sulph.* (itch bleeds easily) *Merc.* (ulcers and eruptions have a raw appearance) *Merc. vivus.* (watery vesicles and blotches, turn yellow and maturate) *Nat. mur.* (nettle rash after violent exercise) *Dulc.* (nettle rash after taking cold) *Rhus tox.*

(Nettle rash after getting wet) *Nit.* acid (mercurial ulcers and caries) *Cal. carb., Phos., Sulph.* (dry herpes) *Bell., Acid phos.* (scarlet like rash) *Merc., Acid phos.* (ulcers itching inveterate or flat with dirty pus) *Bell., Puls.* (measles and their secondary ailment) *Puls.* (eruptions like checken pox from eating pork and fat things) *Rhus tox.* (burning, itching eruptions, with swelling of parts and small yellowish vesicles, which run together and become moist) *Rhus tox.* (herpes alternating with pains in the chest and dysenteric stool) *Rux tox.* (glandular swelling) *Sepia.* (ringworm) *Staph.* (frequent boils) *Sulph.* (dry, husky, scaly skin) *Merc., Rhus., Staph., Sulphur.* (psorasis with violent itching and tingling, burning after scratching) *Cal. carb., Phos., Sulph.* (dry tatter, scurfy, itching violently) *Cham., Graph., Lyco., Merc., Sulphur.* (excoriation of the skin, especially where it is folded upon itself) *Ars., Carbo veg., Heper., Sulph.* (ulcers which bleed easily burn like fire) *Anthracinum* (Malignant ulcer, terrible burning) *Calcarea carb.* (induration in ulcers) *Condorango* (fissures are formed, cracks in the corner of the mouth).

Sleep: *Bella.* (moaning during sleep) *Bryo.* (delirium as soon as awakens) *Ars., Bryo., Nux.* (starting as a fright on falling asleep) *Cal carb.* (horrid visions when opening the eyes from sleep) *Bryo.* (horrid vision when closing the eyes) *Hyos.* (deep sleep with convulsion) Ign., Puls., Sulph. (restless sleep with night mare) *Lyco., Merc., Phos., Sulph.* (drowsiness during the day and sleepless at night), *Bryo., Merc. vivus., Nux vom., Phos.* (great inclination to sleep in day time especially after meals) *Merc. vivus.* (cannot sleep until 3 AM) *Cal. carb., Nux vom.* (cannot sleep after 3 AM) *Sepia, Sulphur* (talks in sleep and very restless) *Opium* (stupefying sleep with eyes half open and loud snoring) *Hyos* (during sleep picking at the bed clothes) *Puls., Merc. vivus, Nux vom., Phos.* (drowsiness in the day time) *Puls.* (restless sleep with tossing about frequent waking), *Puls., Bell., Nit. acid., Phos.* (sleep full of frightful dreams) *Sepia, Nat. mur., Sulphur* (loud talking during sleep) *Puls., Sulph.* (jerking of whole body during sleep), *Bell., Croc., Phos. acid.* (sings during sleep) *Sulph.* (jerks and twitches during sleep).

Sleeping by the painful side and by pressing, the ailment subsides: *Ammon. carb., Puls., Bryo., Ignitia, Nat. mur.*

Sleeping side, becomes painful as if crushed: *Bapt., Aranea d., Pyrogenium, Nux mosh., Ruta.*

Sleeplessness in children: *Aconite* (from fright, feverishness) *Belladona* (frighten vision, cries for no reason) *Coffea* (over active brain, due to pleasant excitement, laughter playfulness) *Hyoscymus* (due to nervous excitement in sensitive children) *Nux vom.* (due to indigestion particularly later part of the night) *Pulsatilla* (due to intake of fatty food) *Cypripedium* (due to any cause).

Sleeplessness, due to business disturbance: *Ambra gra., Actea racemosa, Sepia.*

Sleeplessness: *Aconite* (by agitating events, which causes fever and anxiety) *Coffea* (arises from excessive joy or the use of tea) *Opium* (various figures prevents sleep, severe mental exertion or long continued night watching) *Coff., Gels.* (Q), *Glon., Bella., Ign., Hyos., Acon.* (from pain), *Avena sat., Cimici., Verat alb., Agar., Passiflora* (Q).

Sleeplessness: *Acon., Ars., Bell., Cham* (sleeplessness with restlessness tossing about) *Bell., Ferr., Opi.* (sleepy but cannot go to sleep) *Calc., Chin., Nux vom.*

(sleeplessness from many thoughts crowding in the mind) *Coffea* (sleeplessness from over-excite ness of mind and body) *Hyos.* (nightly sleplessness) *Mag carb.* (sleeplessness at night from oppression in the abdomen) *Merc. vivus.* (excessive restlessness with sleeplessness) *Rhus tox., Bryo., Graph., Phos.* (sleeplessness especially before midnight).

Small pox (varila): *Mercurius* (ulcerated throat with profuse saliva, perspiration without relief) *Antim. tar.* (a remedy for the disease where much irritation of the respiratory organs is present) *Arsenic.* (eruptions are dark, extreme thirst but drinks little, great anguish and fear of death) *Belladona* (starting and jumping during sleep, pain in back as if it will break) *Rhus tox.* (disease assumes typhoid character, great debility and restlessness) *Varolinum* (6 or 30 every 4 hrly), *Ant tar., Apis.* (much swelling and itching) *Merc.* (during suppurative fever) *Ars., Bapt.* (typhoid symptoms) *Kali brom., Acon., Bella., Sulph., Thuja.*

Smell (loss of): *Acon.* (recent) *Puls., Merc., Sepia, Cal. carb., Plumb.* (constipation).

Sneezing: *Merc., Euphr., Ars., Kali iod., Ipecac., Allium cepa.*

Snoring: *Opium* (deep snoring, breathing with open mouth).

Snuffles of infants: *Dulcamara* (nose very dry from exposure to cold air) *Nux vom.* (during night the nose becomes dry, constipation of bowls).

Sole unbearable to touch: *Puls., Antim. crud., Baryta carb., Led., Lyco., Medorihnum.*

Somebody is piercing nail: *Nux., Coffea., Ignitia, Thuja.*

Somnambulism: *Znic., Opi.* (heavy sleep), *Acon., Cup. met. Phos.*

Sore mouth (apathae) of infants: *Arsenic.* (green watery diarrhoea, weakness) *Mercurius* (profuse secretion of saliva, tongue inflamed ulcerated on the edges) *Sulphur* (acrid, slimy or greenish diarrhoea excoriating parts).

Sore nipple: *Calcarea carb.* (sore chapped nipples with deep cracks) *Graphites* (eruption on the breast oozing out a sticky fluid) *Heper sulph.* (burning, stinging in ulcers which bleeds easily).

Sore throat in children: *Aconite* (due to exposure to dry cold air, feverish) *Belladona* (bright red inflamed tonsils, pain on swelling) *Bryonia* (due to taking cold drinks) *Baryta carb* (painful swallowing) *Heper Sulph.* (shooting pain with pus in tonsils) *Lachesis* (purple throat, worse left side) Merc. *sol.* (pus in tonsils, with no or little pain) *Nux vom.* (mild sore throat, scraping rough feeling).

Sore throat: *Belladona* (burning and dryness in throat, sensation of a lump in the throat, soreness of right side) *Lachesis* (soreness is felt at a small spots, sensation of lump or plug in throat worse after sleeping) *Mercurius* (catarrhal sore throat, worse at night and in damp weather).

Sound intolerable: *Aco., Bella., Borax, Caladium, China, Coffea, Colchicum, Ign.atia, Nux vom., Spigellia, Tarentula his., Thiridion.*

Sour smell in children's stool: *Cal., Rheum., Heper., Mag. carb.*

Sour vomiting: *Ferrum met., Lyco., Acid sulph.*

Spams (Convulsion): *Belladona* (starting and jumping during sleep, drowsiness after the spasm, precocious child) *Hyoscymus* (convulsive trembling and foam at the mouth, cough worse when lying down) *Opium* (loudscreaming before or during the spasm, convulsion caused from fright).

Spasmodic Croup in children: *Belladona* (violent attack, delirium) *Heper sulph.* (after attack exhausted, wheezing and hoarseness) *Ipecac.* (wheezing most prominent) *Spongia* (attack in night with voice as if wood is cut with saw) *Chels.idonium* (lamps of mucous which flies from mouth on coughing).

Spasms muscular cillery (spasm of the accommodation): *Jaborandi* (spasm of the accommodation or irritability of the ciliary muscle, everything at a distance is blurred without concave glasses, though near objects are seen distinctly, the vision may be constantly changing, nausea or vertigo on using the eyes) *Physostigma ven.* (has to bring the book near to eyes to read, twitching in the lids and around the eyes) *Agaricus* (spasms of lid or chorea, twitching of the eyelids).

Spasms: *Coloc.* (of the bowels) *Nux vom.* (of the stomach and bowels) *Ver. vir.* (sudden spasms of children from congestion with nausea prostration etc) *Gels., Cocc., Camph.*

Spermatorrhoea: *Arg. met., China, Coni., Ferr., Gels., Dios., Nuphur., Phos., Acid phos., Staph., Dig., Eryng., Sil., Selen., Nat. mur., Iris., Canth., Digit.*

Spinalbifida (cleft spine): *Bryo., Cal. Phos.*

Spinal irritation: *Cimic., China, Ign., Agar., Nux vom., Macrot.*

Spine (concussion of) *Arn., Diosc., Heper., Cicuta.*

Spine (congestion of): *Acon., Ver. vir.* (acute) *Rhus* (rheumatic) *Gels., Nux vom., Bell., Agar.*

Spleen (enlargement of) *Merc. bin iod., China, Ferr., Agar., Kali bromide, Nat. mur., Ceanoth.*

Sprain in body: *Rhus tox., Ruta, Arnica, Nux., Calc. carb.*

Sprain neglected: *Iod., Kali iod.*

Sprain: *Arn., Acon., Rhus tox., Ruta.*

Squinting: *Belladona* (squinting are seen from some disease of the brain, eyes look wild, unsteady wavering) *Hyoscymus* (eyes turned inward and upwards, things look too large or double vision) *Phos.phorus* (difficulty in opening the lids) *Stromonium* (squinting in all directions, pupils unmovable as if paralysed) *Cicuta* (pupils dilated squinted, eyes staring) *Gelsemium* (due to disturbed muscular functioning of the eye).

Stare: *Cup. met.* (eyes fixed, staring, sunken, turned upward, crossed, quick rolling of eye balls).

Sterlity (in females) *Coni., Sepia., Dig., Plat., Borax, Cal. carb., Iod., Helon., Cimici.*

Stiff neck: *Acon., Bella.* (from cold), *Ant. tar., Cimici., Bryo., Bella., Dulcamara* (from damp).

Stings, insect bites in children: *Aconite* (sudden onset of fever, swelling) *Apis.* (painful swelling, stinging pain) *Ledum pal.* (in punctured wound in insect bite).

Stitches in the side or chest: *Bryo., Ran. bulb., Cimici., Acon., Arn.*

Stomach (acidity of) *Cal. carb., Robinia, Lyco.*

Stomach (inflammation of) *Acon.* (acute) *Ant. tar., Ars.*

Stomach (pain or spasm of) *Acon., Nux vom., Cham.* (spasm) *Bismith.* (burning pain vomiting) *Ars.* (pain and vomiting).

Stomach felt full with smallest eating: *Cyclamen, Lyco.*

Stomach is upset, by eating sour items: *Antim. crud., Carbo veg., Drosera, Nat. mur., Acid phos.*

Stomach: *Ant. crud., Ipecac., Nux., Puls.* (derangement from overloading the stomach), *Carb v., Ipecac., Puls.* (derangement from eating fat food, pork etc), *Ant. crud, China, Nux, Puls* (cramp like in the stomach from indigestion) *Ant. crud.* (violent pain and sensitiveness of the stomach) *Ars., Bryo., Lyco., Merc., Nux.* (stomach very painful to touch) *Bell., Chin., Cocc., Nux.* (cramp like pain in the stomach) *Bryo., Ars., Lyco., Merc. Nux* (stomach sensitive to touch or pressure) *Calc. carb., Puls.* (aversion to anything boiled) *Calc., Lyco., Nux.* (cannot bear tight clothing around waist) *Canth., Ars., Nux., Phos.* (gastritis with violent burning pain in the stomach) *Canth., China, Lyco.* (great fullness after eating or drinking) *Caust.* (sensation as if lime has been burnt in stomach) *China* (weak digestion, milk disagree) *Ars., Canth., Phos., Nux.* (inflammation of stomach) *Ars., Ferr., Nux., Puls.* (violent pain in the stomach after eating or drinking) *Carbo veg.* (incarcerated flatulence) *Cimici.* (sinking sensation at the stomach) *Cocculus.* (cramps in the stomach during and after a meal, with oppressed breathing) *Nux., Colchicum.* (stitches in the stomach) *Con., Colo., Nux.* (spasmodic or pinching pain in the stomach) *Croc. sat.* (sensation as if something alive is hopping about in the stomach) *Dig.* (great sense of weakness in the stomach) *Ars., Nux.* (cramps in stomach) *Dul.* (sensation of fullness in the stomach and emptiness in abdomen) *Graph., Ars., Bryo., Merc.* (pressure in the stomach as of a stone after eating) *Condorango* (vomit of food) *Crotalus h.* (vomiting of bloody slimy mucus, black or coffee coloured vomit) *Nitirc acid.* (burning pain, thirst, inability of retaining food), *Phosphorus* (sharp cutting pain, coffee coloured vomit) *Heper., Bryo., Chin., Nux.* (longing for acid, wine and strong food), *Heper., Dig., Nat. mur.* (longing for bitter things), *Heper., Nit. acid., Nux.* (longing for chalk, lime etc.) *Merc., Nux.* (longing for milk) *Cal. carb., Carb veg.* (longing for salty food), *Ipec., Lyco.* (longing for sweet things), *Puls.* (aversion to fat food) *Lyco., Nux.* (aversion to bread), *Ign., Sep., Sulph.* (aversion to meat) *Caust., Graph., Nit. acid.* (aversion to sweet things) *Heper.* (frequent eructation without taste or smell) *China, Lyco., Nux.* (distension of the stomach, compelling to loose clothing) *Ign., Rhus.* (fine stinging pain like pin pricking in the stomach) *Kali bich., Ars., Merc., Nux vom.* (after eating the food lies in the stomach like a heavy load) *Bryo., Merc., Phos., Nux.* (region of the stomach very sensitive to pressure) *China, Heper., Lyco., Nux.* (cannot bear the tight clothing around the waist) *Colo., Nux vom.* (constrictive cramp like pain in the stomach) *Rhus tox.* (cramp like drawing in the umbilical region).

Stomatitis: *Merc. cor., Hydras., Bell., Caps., Heper sulph., Bapt.* (with much saliva) *Kali chol, Arsenium.* (burning, gums turn black) *Carbo veg.* (from absue of mercury or excessive salty food, the gums recede and bleed easily) *Mercurius vivus.* (constant flow of fetid saliva, worse at night, no better from pofuse sweating).

Stomtitis in children: *Merc.* (saliva from mouth) *Borax* (no saliva from mouth, ulcer white coloured) *Bryonia* (dryness in mouth, cannot feed the milk initially but as soon as the mouth becomes wet by milk starts sucking milk) *Arum triphyllum* (due to ulcers the mouth becomes swollen, pricks lips and nose continuously).

Stool spluttering with noisy flatus: *Cal. phos.* (head sweats while sleeping, likes smoked meat) *Arg. nit.* (likes sweats) *Bryo.* (stools dry hard, as if burnt) *Cal. carb.*, *Heper.* (constipation of hard undigested stools clay coloured) *Carbo veg.* (stool hard tough scanty) *Caust.* (hard tough stools covered with mucus and shine like grease) *Con.*, *Lyco.*, *Nux.* (with frequent urging without stool) *Graphites* (large difficult knotty stools, united with mucus thread) *Opi.* (stool hard like black balls) *Phos.*, (stool long like dog's stool, thirst for cold water) *Kali bich.*, *Nat mur.*, *Verat.* (stool dry, knotty with burning at the anus) *Lachesis* (chronic constipation, hard stool resembling sheep dung) *Lyco.* (severe constipation, almost impossible to pass the stool, scanty stool, sensation as if much have remain behind) *Nat. mur.* (stool hard dry, crumbling, difficult to discharge) *Nux vom.* (habitual constipation of large difficult stool with frequent and often ineffectual attempts at stool) *Opi.* (stools composed of round, hard black balls) *Caust.*, *Phos.* (stools long, narrow and long like a dog's stool), *Sabina* (stool difficult and painful, the pain extends from back to pubis) *Silicea* (before and during menstruation stool in hard lump which recedes after having been partially expelled) *Sulph.* (constipation with unsuccessful desire for stool, hard insufficient stool) *Graph.* (constipation before and Diarrhea after menstruation).

Stool very offensive, of children and old people: *Bapt*, *Carb veg.*, *Kali Phos.*, *Podo.*, *Psoranium.*

Stool white coloured: *Cal. carb.*, *Digitalis*, *China.*

Stool: *Acon.*, *Ars.*, *Bell.*, *Colch.*, *Merc.* (frequent scanty stool with tenesmus) *Mag. carb.* (stool like the scum of a frog pond), *Cal. carb.*, *Heper.* (white stool), *Camp.*, *Chin.*, *Verat.* (black stool), *Ant. crud.* (sensation as if copious stool would pass, whereas only flatus is passed, finally a hard stool is voided) *Arnica* (stools slimy, mucus, brown, fermented like yeast) *Ars. alb.* (dark green mucous stools burning in the anus and rectum during and after stool) *Kali brom.*, *Verat. alb.* (dark or black watery stool, very offensive) Cham., Merc., Sulph. (corrosive watery stool), *Acon.*, *Camp.* (sudden and rapid prostration after stool) *Baptisia t.* (very fetid, dark, thin fecal. stools) *Merc.* (before stool severe colic, during and after tenesmus) *Colocyn.*, *Mag. carb.*, *Nux vom.* (stool with thick green mucus and with gripping colic) *Ars.*, *Ipec.*, *Merc.* (stool with thin green mucus), *Bryo.* (stool dry, hard as if burnt), *Calc carb.*, *Nux vom.* (stool too large in size), *Opi.* (stool composed of small hard black balls), *Calc c.*, *Heper.* (stools hard of undigested food, clay coloured) *Canth.* (green or bloody mucus stool before stool violent colic, during stool burning at the anus, after stool tedious, burning, biting stringing at the anus) *Carbo veg.* (stool hard tough, scanty associated with constipation) *Causticum* (hard tough stools, covered with mucus and shine like grease, small shaped), *Phos.* (stool long, narrow, hard like dog's stool) *China*, *Phos.* (difficult passage of feaces even when soft), *Podo.* (prolapsus of anus with every stool white chalk like stool) *Con.*, *Lyco.*, *Nux vom.* (frequent urging without stool, constipation), *Digitalis pur.*, (chilliness before stool), *Ars.*, *Merc.*, *Verat.* (chilliness during stool), *Canth.* (chilliness after stool, cold sweat on the forehead), *Verat.*, *Gels.* (stool yellow fecal, cream coloured bilious), *Graphites* (large, difficult knotty stools, united by mucus thread), *Ignitia* (difficult stool, causing prolapsus anus, after stool or violent stabbing stitch from the anus towards the rectum, bleeding during and after stool), *Sepia* (hard, difficult stools with a sense of weight in the anus, not relieved even by an evacuation), *Silicea* (hard difficult stools as if rectum has no power to expel them, they recede after having been partially expelled or ascarides with the stool), *Rhus tox.* (before stool urging, cutting colic, nausea, after stool remission of the pains, frothy stool) *Canth.*, *Graph.*, *Sulph.* (stool thin with red mucus), *Apis.*, *Cham.* (thin yellow mucus stool), *Colch.*, *Kali bich.* (jelly like mucus stool), *Colocynth*, *Phos.* (bloody stool).

Stove or bonfire is unbearable: *Antim. crud.*, *Apis.*, *Bryo.*, *Allium cepa*, *Chamo.*, *Gels.*, *Glonine*, *Graph.*, *Guiacum*, *Iodium*, *Led.*, *Merc.*, *Nat. carb.*, *Puls.*, *Sabina*, *Secale.*, *Sulph.*

Strabismus: *Gels.*, *Bell.*, *Hyos.*, *Stram.* (from cerebral causes) *Cina* (worms), *Bryo.* (rheumatic) *Nux vom.* (over use of eyes) *Spig.*, *Phos.* (undetermined causes).

Strangury (difficulty in passing the urine): *Aconite* (painful and very scanty emission of a few drops of deep red turbid uringe pains are aggravated on urinating) *Apis mel.* (urine scanty and high coloured) *Belladona* (sensation of a worm in the bladder, discharge of few drops of bloody urine, back ache) *Conium* (difficulty in voiding the urine, the flow intermits) *Digitalis* (pain in the neck of the bladder, as if a straw has been thrust back and forth). *Camp* (urgent and painful) *Nux vom.* (spasm), *Bella.* (nervous and in children) *Acon.* (from cold) *Canth. Apis.* (in children) *Acon.* (from cold), *Canth.*, *Apis.* (in elderly women).

Stye: *Puls.*, *Merc.*, *Thuja*, *Sulph.*, *Staph.* (to prevent re-occurrence) *Merc. iod.*, *Pulsatilla* (stye on the upper lid) *Rhus tox.* (stye on the lower lids) *Staphysagria* (appear often leaving hard spots behind, biting and burning in the corners where dry pus forms) *Heper sulph.* (tendency of recurrence of the complaint) *Apis.* (with swollen eye lids) *Lycopodium* (near internal acanthi) *Pulsatilla* (mostly in lower lids with disturbed stomach) *Staphysaria* (recurring styes, halogen)

Suffocation (feeling of) *Ign.*, *Cimi.* (nervus) *Acon.*, *Dig.*, *Cact.*, *Lilium.*, *Acid hydrocyn.*, *Sambul.* (from head diseases).

Sun headache: *Glonine* (immediate effect of sunstroke) *Lachesis* (to be used when the sun stroke becomes late and chronic, the tongue is protruded with difficulty) *Nat. carb.* (patient is troubled with headache every time he is exposed to sunheat).

Sun heat unbearable: *Antim. curd.*, *Bella.*, *Bryo.*, *Cactus*, *Gels.*, *Glonine*, *Lachesis*, *Nat. carb.*, *Nat. mur.*, *Puls.*, *Selenium.*

Sun stroke: *Bell.*, *Camph.*, *Gels.*, *Veratrum vir.*, *Glon.*, *Cactus Q.* (this is specific for sun stroke).

Suppuration: *Sil.*, *Heper Sulph.*, *Merc.*, *Cal carb.*, *China.* (for debility) *Sil* (profuse discharge), *Cal phos.* (tubercular cases)

Suspicious: *Arsenic.*, *Aurum.*, *Baryta carb.*, *Causticum*, *Kali ars.*, *Rhus tox.*

Sweat (tendency to): *China*, *Merc.*, *Ver. alb.*, *Carbo veg.*

Sweat: *Acid Phos.*, *Phos.*, *Verat. alb.*, *Samb.*, *Cal carb.*, *Merc.* (sour), *Petrol.*, *Carbo veg.* (foetid) *Sil.* (Head).

Sweating fever: *Acon.*, *Bryo.*, *Sambicus.*

Sweets intolerable: *Antim. crud., Argent. nit., Ignitia, Lyco., Medorihnum, Sang., Zincum met.*

Swelling (white): *Bryo., Arn.* (early stage) *Iod., Sil., Cal carb., Sulph.*

Swelling: *Apis mel.* (lids swollen, red, conjunctiva bright red and puffy) *Argentum nit.* (due to acute granular conjunctivitis with swelling) *Arsenic alb.* (around the eyes with burning acrid flow of tears.) *Euphrasia* (swelling of lids in catarrhal conjunctivitis) *Graphites* (eye lids swollen and red, fissured) *Kali carb.* (swelling over upper lid like a little bag) *Merc. cor.* (eye lids swollen red, with severe burning pain in the eyes).

Swimming causes cold: *Rhus tox., Tarax., Zincum.*

Swallowing of solids difficult but can swallow liquid: *Bapt., Baryta carb., Silicea.*

Syphilis: *Merc sol., Acid nit., Thuja, Kali iod., Still., Kali bich., Phyto., Arg. nit., Aurum.*

T

Tabes mesenterica: *Merc. cor.* (when glands are in an inflammatory state) *Bacil, Baryl carb., Iod., Hydras., Sulph., Agar., Ars., Lyco., Cal. carb., Plumbum acetate* (when there is obstinate constipation).

Tarsal ophthalmia: *Hepr sulph., Euph., Clem., Sulph., Cal. carb., Merc.*

Taste lost: *Puls., Merc.* (deprived) *Plumb., Sil.*

Taste: *Acon.,* (bitter taste of everything except water) *Bry., Colo., Chin., Puls.* (all foods and drinks taste bitter) *Arn., Merc., Nux, Puls* (putrid slimy taste) *Bell* (bread taste and smell sour) *Bryo., Chin., Puls* (all food taste bitter) *Sepia, Carbo veg, China* (everything taste too salty) *Stram* (food tastes like straw) *Bryo., Colo., Puls* (all food and drink taste bitter) *Bryo., Hep., Lyco., Nat mur* (loss of taste) *Bryo., China, Lyco* (food and drinks taste sour) *Ars., Bryo., Nit acid., Puls* (bitter taste particularly after eating).

Teeth (caries and decay of): *Merc., Kreso., Phos., Staph., Ars., Sil., Cal. carb.* (soreness and sensitiveness of) *Merc., Bell., Mang., Sulph., Ant. crud.* (decayed teeth ache, worse at night and with cold water) *Coff., Puls., Bryonia.* (toothache better by cold water) *Bell.* (grinding of teeth with moaning soreness of inner cheek) *Bryo., Cal. c., Merc., Puls.* (toothache worse from warm things in the mouth) *Cal. c.* (toothache of pregnant females) *Carb v., Merc.* (looseness of teeth, gums recedes and bleed easily) *China.* (throbbing tooth ache, worse from contact and better from hard pressure) *Cina, Ars., Podo.* (grinding of the teeth especially during sleep) *Nux vom.* (tearing toothache, renewed by cold drink better by warmth) *Bryo., Coff., Puls.* (toothache better from cold drink and worse from warm) *Phos., Arn., Cham., Sepia.* (toothache with swelling of the cheeks) *Sepia.* (drawing or beating toothache, sometimes extend to ears., aggravates by taking hot or cold).

Temperature high and skin hot: *Aconite* (dry skin, restlessness, fear of death, good thrust) *Belladona* (perspiration on the covered part of the body, semi-consciousness, blood circulation in head, imaginary fear).

Temperature high is unbearable: *Antim. crud., Ipecac., Lachesis.*

Tendency of swelling of glands: *Cal. carb., Conium, Psorinium.*

Tendency towards fatiness: *Ant. crud., Cal. carb., Graphites, Capsicum.*

Tendency towards tallness: *Cal. carb., Crocus., Phos., Phos., acid.*

Tendon and muscular rheumatism: *Rhus tox., Bryonia., Aco., Colocynth, Ledum., Puls.*

Tenesmus (straining, difficult evacuation) *Merc., Merc. cor., Aloes.* (dysenteric or with Diarrhoea) *Sulph., Nux vom., Alumina, Podophyllium.*

Testicles (enlargement and inflammation) *Acon., Puls., Bell., Aur., Arn., Clem., Merc. bin. iod.*

Testicles (neuralgia of) *Aur.*

Testicles (wasting of) *Iod., Coni., Kali iod.*

Testicles not descended: *Aurum mur.* (undescended testicle in boys with girlish disposition and apperance) *Clemates* (testicles retracted, pain along spermatic cord, worse right side) *Rhododendron* (testicles drawn up, painful swollen, worse left side).

Testicles: *Apis mel.* (swelling of testicles) *Bell., Merc., Nux.* (orchids with great hardness of the drawn up testicles) *Phos. acid.* (Gnawing in the testicles).

Tetanus: *Hypencum* (when tetanus comes from punctured wound) *Led. pal.* (punctured wound be treated to save tetanus) *Nux vom., Acon., Bell., Acid hydrocynic.*

The ailment does not subside from the perspiration: *Merc., Tilia.*

Thirst in, drinks good quantity of water at a time: *Acetic acid., Bryo., Ars. alb., Nat. mur., Phos., Veratrum album., Sulph.*

Thirst of water lost: *Puls., Apis., Aethusa.*

Thirst: *Ars., Chin., Puls.* (violent thirst, drinks often but little at a time) *Acon., Bell., Nat. mur.* (drinks often and much at a time) *Phos.* (thirst for very cold drinks).

Thread worms: *Cin., Teuc., Merc., Sant., China, Urt, Vren, Ign.*, (nervous debility).

Throat (clergymans) : *Cal. carb., Phos., Phyto.* (1 x), *Kali iod., Caust., Kali bich., Acid nit., Carbo veg., Ars. alb., Acid mur.*

Throat (sore): *Acon., Bryo.* (simple acute with dryness) *Bell.* (scraped sensation, and bright redness of the part) *Arum triph.* (burning roughness, and stinging) *Kali bich.* (dark red) *Merc.* (Swollen sensation, salivation etc.) *Heper sulph.* (chronic cases) *Phyto.* (when much mucus adheres to the membrane).

Throat (with deafness problem): *Puls.* (recent) *Iod.* (chronic).

Throat cleaning while in the morning causes nausea, which expell whatsoever taken in the breakfast: *Bryo., Euphorasia.*

Throat: *Ars., Aco., Bell., Lach., Nit. acid.* (burning throat) *Carb v.*, Verat. (coldness in throat) *Bell., Hyos.* (throat feels constricted) *Caust.* (sensation of something cold arising in the throat) *Merc.* (sensation of hot vapors arising in throat) *Dul., Cham., Merc.* (sore throat after taking cold) *Dig.* (burning sensation in stomach ascending to throat) *Heper.* (sensation as if a foreign body is lodging or splinter in the throat). *Ars., Heper.* (roughness and scrapping in the throat) *Hyos., Bell., Strom.* (constriction of the throat with inability to swallow, especially fluids) *Lach.* (diseases of the throat begin on the left side and move to right) *Gels., Lyco., Podo.* (diseases of the throat begin on the right side and travel to left side) *Lach* (cannot bear the touch on throat). *Merc. v., Ars.. Bapt.* (putrid dark looking ulcer) *Merc., Bell., Con.* (complete loss of speech and voice) *Nat mur., Merc., Nux.* (sore throat feels as if a plug is lodged in it) *Calc c., Caust., Heper.* (as if splinter is lodged in the throat) *Nux vom.* (catarrhal sore throat) *Phos. acid, Bell.* (dryness of the throat and tongue, without thirst) *Podophyllum* (rattling of mucus in the throat) *Puls.* (sore throat, feels too narrow on swelling back part of the throat feels painful as if raw) *Phos. acid., Phos.* (hoarseness and roughness of the throat).

Thrombosis: *Arnica* (skin turns black or blue tightness constriction after over exertion, severe pain in left elbow and in the region of heart) *Bothrops* (with one sided paralysis or with loss of power of expression by speech, writing or signs or of understanding written or spoken language) *Lachesis* (purple appearance of the skin, coagulation of the blood, worse left side facial problem) *Lilium* (thrombosis affecting pelvic region.

Tinea capitis (scaled head): *Graphites* (eruption oozes out a sticky fluid disease extends down behind the ears.) *Rhux tox.* (eruption consist of watery vesicles which itches violently). *Sulphur* (eruption dry and scabby, bleeds easily with offensive smell).

Tolerate (cannot) the slightest contradiction: *Puls., Apis., Antim. crud.*

Tolerate cannot, tight clothe on the waist: *Bovista, Cal. carb., Lachesis, Sulph.*

Tongue (coating): *Ant. crud.* (milky white, offensive breath) *Kali bich.* (yellowish) *Puls.* (roughish white), *Nux vom.* (forepart clean backpart thickly fussed) *Rhus., Bryo.* (brownish) *Merc.* (thick whitish slimy fur., offensive breath) *Ant. tar., Acid mur., Bapt.*

Tongue (cracked or fissured): *Merc. cor., Acid nit., Spigel., Arum triph., Hydrast.*

Tongue (dryness of): *Acon., Ars., Bella., Tereb., Bryo., Merc., Phos.*

Tongue (inflammation and swelling of): *Acon., Merc.* (from cold) *Bell., Heper sulph.* (mercurial) *Apis., Arum triph.* (oedema) *Merc. vivus.*

Tongue (ulcer on): *Merc., Merc. cor., Merc. iod.* (simple non mercurial) *Acid nit.* (mercurial) *Hydras., Phyto.*

Tongue have imprints of teeth: *Merc., Rhus tox., Podo., Chelsidonium., Staph.*

Tongue: *Apis mel.* (tongue dry, swollen, cracked, sore ulcerated, inability to swallow) *Phosphorus* (open sores, hole through tongue tearing and burning pain) *Crotalus h.* (with tendency to bleeding red and sore) *Acon., Bryonia, Cham.* (tongue and mouth dry) *Bell., Lyco.* (tongue dry without thirst) *Ant crud., Arn, Bryo., Nux vom., Sepia.* (thick milky white coating on the tongue) *Merc., Puls.* (coated as with fur) *Apis., Bell., Merc.* (dry swollen inflamed tongue with inability to swallow) *Ars., Lyco.* (tongue bluish or white brown or blackish) *Bapt.* (tongue coated brown and dry particularly in the centre) *Bell.* (tongue red, hot and dry with red edges and white in the middle) *Bell., Merc.* (tremor of tongue, stammering speech, profuse ptyalism) *Bryo.* (tongue coated white or yellow) *Cina.* (tongue slightly coated white with papillae raised and red on the edge) *Dul.* (dry rough tongue) *Hyos.* (paralysis of the tongue) *Ipecac.* (white thickly coated tongue) *Kali bich.* (tongue coated with thick yellowish brown fur like felt) *Lach.* (interior of the tongue red, smooth and shining, trembles on protruding out) *Merc. v., Colo.* (tongue feels as if burnt) *Nat. mur.* (white coated or map tongue or vesicles on the tongue) *Colch., Nat. mur.* (tongue feels heavy) *Ars., Lyco., Merc., Verat.* (tongue dry becomes black and cracked).

Tonsil (chronic enlargement of) *Bart carb., Sep., Cal. phos., Merc. iod., Cal. iod., Silicea* (tubercular patient) *Kali iod.* (syphilitic patient).

Tonsillitis and gland enlargement: *Baryta carb.* (the tonsils inflamed usually and become hard) *Calcarea carb.* (due to inflammation of tonsils there is sensation that the throat is constricted, pain from tonsils goes into the ear) *Calcarea phos.* (tonsillitis is associated with middle ear inflammation pain in throat while taking inside anything) *Calcarea iod.* (chronic tonsillitis develops hypertrophy of the tonsils, they become enlarged and hard) *Conium.* (no pus formation in the tonsils but they remain hard) *Heper sulph.* (tonsillitis is associated with hard of hearing, sensation of pin pricking in the throat) *Ignitia.* (pain while not swallowing anything and no pain while swallowing) *Lachesis.* (bluish colour especially of left side tonsil, pus of foul smell difficulty in swallowing liquid rather than solid) *Merc. sol.* (tonsils inflamed tendency towards pus and ulcer formation) *Silicea.* (to dry up the pus of tonsils).

Tonsillitis from hard of hearing develops: *Baryta carb., Heper., Lyco., Pulumbum, Psoranium.*

Tonsils: *Bell., Hyos.* (inflammation of tonsils with great difficulty of swollen the liquid) *Heper., Silicea.* (impending suppuration) *Kali bich., Phyto.* (dark coloured pseudo-membrane) *Apis.* (dirty gray coloured membrane) *Lyco., Bell., Podo.* (ulceration of tonsils begins from right, left latch).

Toothache (during pregnancy): *Bell., Cham., Coff., Nux vom.*

Toothache goes up to ear aggravates by cold drinks: *Manganum acetate.*

Toothache is relieved by keeping the cold water in the mouth: *Bismith, Coffea, Puls., Causticum, Sepia, Nat. Sulph.*

Toothache of childtren: *Aconite* (caused by exposure to dry cold wind, feverish) *Belladona* (pain extending to temples, throbbing pain) *Bryonia* (due to taking of bold or cold food) *Chamomilla* (spasmodic pain one chick red the other pale, worse at night) *Hypericum* (pain in exposed roots of the teeth) *Kreosotium* (in caries teeth).

Toothache with saliva in mouth: *Manganum.*

Toothache: *Acon., Bell.* (burning, throbbing) *Merc.* (gnawing, aching, swollen gums, decayed teeth, flow of saliva, gum boil) *Kreos.* (from decayed teeth) *Bryo., Merc. vivus* (worse at night tender to touch) *Glon.* (pains extending to the back) *Cham.* (neuralgic, pain unbearable with swelling of the face especially in females and children) *Coffea.* (relieved by cold, nervous excitability etc.) *Puls., Staph., Plantago., Phos.* (tendency to) *Arnica.* (toothache after an operation, cheek swollen red and hard) *Arsenic.* (jerking pain extending to the teeth, prostration, restlessness drinks often but little) *Bryonia.* (sensation of elongation in the teeth, worse at night or from taking warm anything, constipation) *Calcarea carb.* (pain aggravates by taking anything warm or cold) *Chamomilla* (pains beating or stitching) *China.* (aggravagtes from slightest contact, relieved by pressing the teeth together) *Coffea.* (pains relieved by cold water) *Hepe.* (pain worse when pressing the teeth together or at night) Mercurius much saliva in the mouth) *Nux vom.* (aggravation at night or early in the morning) *Pulsalitta* (better from cold things and worse from warm, scanty or suppressed menses) *Rhus tox.* (painful soreness of the face) *Sepia.* (during pregnancy, swelling of cheeks and submaxillarly glands, profuse leucorrhea) *Staphysagria* (pale, white ulcerated swollen and painful gums) *Sulphur* renewal of pain from cold water) *Chamomilla* (caused or increased if any thing warm is taken and also not relieved by taking cold gargle) *Puls.* (toothache better by taking and keeping cold water in the mouth but returns again when water becomes warm) *Nux vom.* (caused or increased by taking cold in the mouth) *Coffea.* (better by keeping cold in the mouth).

Trachoma: *Apis mel.* (gives early relief).

Tremors (nervous) *Acon., Coff., Bella., China, Gels.*

Tuberculosis of vocal chord: *Argent. nit., Ars. iod., Cal. carb., Causticum, Drosera, Iodium, Manganum acetate, Phos., Selenium, Spongia, Stannum., Tuberculinum.*

Tuberculosis: *Bacil., Iod., Phos., Cal. carb., Ferr. iod., Cal. iod.*

Tumor of brain: *Calcarea carb.* (vertigo and headache on turning the head, piercing stitching pain in the scalp, icy coldness in or on the head, worse from cold and wet weather) *Conium* (headache with nausea and vomiting, vertigo on turning the eyes, staggering, loss of strength while walking) *Merc. iod.* (arrest the tumor of the brain) *Thuja* (intense migraine and pain, sweating on forehead and arm, emotional, sensitive and irritable).

Tumors orbital (tumor both benign, or Malignant of orbit): *Electricity* (of great value in removing vascular tumors of the orbit).

Twitching of eyes: *Agaricus* (of eyelids and eye balls)

Tympanites (distension of bowels) *Coloc., China., Hyos., Iris., Terebenth., Nux.*

Typhoid fever of children: *Arsenic alb.* (restlessness, prostration, thirst for small quantity of water) *Baptisia* (with diarrhoea, sour smelling stool) *Bryonia* (headache, dry mouth, tongue coated, great thirst, worse by warmth) *Terentula* (feted dark stool, great prostration) *Pyrogenium* (high temperature touching 104°C).

Typhoid in, the jaw hangs down: *Muratic acid., Opium., Lyco.*

Typhoid or Typhus fever: *Baptisia* (head feels as if scattered around, sweat, urine and stools are extremely fetid) *Belladona* (throbbing headache with violent pulsation of carotids intolerance to noise and light, wishes to strike, bite or quarrel, sleepiness but cannot sleep) *Bryonia* (lips dry and brown, oppressive, stupefying headache, worse from least motion, delirium day and night, sleep with strange dreams, constipation) *Carbo veg.* (great prostration, extremities cold and covered with cold perspiration) *Hyoscymus* (furious delirium which continues while awake, loss of speech and consciousness, twisting and jerking of the limbs, twisting of the tendons paralysis of splinter and vesicle) *Lachesis* (stupor and muttering delirium cannot bear anything to touch the throat, symptoms all worse after sleeping) *Mercurius* (region of stomach and liver very sensitive, copious perspiration, symptoms all worse at night) *Rhus tox.* (tongue red at top in the shape of triangle, oppression of the chest, severe pains in the limbs, involuntary stool worse after mid night) *Stromonium* (ceaseless talking, repeated jerking of head up from the pillow, thirst less, blackish diarrhea) *Acon., Bry., Bapt.* (most stages bewilderment).

U

Ulcer (gastric): *Sulphur* (great burning), *Carbo veg.* (flatus with foul smell, burning patient wants to be fanned) *Anacardium* (pain relieved by eating, weakness, bad memory), *Ars. alb.* (Burning, weakness, frequent vomiting, putrid odor, fear of death) *Graphites* (patient overweight, unhealthy skin, ulcers arising after grief and sorrow) *Phosphorus* (vomiting, haemorrhages, thirst) *Nux vom.* (ulcer caused by business, tension, worries and by drugs), *Secale cor.* (haemorrhage severe and patient is in collapse condition).

Ulcerated sore throat: *Lachesis* (dryness of throat, hawking up of mucus) *Mercurius* (pain in throat as if too dry) *Nitric acid* (dryness, putrid smell from the mouth).

Ulceration and ulcers (Vericose): *Ars.* (burning, debility) (Urethra-inflammation of) *Cann. sat.*, *Gels.* (Urethra-stricture of) *Gels.*, *Camph.* (especially when caused by blister fly) *Canth.*, *Acon.* (urging with cutting and tearing pains) *Merc.* (purulent discharge) *Nux vom.*, *Sulph.*, *Clem.*, *Silicia*, *Phos.*, *Cann.*, *Hydras.* (organic stricture and after repeated attack of gonorrhea) *Kali bich.*, *Hydras.*, *Rhus.*, *Ars.*, *Phos.* (small punched out ulcers, chronic with debility) *Bella.* (eryseplatous appearance) *Caust.*, *Sil.* (of lower extremities), *Merc.*, *Merc iod.*, *Kali iod.*, *Acid nit.* (syphilis) *Sil.* (torpid) *Merc. iod.*, *Phos.*, *Sulph.*, *Cal carb.* (tubercular) *Acid carbolic* (torpid or fungus ulcers) *Arsenic* (the parts burn, discharge scanty thin offensive bloody or blackish) *Belladona* (scrofulous and mercurial ulcers, burning when touched, black crust of the blood) *Carbo veg.* (the ulcer bleeds readily have putrid smell) *Graphites* (the discharge is glutinous sticky) *Heper sulph.* (bleeds easily and has sour smell like that of old cheese) *Lachesis* (old sores on lower limbs) *Lycopodium* (mercurial ulcers) *Mercurius* (syphilitic ulcers, reddish look like a raw beef) *Silicea* (old unclean ulcers) *Arsenic alb* (ulceration of eye lids) *Heper sulph.* (ulceration of cornea).

Ulcer cornea (corneal ulcers): *Heper sulph.* (redness of cornea, severe pain with throbbing, better by warmth, worse by cold or uncovering and in the evening, sensitive to touch, lids bleed upon opening), *Merc. sol.* (dread of light, profuse lachrymation, burning and excoriating, discharge thin and acrid, worse at night and warmth better by cold, lids thick red swollen. *Calcarea carb.* (pains, redness, photophobia and lachrymation variable). *Calcarea hypophos.* (deep sloughing ulcers in depilated persons. *Arsenicum* (photophobia excessive, lachrymation hot, burning acrid and profuse, burning and sticking pain worse after mid night, soreness of internal surface of the lid, often excoriated by acrid discharges) *Rhus tox.* (superficial hepatitis with excessive photophobia and lachrymation so that the tears gush out upon opening the spasmodically closed lids, profuse flow is an important symptom, superficial ulceration of the cornea with glandular lids, caused from exposure in the water). *Conium* (intensive photophobia, no redness of conjunctiva). *Sulphur* (pus is present in interior chamber, scrofulous diathesis, sharp shooting pain through the eyes into the head from 1 to 3 AM, photophobia and profuse lachrymation) *Mercurius prot.* (ulceration of cornea especially the upper part with pain at night, thick yellow coating at the base of the tongue) *Kali bichrom.* (indolent ulceration, photophobia and no redness, stringy discharge) *Graphites* (superficial ulceration resulting from pustules, intense photophobia, bleeding of external acanthi in opening the eyes, profuse acrid burning lachrymation, yellowish acrid mucous purulent discharge from the eyes, blurring of eyes, relieved by winking) *Pulsatilla* (thick bland white or yellowish discharge from the eyes, better in open air) *Silicea* (small round ulcer, worse in the cold) *Cinnabaris* (pain above the eye, extending from the internal to external acanthus or running around the eye) *Argentum nit.* (ulceration of cornea of infants or from any form of purulent ophthalmia with profuse discharge from the eyes of white yellow colour) *Aconite* (ulceration caused due to exposure in the open air, eye dry, hot and burning) *Apis.* (shooting or stinging pains, edematous condition of the lids) *Arnica* (Haemorrhages into the anterior chamber) *Asafoetida* (iritic pains extend from within outward and relieved by rest and pressure) *Chininum mur.* (due to malaria or anemic condition, pain in or above the eye periodic in character) *Cimicifuga* (sharp neuralgic pain through the eye into the head) *Croton tig.* (vesicular eruption on the face and lids) *Mercurious cor.* (photophobia, acrid lachrymation discharges, pains, burning and excoriation of the lids in excess) *Natrum mur.* (lachrymation acrid discharges thin and excoriating shining eruptions on face or around the eyes, sharp and piercing pain above the eye on looking downward) *Spigelia* (symptoms are aggravated by bathing the eyes-Iritis: inflammation of the iris) *Mercurius* (for all types of iritic pains are severe of tearing, boring, cutting burning nature, around the eyes in the forehead and temples, worse in the night and damp weather great sensitiveness to heat, cold, light especially glare of fire, pupil contracted) *Kali iod.* (a good remedy for syphilitic iritic much pain which seems to be in the bones surrounding the eye, pressing pain usually from downward and not inward, bone pain in other parts) *Cinabaris* (pain commences at the inner acanthus and extends across the brow or even passes around the eye, worse at night) *Heper.* (supportive iritic, purulent irido-capsulitis after cataract extraction, throbbing in the eye ameliorated by warmth, eye tender to touch) *Rhus tox.* (caused by exposure to wet or if found in rheumatic patient, lids are edematous swollen spasmodically closed and upon opening them a profuse gush of tears. take place, worse at night) *Bryonia* (from exposing to cold, pains shooting extending to head and face, sensation as if eye has been forced out of the socket, aggravation by moving the eyes or upon exertion and at night) *Asafoetida* (especially syphilitic patient or abuse of mercury, pains throbbing pulsating, pressing, burning above the eyes, better by rest and pressure).

Uncomfortable in crowd: *Aurum.*, *Kali ars.*, *Nux vom.*

Unconsciously moving, head and hand continuously: *Apocynum*, *Bryo.*, *Helleborus*, *Zinc. met.*

Understand only, when read twice: *Agnus cast.*, *Lyco.*, *Acid phos.*, *Sepia.*

Urethra: *Hep.*, *Sulph.* (inflammation of the orifice of the urethra, with mucous discharge) *Canth.*, *Merc.* (Haemorrhages from the urethra with severe pain) *Nat. mur.* (severe cutting pain in the urethra after micturation, involuntary micturation when coughing).

Urinary bladder: *Canth.* (inflammation of the neck of the bladder) *Taraxacum.* (Cancer of the bladder)

Urine (abnormal condition of): *Canth.*, *Tereb.*, *Hamm.* (bloody) *Tereb.*, *Dulc.*, *Acid nit.* (foetid) *Acid benzoic* (dark coloured, smell like horses), *Lyco.*, *Nux vom.*, *Ant. crud.* (gravelly) *Lyc.* (Lit hates) *Acon.* (with fever) *Bryo.* (high coloured) *Acid phos.* (milky especially in children) *Chim.* (difficult urination with mucous sediments) *Aur. iod.*, *Eupatpura*, *Dulc.*, *Ant. crud.*, *Acid nit.*, *Puls.* (mucours), *Uva.* (thick and ropey) *Canth.*, *Clem.*, *Puls.*, *Chem.*, *Sabina* (purulent) *Lyco.*, *Puls.* (purulent with nauseous smell and gastric derangement) *Cina* (thick and turbid, whitish, warm etc) *Merc.*, *Acid phos.* (symptoms worse in the morning) *Sabad.*, *Rhus.*, *China*, *Phos.*

Urine (burning or scalding during passing of): *Canth.*, *Copovia*, *Cann. sat.*, *Merc. cor.*, *Gels.*, *Acon.*, *Bella.*, *Apis.*, *Lyco.*, *Nux vom.*

Urine (excessive): *Scill.* (pale watery) *Murex* (very pale and excessive) *Ign.*, *Hyos.* (hysteric patient), *Ars.*, *Acid phos.* (diabetic).

Urine (in continuance of): *Cina.* (from worms) *Acid phos.* (especially in old persons) *Podophy.* (in women with sense of prolapsus) *Bella.* (copious nocturnal discharges) *Acid benz.* (in children with dry rough skin, particularly with offensive odour) *Uran. nit.*, *Gels.*, *Acid benzoic* (in the aged) *Acid. phos.*, *Canth.* (nocturnal in children), *Ferr. phos.*, (diurnal only) *Acon.*, *Canth. Arg. nit.*, *Apis.*, *Eup. pur.*, *Lyco.*

Urine (retention of): *Camp.* (sudden spasmodic) *Nux vom.* (spasmodic); *Gels.*, *Ign.* (hysterical.) *Canth.*, *Opi.*, *Arn.*, *Hyos.* (in typhoid), *Coleus* (Q).

Urine (scanty): *Acon.*, *Bryo.*, *Canth.*, *Apis.*, *Colch.*, *Dig.*, *Hello.*, *Ruta.*, *Staph.*

Urine (suppression of): *Tereb.*, *Acon.* (from cold-Urticaria: simple), *Apis.*, *Rhus tox.*, *Crot ting.*, *Ant. crud.*, *Urtica urens.*, *Ars.* be alternate with *Apis.*

Urine cannot be controlled, has to run immediately to pass the urine: *Apis*, *Kreosotum*, *Petro selenium.*

Urine incontinence: *Causticum* (frequent desire to urinate, a small portion passes involuntarily) *Pulsatilla* (involuntary emission of urine when sitting or walking, frequent desire to urinate).

Urine passes uncautiously: *Belladona* (during sleep uncomfortable and wets the bed) *Causticum* (during first sleep wets the bed, during winter season aggravation but better during summer season) *Sepia* (thin young girls wet the bed in first sleep) *Calcarea carb.* (flabby children habitual of bed wetting) *Ferrum phos.* (during day time urine passes with coughing).

Urine passes, while cleaning the nose, coughing or sneezing: *Causticum*, *Puls.*, *Squilla*, *Rumex*, *Nat. mur.*, *Silicea*, *Veratrum album.*

Urine: *Acon.* (retention of urine with stitches in the kidney, difficult and scanty emission of bright red urine) *Canth.* (while urinating burning and stinging pain), *Colch.*, *Nat. mur.* (brownish, blackish urine), *Apis.*, *Bell.*, *Lyco.*, *Acid nit.* (Stranguary, dark coloured and scanty urine) *Caust.*, *Puls.*, *Verat.* (involuntary emissions of urine when coughing, sneezing etc.) *Arnica* (brown urine, brick red sediments) *Cal. carb.*, *Sepia* (white sediment) *Ipec.*, *Acid nit.* (bloody urine), *Bell.* (frequent desire to urinate, urine normal but in small quantity) *Con.* (turbid with reddish sediment in urine) *Lach.* (sensation as if ball is in the bladder), *Digital. pur.* (continual desire to urinate only few drops being emitted each time, urine dark brown, hot and burning with sharp cutting pain at the neck of the bladder), *Cina.* (urine turns milky after standing a little while), *Acid nit.* (urine fetid), *Dulcamera* (stranguary, painful micturation, urine turbid and white), *Heper sulph.* (urine corrode the prepuce) *Ars.*, *Bell.*, *Cina*, *Puls.* (involuntary micturation, as if paralysis of bladder), *China*, *Nux vom.* (dark urine with brick dust sediments) *Sil.* (yellow sandy sediments) *Acid nit.* (badly smelling urine like that of horse urine) *Acid phos.* (urine like milk, mixed with jelly like bloody pieces, pain in the kidney).

Urticaria (chronic): *Ars.*, *Sulph.*, *Apis.*, *Nat. mur.*

Urticaria (from cold): *Acon.*, *Dulc.* (from damp).

Urticaria (from gastric disorder): *Ant. crud.*, *Nux vom.*, *Puls.*

Urticaria (nettle rash): *Apis mel.* (eruptions red and shining with stinging, burning in parts, urine dark colored and scanty) *Pulsatilla* (if caused by eating wholesome food delayed and scanty mucus, diarrhoea at night) *Rhus tox.* (if caused from getting wet, worse in cold air, violent itching and burning of the skin).

Urticaria after physical exertion: *Apis.*, *Cal. carb.*, *Heper.*, *Nat. mur.*, *Sanicula*, *Urtica urens.*

Urticaria of children: *Aconite.* (due to exposure to dry cold weather) *Antim. crud.* (from eating rich food or overeating) *Apis mel.* (sensation of stinging, burning and pricking pain) *Bovista.* (with rheumatic lameness and diarrhoea, worse by warmth) *Dulcamara* (in damp weather) *Heper sulph.* (recurring sensitive to touch) *Pulsatilla* (due to intake of fatty foods) *Rhus tox.* (flea bite like spot with purplish swelling, worse on joints) *Sulphur* (intense itching worse by warmth of the bed).

Uterine displacement: *Puls.*, *Sepia*, *Bella.*, *Nat. mur.*, *Nux.*, *Secale.*

Uterus (antoversion of): *Lilium.*

Uterus (congestion of): *Bella.*, *Murex.*, *Lilium.*, *Vert. vir.*, *Gels.*, *Caulo.*, *Cemicifuga.*, *Bella.*, *Merc. sol.*, and *Sepia* (are most reliable).

Uterus (haemorrhages from): *Hamm.*, *Ipec.*, *Trill.*, *Crocus.*, *Secale cor.*, *Sabina*, *China*, *Erigerm.*

Uterus (indurations of): *Merc. cor.*, *Plat.*, *Aur.*, *Iod.*, *Sil.*

Uterus (inflammation of): *Acon.*, *Bell.*, *Nux vom.*, *Iod.*

Uterus (irritability and neuralgia of): *Acon.*, *Cimici.* (especially rheumatic), *Bell.*, *Plat.*, *Xanth.*, *Gels.*, *Verat vir.*, *Caulo.*

Uterus (prolapsus of): *Fraxinus amer.* (Q) *Podophy.*, *Bell.*, *Sepia*, *Arn.*, *Stann. Secale*, *Nux vom.*, *Aletris.*, *Merc. sol.*

Uterus (retro version of): *Ferrum iod.*, *Sepia.*, *Aletrus.*

Uterus (spasm or colic of): *Cocc.*, *Caulo.*, *Nux vom.*, *Ign.*, *Secale.*, *Cham.*, *Gels.*

Uterus (ulceration of): *Merc. cor.*, *Sep.*, *Hydras.*

Uterus displacement due to lifting heavy weight: *Aurum.*, *Podo*, *Rhus tox.* (as per symptoms)

Uterus: *Aurum.*, *Arsenic* (with inflammation of ovaries, sexual desire increased, irregular menses) *Caltha palustris* Q (a palliative) *Carbo anamalis* (burning pain down thighs, lancinating pain) *Carciniosin* (offensive discharge haemorrhage and pain) *Kali carb.* (severe pain from hip to knees, worst on the right side) *Kali iod.* (womb packed with fibroid tumors, hot burning feet) *Kreosotum* (of uterus especially of cervix) *Lapis albus.* (fibroid tumors of uterus with burning pain and profuse haemorrhage) *Pulsatilla* (fibroid tumors of the uterus). *Carbo animalis* (great exhaustion, burning pain extending down the thigh) *Crotalis h.* (with discharge of dark fluid and offensive blood) *Arsenic iod.* (corrosive discharge) *Kreosotum* (intermittent haemorrhages, during confinement the haemorrhages will be associated with lochia, ulceration in uterus, burning in the pelvis like hot coal, discharge clots and foul) *Terebintha* (burning in uterus, haemorrhage) *Carboneum sulph.* (excitable, frighten easily, weak memory, dwarfish body, restlessness in the night) *Ign.*, *Cocc.* (uterine cramps with cutting stitches) *Calc c.*, *Nux.*, *Sepia.* (prolepses of uterus) *Nux.*, *Rhus tox.* (prolepses of uteri from over-lifting or straining) *Phos. acid.*, *Heper.* (uterine ulcers, copious, putrid bloody discharge, itching, corroding pain) *Rhus tox.* (abortion from strain or over-lifting also prolepses of uteri) *Sabina* (uterine Haemorrhages the blood is partially clotted and partially fluid with pain extending from back to pubis) *Sepia.* (burning shooting pains in the neck of the uterus).

V

Vagina: *Lyco.*, *Bell.* (heat and dryness of vagina) *Cal. carb.* (constant aching in the vagina) *Cham.*, *Sulph.* (burning in vagina, as if excoriated with yellow smarting leucorrhoea) *Lyco.* (discharge of wind from vagina) *Merc. vivus.*, *Sepia.* (prolapsus of the vagina with sensation of great rawness) *Sulph.*, *Canth.*, *Lyco.* (burning in the vagina).

Varicocele: *Puls.*, *Ham.* (internally and externally) *Acid flour.* (chronic cases), *Ferr. phos.*, *Plumb.*, *Phos.*, *Arum.*

Varicose veins: *Carbo veg.* (in pregnancy, varicosity with offensive, excoriating discharge) *Lachesis* (purple, sensitive to touch, pressure relieves) *Lycopodium* (on vulva, swelling and enlargement of veins particularly of right leg) *Pulsatilla* (with ulcers, bleeding black blood which easily coagulates) *Calcarea flour* (chronic cases, cases of old persons and women who have given birth to many children, disease of lower extremities) *Hamamelis* (veins enlarged, parts sore, stringing pricking pain) *Millefolium* (the capillaries are spongy and enlarged, congested veins break easily, wounds bleed much easily) *Sulphur* (veins ulcerate, rupture and bleed, varicose veins of extremities) *Arsenic album* (chronic, burning like fire at night) *Fluoric acid* (of legs, cures varicose ulcers as well).

Veins (inflammation of): *Acon.*, *Puls.*, *Hamm.* (varicose condition) *Phos.*, *Lach.*

Vertical. hemiopia: *Cal. carb.*, *China*, *Sulphur*, *Mur. ac.*, *Nat. mur.*, *Rhus.*, *Sepia* and *Stram* (as per symptoms of the remedy).

Vertigo and headache: *Aconite* (faintness on rising, fullness and heaviness in the forehead) *Belladona* (vertigo with vanishing of sight, throbbing headache) *Nux vom.* (tearing, drawing and jerking pain in the head, habitual constipation, leads a sedentary life, addicted to the use of strong coffee and drug) *Opium.* (sensation of lightness in the head great heaviness of the head) *Sepia.* (violent beating headache, empty feeling in the stomach, constipation with a sense of weight in the anus).

Vertigo on rising from the seat stooping or looking up: *Aco.* (fullness and heaviness in the forehead), *Bryo.*, *Cocc.* (sensation of emptiness in the head with great difference) *Croc.* and *Gels.* (as if intoxicated, confusion of the head with pain, after watching anything) *Puls.* (when stooping, lifting up the eyes, after eating, feeling of chilliness). *Bryo.*, *Podo.*, *Puls.* (vertigo from rising from seat, stopping or looking up), *Apis.* (with nausea and headache) *Ant. crud.* (with nausea and bleeding from nose) *Gels.*, *Nux vom.*, *Puls.*, *Cal. carb.*, *Kali carb.*, *Bella.*, *Acon.*, *Acid hydrocyn.* (with headache), *Cact.* (from heart disorder) *Cocc.* (with sickness), *Iod.* (in old persons) *Dig.* (with feeble heart action), *Glon.* (with occipital pain), *Sulph.*, *Acid phos.* (brain fag).

Voice (hoarse, loss of, weakness of etc): *Caust.* (recent from cold or over use of the voice) *Arn.* (from overuse), *Acon.*,

Bell. (acute case with dry hard cough), *Phyto.* (constant dryness and roughness with cough and dark redness of the faces) *Heper sulph., Rumex.* (chronic hoarseness, wheezing breathing loose cough etc.), *Nux vom.* (from spinal irritation), *Graph.* (dry, rough voice cough etc), *Ign.* (hysterical), *Ant. crud.* (when heated); *Kali bich.* (especially in tenor voices or in beer drinkers with dark redness of faces) *Phos., Carbo veg.* (in elderly men), *Spong.*

Voice lost, in the morning and there is no pain in the throat: *Cal. carb., Nux vom., Ars., Lyco., Carbo veg., Asaf.*

Vomiting (chronic) *Kreos., Ipecac.* (with retching) *Ver. vir.* (violent prolonged vomiting and hiccough and sensation as if a ball rising in the throat) *Cocc., Petrol.* (from the motion of a carriage) *Hydras., Kreos., Ars.* (from ulceration or cancer of the stomach with wasting, gastritis etc.) *Zinc.* (without retching) *Acid sulph.* (empty retching), *Coni.* (chocolate coloured in cancer symptoms) *Arg. nit.* (with great sourness) *Lyco.* (greenish masses), *Ant. tar.* (whitish rice water vomit with Diarrhoea of similar fluid), *Nux vom.* (from gastric causes preceded by spasmodic pains) *Ver. alb.* (prostration and cold sweats) Puls. (mucous), Apomorphia (cold compression over stomach or from spinal irritation).

Vomiting (curd like): *Aethusa.*

Vomiting (general): *Ant crud., Ant. tar.* (terrible vomiting which nothing can stop) *Arn., Ipecac.* (vomiting coagulated blood renewed by eating or drinking), *Ars.* (vomiting after drinking sometime later) *Bryo., Nux., Puls., Verat.* (vomiting, especially after eating or drinking) *Ipecac., Sec., Verat.* (vomiting black bile and blood) *Ant. tar., Verat., Ars.* (vomiting with Diarrhoea and great prostration) *Bell., Ipecac.* (vomiting undigested food or mucus and bile) *Canth.* (vomiting with violent retching) *Cimi.* (nausea and vomiting due to nervous or sympathetic irritation of the brain Cina. (vomiting worms, food, mucus and bile) *Cocc.* (nausea and vomiting while riding in a carriage) *Antimonium crud.* (nausea and vomiting from over loading the stomach, milky white tongue) *Arsenic* (vomiting especially after eating or drinking, vomiting of brownish, blackish substances) *Bryonia* (bitter bilious vomiting) *Coculus* (nausea and vomiting from riding in a carriage on a boat, sea sickness, nausea) *Ipecac.* (constant and continual nausea, horrible pain and sick feeling in the stomach) *Nux vomica.* (nausea after eating, vomiting of sour smelling mucus, frequent hiccough) *Pulsatilla* (vomiting after eating pork or greasy food) *Veratrum album.* (vomiting black bile and blood, vomiting whenever patient moves or drinks, cold sweat on the forehead, sudden sinking of strength) *Colchicum* (the smell of fish, eggs, fat meals causes nausea and vomiting even to faintness) *Dig., Ipec., Ant. tar.* (vomiting of large quantity of mucus) *Puls.* (vomiting of bitter sour fluids) *Hyos.* (eating produces vomiting, colic relieved by vomiting) *Rhus tox.* (sudden vomiting when eating).

Vomiting (of bile) *Iris., Podoph., Ipecac., Bryo., Merc.*

Vomiting (of blood): *Ipecac., Hamm., Kreos.*

Vomiting (of milk in children) *Nux vom., Acid sulph., Ipecac., Silicea.*

Vomiting immediately after drinking: *Ars. alb., Bismith, Bryo., Cadmium.*

Vomiting instantly, as soon as water reaches in the stomach: *Ars. alb.*

Vulva: *Carbo v.* (apathies of the vulva).

W

Warts: *Dulcamara* (on the back of the fingers, delicate skin, sensitive to cold) *Thuja.* (warts are fig like or cauliflower like shape) *Causticum* (warts are generally on face and are of big size and solid) *Antim. crudum.* (warts long and pointed generally formed on palm and sole) *Staphsagaria* (generally found on eyelid) *Nat. mur.* (warts hard and in the palm) *Thuja, Antim. crud., Sabina, Causticum, Thuja., Cal. carb.* (small, soft) *Sep.* (large hard) *Sil., Sulph., Kali bich.*

Water brash: *Lyco., Nux vom., Iris., Acid chrom., Bryo., Carbo veg., Rob., Ars., Acid sulph.*

Weakness after long suffering: *Carbo veg., China, Phos., Psoranium, Kali carb.*

Weakness and anemia: *China.* (from loss of vital fluid) *Arsenic alb.* (from excessive labour or climbing the mountain) *Ferrum met.* (anemia from blood accumulation) *Phosphorus* (weakness of nervous system causes sleepiness suddenly and also weakness) *Phosphoric acid.* (sudden nervous weakness without pain, deep sorrowness, unsuccessful in love matters or excessive indulgence in sex causes weakness, burning in spinal column and hand and feet, cannot sleep during night due to various thoughts in mind) *Coccolus* or *Colchicum* (weakness caused due to continuous work for several nights).

Weeps loudly from happiness: *Coffea.*

Weeps loudly from music: *Graphites.*

Weeps loudly, when asked about his/her illness: *Puls.*

Weeps loudly, when given thanks: *Lyco.*

Weeps when thinking about future: *Lyco.*

Weeps whenever desires: *Actea racemosa, Aurum mur, Cal. carb., Lac can., Lacheses.*

Wens (operation): *Baryt. carb., Kali iod., Sil., Cal. carb., Graph., Lyco.*

Whitlow: *Sil., Bell., Heper sulph., Lach., Mer., Stram.* (intolerable pain) *Myristica.*

Whole body parts are scattered, tries to assemble them: *Bapt., Petrolium.*

Whooping cough associated with discharge of blood: *Arnica., Bella., Corallium, Crotalus h., Droseara, Cocinallea, Ipecac., Bromium, Cina.*

Whooping cough in children: *Drosera* (violent cough) *Aconite* (with fever) *Belladona* (with sore throat flashed face) *Cuprum met.* (paroxysms with suffocation, rattling noises) *Ipecac.* (constant nausea, vomiting).

Whooping cough: *Acon.* (at commencement) *Ipecac.* (with gastric symptoms, vomiting of mucus) *Dros.* (severe paroxysms of hoarse cough and vomiting) *Coccus cacti.* (violent spasmodic cough with copious expectoration of stringy mucus), *Arn.* (child cries before the fit of coughing comes on) *Cup. act.* (croup like cough with convulsive movements, collapse from closing of air cells of the lungs), *Bella.* (sudden and violent paroxysms with sore throat, worse at night child cries with cough) *Petrol.* (great sickness) *Phos.* (Lung complication) *Cina.* (worm symptoms) *Coral., Veret. alb., Gels., Verat vir., Nux vom.*

Wind passing relieves the ailment: *Lyco.*

Worm (tape): *Filix mas.* (Q)

Worm (thread) *Cina.* (children) *Filix mas, Teuc.* (in adult) *Merc., China, Ign., Sulph. Sant* (1 x).

Worm affection: *Cina* (constant boring of nose, the urine turns milky after standing short time) *Lycopodium* (ascarides with much itching about the anus, red sandy sediment in the urine) *Mercurius* (ascarides with much troublesome itching of the anus continual greediness for eating yet grows weaker) *Sulphur* (gets very hungry about 11 A.M., frequent weak faint spells throughout the day).

Worms (long or round): *Merc., Sant., Ign., Spig., Sulph., Cina* (Q)

Worms in children: *Cina.* (for thread or round worms or ascardis, tossing in bed, itching of nose, bores it till bleeds, vomiting) *Sabadilla* (pin worms, round worms and tape worms, itching at anus, constant cutting and diarrhoea, liking for sweets, nausea and vomiting) *Terebintha* (round or tape worms, foul breath, dry hawking cough, itching at anus) *Spigellia* (pain at navel, itching at anus, foetid breath, eye complaints).

Worry for others: *Arsenic., Phosphorus.*

Wounds: *Calend.* (lancerated and incised), *Led.* (punctured) *Arn.* (contused) *Ham.* (much discolouration).

Wry neck: *Cimic., Macrot., Rhus., Ign., Bella., Nux vom., Merc., Acon.*

Y

Yawning: *Ign.*, *Plat.*, *Rhus.* (convulsive) *Acon.* (with chilliness and excessive and continuously recurring flatulence) *Nux vom.*, *Lyco.*, *Zinc.*

Yellow fever: *Arsenic.* (violent vomiting immediately after eating or drinking, vomiting of brown and black substance, burning in the stomach, rapid prostration) *Camphor.* (long lasting chill, coldness of the skin, yet cannot bear to be covered, prostration) *Veratrum album.* (face cold covered with cold perspiration, violent vomiting of green or black bile, intense thirst for cold drinks, cramps of the limbs with cold sweat) *Nux vomica.* (yellowish face especially around the nose and mouth, very irritable and wishes to be alone, intemperate habits) *Camph.* (chill stage) *Acon.*, *Bell.* (fever) *Crotal.*, *Phos.*, *Bryo.*, *Ipecac.* (gastric symptoms) Canth. (suppressed urine) *Arg. nit.* (black vomit) *Ars. alb.*

Yellow skin: *Chelidonium* (in liver problems, enlarged, jaundiced skin, tongue yellow, bitter taste, nausea yellow urine) *Chionanthus* (in jaundice, liver enlarged with constipation, urine full of bile and sugar) *Crotalus hor.* (in malignancy, cancer of the stomach, vomiting of bloody slimy mucus, pain in the region of liver) *Myrica* (bronze yellow skin, appetite lost, urine scanty, dark, frothy with bile, pain in the region of liver) *Phosphorus* (large yellow spots on abdomen, hepatitis, cirrhosis, fatty degeneration of liver).

Glossary

Abscess: A collection of pus formed by tissue disintegration and surrounded by an inflamed area.

Achalasia of the cardia: The oesophagus muscles do not work properly causing difficulty in swallowing both liquid and solid.

Acrid: Biting, sharp to taste or smell.

Acrocyanosis: Cyanosis of the extremities with mottled blue or red discoloration of the skin of the digit, wrist and ankles.

Ague: Malarial or intermittent fever.

Albuminaria: The presence of albumin in the urine, sometimes an indicative of kidney disease.

Alopecia: Loss of hair, baldness.

Amblyopia: Dimness of vision.

Amenorrhea: Abnormal suppression or absence of menstruation.

Amnesia: Loss of memory due to various causes.

Amoebiasis: A digestive tract infection caused by amoeba.

Amoebic dysentery: An infection, inflammatory disease of the colon, resulting in severe pain and diarrhoea.

Aneurisms: A sac is formed by the dilation in the wall of an artery.

Angina pectoris: A syndrome characterized by paroxysmal pain below the sternum most easily precipitated by exertion or excitement and caused by ischemia of heart muscle, usually due to coronary heart diseae such as arterial selerosis.

Anorexia nervosa: A substantial weight loss in adolescents.

Aortic incompetence: Aortic value of the heart gets thickened and does not close properly causes shortness of breath due to leakage of blood.

Aortic valve steno sis: The opening of the aortic valve becomes narrow causing obstruction to the forward flow of the blood to the brain, there is difficulty in breathing and vertigo while standing up from a sitting position.

Apathae: Small ulcers, especially the whitish or reddish spots in the mouth.

Aphonia: Loss of speech or voiceless ness as a result of disease or injury to the organ of speech.

Apoplexy: A sudden, usually marked loss of bodily function due to rupture or occlusion of a blood vessel.

Arterial thrombosis: Formation of a blood clot in an artery of the brain, the heart or a leg or other arteries.

Arterio sclerosis: Hardening and narrowing of the artery wall due to degeneration.

Ascites: Dropsy of the abdomen.

Atrial fibrillation: Irregular breathing of the heart associated with shortness of breath and palpitation.

Atrophy: A wasting away of tissues, organs or the entire body.

Banalities: Inflammation of the glans penis.

Bell's paralysis: One side of the face drops on account of an inflammation of the facial nerve.

Biliary colic: Paroxysms of pain from the passage of the gall-stones through the gall duct.

Biliousness: The condition marked by constipation, adrenal discomfort, headache and anorexia due to excess of bile.

Billadry calculus: Billadry concentrations composed of thickened bile or chiefly of cholesterol found in the gall bladder.

Blepharitis: Inflammation of the eye lids.

Blepharospasm: Spasm of the orbicular acute muscle producing more or less complete closure of the eye.

Branny tettr: A superficial cutaneous affection in which there is desquamation - the skin falling off in whitish bran like scales. Also more or less redness, itching and heat.

Bright's disease: A genetic term for acute and chronic disease of the kidneys usually associated with dropsy and albuminaria.

Brow ague: Frontal neuralgia, of an intermittent nature.

Bruise: An injury on the surface of unbroken skin, due to hemorrhage into tissue from ruptured vessels.

Bubo: An inflammation and swelling of the lymphatic glands of the groin, axilla due to infection like gonorrhea, syphilis, plague, tuberculosis, chancroid.

Bursitis: An affection of the elbow or the knee cap. The affected part is swollen and hot.

Callosities/corn: Corns formed on the sole of the foot due to pressure or friction on a part of the skin. The skin turns hard, thick and losses sensitivity.

Caries/Dental Cavities: Due to decay of tooth a cavity is formed in it. The tooth becomes sensitive to heat, to cold or to sweets.

Cataplexy: A condition marked by abrupt attack of muscular weakness.

Cerebral palsy: A movement disorder resulting from an injury to the brain or by birth.

Cerebra-spinal meningitis: Inflammation of meninges or pertaining to the brain and the spinal cord.

Cervical spondylosis: Pain and stiffness in the spinal column of the neck.

Cervicitis: An inflammation of the neck of the uterus with infection. There is pain low down the back.

Chancre: A dull red, hard, insensitive lesion that is the first manifestation of syphilis.

Chlorosis: Pallor of anaemia with a yellowish green aspect, peculiar odour of breath, irregularity or suppression of menstruation, shortness of breath with a peculiar sound.

Cholera infantum: Infantile diarrhoea.

Cholesterol: A glistening white, soapy, crystalline substance occurring notably in bile, gall stones, the brain, blood cells, plasma, egg yolk and seeds.

Chorea: A nervous disorder, especially of children, marked uncontrollable and irregular movements of the muscles of the arms, legs and face.

Cirrhosis of the liver: Serious disorder of the liver.

Colitis: A disease caused by inflammation of the lower bowel, causing severe cramping pain in the abdomen, constant pressure on the rectum and diarrhoea.

Concussion: Violent shaking or shock to a soft structure especially of the brain.

Condyloma: A wart like excrescence on the skin, usually in the region of anus and genitals.

Conjunctivitis: Inflammation of conjunctiva

Contusion: A bruise from a blow by a blunt object.

Coronary thrombosis: Coagulation of blood in a coronary artery often leading to distraction of heart muscles.

Crick in the neck: A pain of rheumatic affection of the muscles of the neck, causing the head to be held on one side.

Crista lactea: Seborrhea of the scalp in infant.

Cyanosis: A bluish discoloration of the skin resulting from inadequate oxygenation of the blood.

Cystitis: Lining of the urinary bladder is inflamed.

Dacryoadentis: Inflammation of lachrymal gland.

Debauchery: Over indulgence in harmful or immoral pleasure.

Delirium: Disordered state of mind, especially during fever.

Dementia: Marked deterioration in the intellectual and physical condition in old age such as forgetfulness of recent events and names loss in the sense of time and confusion. At times limbs become stiff.

Detachment of the retina: Separation of the inner layer of the retina from the pigment layer.

Diabetes mellitus: A disease characterized by insulin deficiency in which sugar and starch are not properly metabolized by the body.

Diastolic pressure: Blood pressure during the normal rhythmic dilation of the heart during which its chambers are filling with blood.

Diphtheria: Infectious disease with inflammation of the throat.

Dropsy: Disease in which fluid collects in the body.

Dysmenorrhea: Painful menstruation

Ecthymae: An ulcerative pyodermia usually caused by streptococci at the site of minor trauma. Heals with scar formation.

Ectropion: Eversion of the eye lids; most commonly the lower one is turn down.

Emphysema: A disease in which there is a progressive loss of lung elasticity. The air sacs of lungs get inflated and distended. The walls of the air sacs become rupture.

Encephalitis: Inflammation of the brain and its membranes.

Endocarditic: Inflammation of the lining of the heart cavity and of the heart valves on account of infection.

Ennui: A feeling of weariness with life, a result of boredom, satiety or lack of interest in life.

Enteritis acute: Inflammation of the intestine.

Enuresis: Involuntary urination.

Epistaxis: Nose bleeding.

Erysipelas: An acute skin disease marked by spreading and shifting inflammation.

Erythema: Non contagious superficial hyperemia of the cutaneous surface; redness and swelling of the skin.

Excoriate: To tear or wear off the skin, chafe.

Excrescence: An abnormal disfiguring out growth or enlargement.

Fauces: The space on the two sides of the arch of the palate; the throat.

Febricula: A mild fever of short duration

Felon: Infection of the finger usually terminating in an abscess

Fester: To discharge a thin fluid as the result of irritation.

Fibro adenoma: A benign tumor of gland like structure full of fibrous matter.

Fibroid tumor: A tumor largely composed of smooth muscle.

Fibroids: Benign tumors consisting of fibrous tissue.

Fissure: A groove or furrow in skin.

Fistula lachrymalis: An abnormal passage communicating with the lachrymal sac or duct.

Fistula: An abnormal duct or passage from an abscess, cavity or hollow organ to the body surface or to another hollow organ.

Freckles: A benign small tan to brown macule occurring on the skin exposed to the the sun usually in children fading in adult life.

Gall stones: Calcareous concentrations in the gall bladder and its ducts

Ganglion: An encysted tumor on a tendon.

Gangrene: Decay of body tissue, due to failure in the blood supply due to injury or disease.

Gastralgia: Gnawing or burning in the stomach with loss of appetite, spasm of the stomach.

Gastric ulcers: An erosion of the inner wall of the stomach caused imparity by the corrosive action of the gastric juice on the mucus membrane.

Gastro enteritis: Inflammation of the mucus membrane of the stomach and intestine.

Gastrodynia: Neuralgic pain in the stomach; flatulent colic.

Gastrolgia: Neuralgia of the stomach, any stomach pain.

Gingivitis: Inflammation of the gums.

Glaucoma: Condition caused by increasing the presence of fluid within the eyeball.

Gleets: Chronic stage of gonorrhea with mucus purulent discharge.

Goiter: Unhealthy enlargement of thyroid gland.

Gout: Disease causing inflammation of the joints.

Haematesis: Vomiting of blood

Haematuria: Passing of blood in urine.

Haemoptysis: The spitting of blood

Hallucination: Illusion of seeing or hearing something which is actually not present.

Hay asthma or hay fever: Summer catarrh caused by the seeds of grasses.

Headache anemic: Due to anemia.

Headache chronic: Long standing with a tendency to recur.

Headache congestive: Headache ascribed to hyperemia or congestion.

Headache sick: A headache accompanied by a stomach disorder.

Heart attack: Sudden failure of the heart not functionally normally.

Heat stroke: Illness caused by over exposure to sun, or to heat.

Hectic fever: The protracted fever of phthisis

Hemi crania: One sided headache.

Hemianopia: Defective vision or blindness in half of the visual field.

Hemiplegia: Paralysis of one side of the body

Hemorrhoids: Piles. A varicose dilation of a vein resulting from a persistent increase in venous pressure in the anus.

Hepatitis: Inflammation of the liver accompanied by jaundice and fever.

Hernia femoral: Protrusion of a loop of the intestine into the femoral canal.

Hernia inguinal: Hernia into the inguinal canal.

Hernia umbilical: Hernia of the part of the umbilicus.

Herpes: A skin disease with patches of distinct vesicles along the course of a nerve. An acute non-contagious inflammatory disease with burning and pain.

Hydrocele: Accumulation of serious fluid in a bodily cavity, especially the testis.

Hydrocephalus: A collection of water in the head, dropsy of the brain.

Hydrothorax: Dropsy of the chest.

Hypertension: Abnormally high arterial blood pressure; a state of high emotional tension.

Hypertrophy of heart: Abnormal enlargement of the heart

Hypochondria: Morbid anxiety about ones own health with complaint of imaginary disorder.

Hypochondriasis: Extreme depression with morbid anxiety regarding the health.

Impetigo: An acute pustules disease of skin, characterised by the formation of discrete round or oval pustules situated on a slightly inflamed base.

Influenza: Viral disease causing fever, muscular pain, catarrh.

Intermittent fever: A fever with a period of a pyrexia.

Intertrigo: Erythema from friction.

Iritis: Inflammation of the iris of the eye.

Jaundice: Yellowish discoloration of tissues, skin and bodily fluid with bile pigments, caused by any of several pathological conditions in which normal processing of the bile is interrupted.

Laryngitis: Inflammation of the larynx.

Lead colic: Colic from lead poisoning.

Leprosy: An endemic, chronic, malignant disease with cutaneous and other lesions.

Leucorrhoea: A vaginal discharge containing mucus and pus cells.

Lichen: Aggravated or obstinate eczema.

Lienteria: Diarrhoea with undigested food

Lochia: A vaginal discharge after labour

Locomotar ataxia: Disease of posterior columns of spinal cord

Lumbago pain: Rheumatic pain in the lower back.

Lupus: Localized degeneration of the skin caused by various cutaneous diseases.

Lymph nodes: Number of oval or round bodies located along the lymphatic vessels that supply lymphocytes to the circulatory system and remove bacteria and foreign particles from the lymph.

Measles: An exhanthematous contagious disease in children

Meningitis: Inflammation of the membranes covering the brain and spinal cord.

Menopause: Time in the life of a woman when she ceases to menstruate.

Menorrhagia: Abnormally heavy menstrual flow.

Metrorrhagia: Uterine hemorrhage between menstrual periods.

Migraine: Headache confined to one side only.

Miliaria: A disorder of sweat glands with obstruction of their ducts.

Milk fever: Fever attending the establishment of lactation after delivery.

Milk leg: An acute oedema, especially of the leg from venous obstruction.

Morning sickness: Morning nausea and vomiting of pregnancy.

Mumps: An acute infectious disease marked by swelling of the parotid glands.

Muscae volitantes: Floating spot in visual field

Myalgia: Pain in the muscles.

Myasthenia gravis: Abnormal muscular weakness.

Myelitis: Inflammation of the spinal column or the bone marrow.

Myocarditis: Inflammation of the muscle tissue of the heart.

Nephritis: Various acute (any) inflammation of the kidneys.

Nervousness: The state of having the nervous affected, nervous weakness.

Nettle rash: Spots of different colours, disappearing in warmth and appearing in cold, appearing suddenly and continually changing their place.

Neuritis: Inflammation of a nerve causing pain

Nevus: A birthmark.

Night terrors: Excessive nightmares, especially in children.

Nodes: A small mass of tissue in the form of a swelling knot or protuberance either normal or pathological.

Oedema: An excessive accumulation of serous fluid in the tissues.

Ophthalmia: Inflammation of the eye.

Osteomyelitis: Inflammation of the bone marrow.

Otitis media: Pain and inflammation in the middle ear.

Ozaena: A condition of the nose associated with a foul smelling discharge.

Pancreatitis: Inflammation of the pancreas.

Peethora: Over fullness of the blood vessels in a part or in the system.

Pemphigus: A chronic skin disease characterized by a successive formation of irregulary scattered variously sized vesicles.

Pericarditis: Inflammation of the pericardium.

Periostitis: Inflammation of periosteum

Phimosis: Constriction of the orifice of the prepuce so that it cannot be drawn back over the glans.

Phthisis: Emaciation with consumption of lungs.

Pimple: A very small boil or inflamed spot or papula.

Pityriasis: A scaly skin disease with hypopigmented patches, usually involving the face especially the cheeks and the area around the mouth.

Plica polonica: Verminus matting of hair.

Poliomyelitis: An infectious viral disease occurring mainly in children, in its acute forms attacks the central nervous system producing paralysis.

Polyps: A growth protruding from the mucous lining of an organ such as nose etc.

Porrigo: Scald in the head, ring worm.

Prostatitis: Inflammation of the prostrate.

Prostatitus: Itching or heat often disturbing in old people.

Pruritis vulvae: Intense itching of vulva.

Pruritis: Severe itching of undamaged skin.

Psoriasis: A chronic inflammatory skin disease with scale formation.

Pterygium: Chronic thickening of the conjunctiva, usually triangular and situated at the inner acanthus.

Ptosis: Drooping of the upper eyelid due to paralysis Puerperium disorders: The period from delivery to the completion of involution.

Purpura: Small livid spots under the skin from effused blood.

Pyelitis: Inflammation of the interior of the kidney.

Pyorrhea: Inflammation of the gum and tooth socket.

Pyrosis: Gastric burning pain with eructation; heartburn.

Quinsy: Inflammation of the tonsils and the surrounding tissue, often leading to the formation of an abscess.

Rachitis: Inflammatory disease of the vertebral column.

Ranula: A cystic tumor beneath the tongue.

Relapsing fever: A fever recurring during convalescence.

Remitted fever: Fever alternately abating and returning.

Renal colic: Pain due to calculus in the ureter

Retinitis: Inflammation of the retina.

Rheumatism gonorrheal: Arthritis associated with gonorrheal urethritis.

Rheumatism: Pain in the muscular, joints tendons or covering of the bone, the result of cold, damp or wet, often shifting and increased by changes of weather or storms.

Rickets: Children's disease causing softening and deformity of the bones.

Ringworm: Ring shaped configuration of lesions.

Roseola: Rose coloured rash on the skin.

Rubella: Infectious fever of childhood, resembling measles.

Rubia: A syphilitic eruption with dark encrusted foul ulcers

Rupia: An erupton of large flat blebs or vesicles.

Sarcitis: Inflammation of muscle tissue.

Scabies: The itch.

Scalding: Injury or pain caused by hot liquid or steam.

Scarlatina: An epidemic fever accompanied by sore throat, small reddish continuous spots and often followed by glandular swellings.

Scarlet fever: An epidemic exanthematous contagious disease with fever and a erythematous rash.

Sciatica: A nerve pain affecting the nerve.

Scirrhus: Hard stony cancer, principally affecting the breast.

Sclerosis: Abnormal hardening of the tissue.

Sclerotitis: Inflammation of the sclerotic coat of the eye.

Scrofulosis (Scrofula): A constitutional condition with glandular tumors and a tuberculosis condition.

Scurry: A form of purpura due to deficiency of ascorbic acid.

Senile: Weakness in the body or mind due to old age.

Septic: Capable of producing putrefaction.

Smallpox: A specific infection with fever followed by vesicles, pustules and pits

Snuffles: Breathing with difficulty through the nose from accumulation of mucus.

Somnambulance: Walking in the sleep.

Spasm: A morbid or forcible contraction of one or several muscles.

Spasmodic: Condition occurring in spasms.

Spermatorrhea: Involuntary discharge of semen.

Spinal bifida: A cleft of the spine, a congenital anomaly.

Spondylosis: Vertebral immobility and fusion of a joint due to disease, injury or surgery.

Sprain: The twisting of a joint by violence or accident, as the knee, ankle, wrist or elbow especially and lameness which results.

Staphyloma: Protrusion of the sclera or cornea.

Stomtitis: Inflammation of the mucus tissue of the mouth.

Strabismus: Squintness.

Strangury: Slow, painful urination with spasms of the urethra and bladder.

Styes: Inflamed swelling on the edge of the eyelid.

Sunstroke: Illness caused by the exposure to sun.

Systolic pressure: Blood pressure during contraction of the heart.

Tabes mesenterica: Infantile tuberculosis of the mesenteric glands.

Tenea capitas: Ring worm of the head, scald head.

Tenesmus: Continuing urge.

Tetanus: A disease with spasmodic and continuous contraction of the muscles.

Thrombosis: Formation of a clot of blood in the blood vessel or organ of the body.

Tonsillitis: Inflammation of the tonsils.

Trachoma: A contagious viral disease of the conjunctiva of the eye characterized by inflammation, hypertrophy and swelling.

Tumor: A permanent swelling of some part of the body, they are fleshy, fibroid, fibre cellular, fatty, vascular, bony or cancer one.

Tympanites: Gaseous distension of the abdomen.

Urethra affections: Affections to the excretory canal of the bladder.

Urticaria: A skin condition characterized by intensely itching welts.

Vertigo: Giddiness, dizziness.

Warts: Small, hard, abnormal growth on the skin.

Wen: A swelling on the head, of variable size, without change of colour or inflammation.

Whitlow: Small abscess under or affecting a nail.

Whooping cough: Infectious disease especially of children with a violent convulsive cough.

Wry neck: Torticollis.

Yellow fever: The gastric and malignant bilious remittent fever of the tropics.

List of Drugs

Abbreviations used for drug	Drug full name
Acalpha ind.	Acalypha indica
Ac. benzoic.	Benzoicum acidum
Acid flour.	Fluoricum acidum
Acid hydrocyn	Hydrocyanicum acidum
Acid mur.	Muriaticum acidum
Acid nit/Acid nitric	Nitricum acidum
Acid. phos.	Phosphoricum acidum
Acid picr.	Picricum acidum
Ac.Sulph/Acid.Sulp	Sulphuricum acidum
Aco/Acon.	Aconitum napellus
Aesculus.h.	Aesculus hippocastanum
Aesthusa cyn.	Aethusa cynapium
Agac/Agaricus.	Agaricus muscaris
Alt/Aletris/Aletrus	Aletris farenosa
Aloes	Aloe soctrina
Alumen	Alumen
Alum.	Alumina
Ambra/Ambra gr.	Ambra grisea
Amm.carb./Ammon.carb.	Ammonium carbonicum
Ammon.Cast.	Ammonium causticum
Ammon. mur.	Ammonium muriaticum
Amyl nit.	Amylenum nitrosum
Ana/Anac./Anacard.	Anacardium orientale
Anthrac.	Anthracinum
Ant.crud./Antim crud.	Antimonium crudum
Ant. tar./Antim tar.	Antimonium tartaricum
Apis./Apis.mel.	Apis mellifica
Apoc/Apocy.can.	Apocynum cannabinum
Apom/Apomorph.	Apomorphinum hydrochloricum
Aralia.r.	Aralia racemosa
Argn. nit./Argent.nit.	Argentum nitricum
Ars./Arsenic/Ars.alb.	Arsenicum album
Ars. iod.	Arsenicum iodatum
Arnia.	Aranea diadema
Arn./Arnic.mont.	Arnica montana
Arum. sulph.	Aurum sulphuratum
Arum triphy.	Arum triphyllum
Asaf.	Asafoetida
Asarum.	Asarum canadense

Abbreviations used for drug	Drug full name
Asclep.	Asclepias cornuti
Astac.	Astacus fluviatillis
Aster.rubens.	Asterias rubens
Aur.iod.	Aurum iodatum
Aur./Aurum./Aur.met.	Aurum metallicum
Aur.mur./Aurum.mur.	Aurum muriaticum
Avenà.sat.	Avena sativa
Bacil.	Bacillinum burnett
Bar.c./Bary.carb.	Baryta carbonica
Bapt.	Baptisia tinctoria
Baryta.mur.	Baryta muriatica
Bell./Bella.	Belladonna
Bellis.	Bellis perennis
Berb./Berb.vul.-Berberis.vul.	Barberis vulgaris
Bor.	Borax veneta
Bryo.	Bryonia alba
Bufo./Buffo.	Bufo rana
Cacts.	Cactus grandiflorus
Caland.	Calendula Officinales
Cal/Cal.carb./Cal.carbo.	Calcarea carbonica
Calcarea hypophos.	Calcarea hypophosphorosa
Calcarea flour.	Calcarea fluorica
Cal.iod/Calcarea iod.	Calcarea iodata
Cal.phos.	Calcarea phosphorica
Calcarea pic.	Calcarea picrica
Camp.	Camphora officinalis
Cann. ind.	Cannabis indica
Cann.sat/Canna sat.	Cannabis sativa
Canth.	Cantharis vesicatoria
Caps.	Capsicum annum
Carbo ani.	Carbo animalis
Carbo veg.	Carbo vegetabilis
Carboneum sulph.	Carboneum sulphuratum
Cardus. mar.	Cardus marianus
Caulo.	Caulophyllum thalictroides
Caust.	Causticum
Cedr.	Cedron
Cham.	Chamomilla
Cheli/Chelid.	Chelidoninum
Chin.	China
China sulph.	Chininum sulphuricum
Chinunum ars.	Chininum arsenicosum
Chlor. hyd.	Chloralum hydratum
Cic.	Cicuta virosa
Cimic/Cimicig.	Cimicifuga racemosa

Abbreviations used for drug	Drug full name
Cinnab.	Cinnabaris
Cistus. can.	Cistus canadensis
Cocculus ind.	Cocculus indicus
Cof./Coff.	Coffea cruda
Colch.	Colchicinum
Collin.	Collinsonia canadensis
Colo/Coloc.	Colocynthis
Conium.	Conium maculatum
Copa.	Copavia officinalis
Coral.	Corallium rubrum
Cratagus. ox.	Crataegus oxycantha
Crocus.	Crocus sativus
Crot.h/Crotalus.	Crotalus horridus
Crot.tin/Crotn tingl.	Croton tiglium
Cup. acet.	Cuprum aceticum
Cup./Cup.met./Cuprum met.	Cuprum metallicum
Cycl/Cycla.	Cyclamen europhaeum
Cyprip.	Cyripedium pubescens
Daphna ind.	Daphne indica
Dig/Digi/Digit/Digitalis pur.	Digitalis purpurea
Dioscor/Diose.	Dioscorea villosa
Dipth.	Diphtherinum
Dulc/Dulcam.	Dulcamara
Erige/Erigerin.	Erigeron canadense
Eryng.	Eryngium acuaticum
Eup.pur.	Eupatorium purpureum
Eupha/Euphr.	Euphrasia officinales
Eupion.	Eupionum
Ferr. acet.	Ferrum aceticum
Ferr./Ferrum.met.	Ferrum metallicum
Ferrum mur.	Ferrum muriaticum
Ferr.phos/Ferrum phos.	Ferrum phosphoricum
Gels.	Gelsemium sempervirens
Glon.	Glonoinum
Graph.	Graphites
Ham/Hamma.	Hamamelis virginiana
Hellob./Hell.	Helleborus niger
Helon/Halonias.	Helonias dioica
Heper/Heper. sulph.	Heper sulphuris calcareum
Hydras.	Hydrastis canadensis
Hydrophs.	Hydrophobinum
Hyos.	Hyoscyamus niger
Hypericum. perf.	Hypericum perforatum
Ign.	Ignatia amara
Iod./Iodin.	Iodium

Abbreviations used for drug	Drug full name
Ipecac.	Ipecacuanha
Iris/Iris. vers.	Iris versicolor
Juglans.	Juglans cinerea
Justica adha.	Justicea adatoda
Kali bich./Kali bichrom.	Kalium bichromicum
Kali brom.	Kalium bromatum
Kali carb.	Kalium carbonicum
Kali hydroiod.	Kalium hydroiodicum
Kali iod.	Kalium iodicum
Kali. mur.	Kalium muriaticum
Kali. sulph.	Kalium sulphuricum
Kalmia.	Kalmia latifolia
Kreos.	Kreosotum
Lac. can.	Lac. caninum
Lac. delf.	Lac defloratum
Lach.	Lachasis mutus
Lapis alb.	Lapis albus
Lappa.	Lappa arctium
Lauro.	Laurocerasus
Ledum/Led.pal.	Ledium palustre
Lept.	Leptandra virginica
Lilium tingl.	Lilium tigrinum
Lob./Lobell.	Lobelia inflata
Lyco.	Lycopodium clavatum
Lycopus virg.	Lycopus verginicus
Macrot.	Macrotinum
Mag.acet./Manganum.acet.	Manganum aceticum
Mag.c./Mag. carb.	Magnesium carbonica
Mag. mur.	Magnesium muriaticum
Mag. phos.	Magnesium phosphoricum
Mag. sulph.	Magnesium sulphuricum
Magnet. austral.	Magnetipolus australis
Merc.	Mercurius
Merc. bin. iod	Mercurius bin.iodatus
Merc. cor.	Mercurius corrosivus
Merc. cyanatus.	Mercurius cyanatus
Merc. dulsis.	Mercurius dulcis
Merc. iod.	Mercurius iodatus flavus
Merc. iod ruber.	Mercurius iodatus ruber
Merc. proto iod.	Mercurius proto iodatus
Merc. prot. ruber.	Mercurius praecipitatus ruber
Merc. sol.	Mercurius solublis Hahnemanni
Merc. vi.	Mercurius vivus
Mosch.	Moschus
Myristica.	Myristica sebifera
Nat. carb.	Natrium carbonicum

Abbreviations used for drug	Drug full name
Nat. mur.	Natrium muriaticum
Nat. salicycl.	Natrium salicylicum
Nat. sulf/Nat. sulph.	Natrium sulphuricum
Niccolum. met.	Niccolum metallicum
Nictit	Nicotinum
Nuphur	Nuphar luteum
Nux mosh/Nux moashi	Nux moschata
Nux/Nux vom.	Nux vomica
Ocimum can.	Ocimum canum
Olender.	Oleander
Op/Opi.	Opium
Paris quad.	Paris quadrifolia
Petro/Petrol.	Petroleum
Petro sel.	Petro selinum sativum
Phell.	Phellandrum aquaticum
Phos.	Phosphorus
Phos. acid.	Phosphoricum acidum
Phyos.	Physostigma venenosum
Phyto.	Phytolacca berry
Plat.	Platinum metallicum
Plumb.	Plumbum metallicum
Podo.	Podophyllum peltatum
Prunus spin.	Prunus spinosa
Puls.	Pulsatilla
Pyro.	Pyrogenium
Rad. brom.	Radium bromatum
Ran bulb/Rananculus bulb.	Ranunculus bulbosus
Rheum.	Rheum palmatum
Rhod.	Rhododendron chrysanthum
Rhus/Rhus tox	Rhus toxicodendron
Rhus.ven.	Rhus venenata
Rob.	Robinia pseudacacia
Ruta.	Ruta graveolens
Sabad.	Sabadilla
Sabi.	Sabina
Sambucus.nig.	Sambucus nigra
Sangu/Sangunaria.can.	Sanguinaria canadensis
Sarsa.	Sarsaparilla officinalis
Sant.	Santalum album
Scill.	Scilla maritima
Scutel/Scutell.	Scutellaria laterifolia
Sec/Secale/Secale cor.	Secale cornutum
Selen.	Selenium metallicum
Senec.	Senecio aureus
Sel.	Selenicereus spinulosus
Spig.	Spigellia anthelmia

Abbreviations used for drug	Drug full name
Spon/Spongia.t.	Spongia tosta
Stann.	Stannum metallicum
Sticta.p.	Sticta pulmonaria
Stram.	Stramonium
Stronsia.	Strontium carbonicum
Strophanthus.	Strophanthus hispidus
Strych/Strych. nit.	Strychninum nitricum
Sulphur iod.	Sulphur iodatum
Syzgium.	Syzygium jambolanum
Tabac.	Tabacum
Tarax.	Taraxacum officinale
Tarentula his.	Tarentula hispanica
Terebinth.	Terebinthi niae oleum
Teuc./Teucar.	Teucrium marum verum
Thuja.	Thuja occidentalis
Tilia.	Tilia europaea
Tric.	Trichosanthes dioica
Trill.	Trillium pendulum
Tuber.	Tuberculinum bovinum-Kent
Uran nit.	Uranium nitricum
Urt. urens.	Urtica urens
Uva.	Uva urse
Verat/Veratrum alb.	Veratrum album
Ver. vir.	Veratrum viride
Viburum Op.	Viburnum opulus
Viola. tric.	Viola tricolor
Viscum alb.	Viscum album
Voila/Violoa.	Viola odorata
Xantho.	Xanthoxylum fraxineum
Zinc. ox.	Zincum oxyalatum
Zinc/Zincum/Zincum met.	Zincum metallicum
Zincum. Sulph.	Zincum sulphuricum